work based learning

learning

Journeys to the Core of Higher Education

work based learning

Journeys to the Core of Higher Education

edited by

Jonathan Garnett
Carol Costley
Barbara Workman

Middlesex
University
PRESS

First published in 2009 by Middlesex University Press

Copyright © Middlesex University Press

Authors retain rights to individual chapters

ISBN 978 1 904750 19 2

A CIP catalogue record for this book is available from
The British Library

Design by Helen Taylor

Printed in the UK by Ashford Colour Press

Middlesex University Press
Tel: +44 (0)20 8411 4162
Fax: +44 (0)20 8411 4167

www.mupress.co.uk

Foreword

Middlesex University has been at the forefront of the development and operation of work based learning at higher education level for over sixteen years. While Middlesex has a much longer track record of highly successful vocational education the origins of the distinctive Middlesex approach to work based learning can be traced back to a 1992 Employment Department funded project to investigate the possibility of identifying and accrediting a "curriculum in the workplace". This was a radical step for a higher education institution and Middlesex showed equal boldness in establishing the National Centre for Work Based Learning Partnerships and recognising work based learning as a field as well as a mode of study. (The Centre was created as the Institute for Work Based Learning (IWBL) in August 2007). This paved the way for the validation of programmes "in" Work Based Learning Studies at undergraduate and postgraduate level and the subsequent development of a Doctorate in Professional Studies.

Work based learning is now a common, if far from universally accepted, feature of the UK higher education landscape. There are an increasing number of forms of work based learning as higher education institutions seek to engage with employers and demonstrate their worth in the knowledge driven economy. At Middlesex we particularly value the potential of work based learning to make a direct impact upon practice through real life work based projects facilitated by the university. Recognising learning at, through and for work makes new demands of higher education concepts, practices and structures. Work based learning requires educational practitioners to question not only their practice but also their underpinning epistemological beliefs.

In 2005 Middlesex was awarded a Centre for Excellence in Teaching and Learning in the area of work based learning by the Higher Education Funding Council for England. A main aim of the Centre is to disseminate work based learning in and beyond Middlesex University. This book provides timely insights into the ways in which work based learning has been adapted and developed across the university and by some of our partner organisations. Consideration of these many journeys sheds light upon core concerns of higher education: learning, teaching and assessment, quality assurance and curriculum development. Work based learning at Middlesex has developed from bold innovation to a distinctive and growing resource for the whole university.

Professor Margaret House
Deputy Vice-Chancellor Academic
Middlesex University
December 2008

Contents

Section A: Introduction

1   *Chapter 1*   The Development and Implementation of Work Based Learning at Middlesex University
Barbara Workman and Jonathan Garnett

Section B: Case Studies of the Middlesex Approach to Work Based Learning

16   *Chapter 2*   Developments in Practice-based Arts Education
Alan Durrant

27   *Chapter 3*   Middlesex University Business School: Returning to Vocational 'Routes'
Peter Critten

38   *Chapter 4*   Work Based Learning in the School of Computing Science
Muthana Jabbar

51   *Chapter 5*   Using Work Based Learning in the School of Health and Social Science
Barbara Workman and Katherine Rounce

62   *Chapter 6*   Articulating the Learning from Part Time Work
Philip Frame

73   *Chapter 7*   Improved Qualifications and Career Opportunities of Early Years Practitioners
Gillian Hilton

86   *Chapter 8*   The Undergraduate Curriculum: Echoes and Traces of Contemporary Cultures of Work
Molly Bellamy

102   *Chapter 9*   Developing Work Based Learning at Doctoral Level
Pauline Armsby and Carol Costley

118   *Chapter 10*   Combining Academic Study and Professional Practice: The Story of the Doctorate in Psychotherapy
Derek Portwood

131 *Chapter 11* The Development of a CPD Framework for GP
Vets by Experienced Practitioners
Annette Fillery-Travis, David A Lane and
Jonathan Garnett

143 *Chapter 12* Transnational Corporations: The Irish Centre
Experience
Nick Hodgers and Andrew Hodgers

153 *Chapter 13* Negotiating Learning with SME Managers
Barbara Light

Section C: Themes in Work Based Learning Development

164 *Chapter 14* Partnerships in Higher Education
Katherine Rounce

173 *Chapter 15* The Quiet Revolution: Developments in Europe
Barbara Light

189 *Chapter 16* The Core Components: Teaching, Learning and
Assessing
Barbara Workman

204 *Chapter 17* Enhancing Quality Assurance
Jonathan Garnett

213 *Chapter 18* The Role of Research
Carol Costley and Paul Gibbs

226 *Chapter 19* Contributing to the Intellectual Capital of
Organisations
Jonathan Garnett

239 **Biographies of contributors**

section A

Introduction

1

The Development and Implementation of Work Based Learning at Middlesex University

Jonathan Garnett and Barbara Workman

***

Middlesex University has pioneered the development of Work Based Learning (WBL)[1] at higher education level since the early 1990s. Since publishing our previous book about WBL (Portwood and Costley 2000) there has been increasing interest in WBL in its many different forms throughout the UK, Europe and internationally. Middlesex University has led on several national and international developments within the field. This has been possible because the programmes have been successful with both students and employers since starting in 1993. The University has given WBL significant support and enabled these new-style programmes to be structured within a higher education approach that is inclusive and responsive to the demands of work based learners and a range of other stakeholders including employers. All WBL programmes from undergraduate Certificate to Professional Doctorate level have been made available to individuals or organisations through cohorts linked to employer or professional development initiatives.

Learning from work is not a new concept. Indeed, it formed the basis of many professional programmes from the middle ages where professions such as medicine and law developed their skills in practice and then took their learning into the academy to inculcate into new recruits coming into the profession and into the body of professional knowledge. Since then it has been taken up by other professions such as engineers, nurses and teachers, often starting as an apprenticeship model, but increasingly moving into delivery by higher education with academia defining the curriculum and mode of study. In the latter part of the twentieth century other forms of WBL began to emerge, largely in the form of continuing professional development training for post qualifying professionals, such as in management, but with the curriculum being determined by professional bodies or advances in technology. Whilst the commonest application has

---

1 Portwood D. & Costley C. (2000) Work Based Learning and the University: New Perspectives and Practices SEDA paper 109. Available on line at:
http://www.mdx.ac.uk/wbl/research/pubs.asp

been within vocational subjects, the distinctive work of Middlesex University has demonstrated WBL at higher education level can be seen as grounded in the context, nature and imperatives of work.

WBL at Middlesex University stemmed from a research project which explored the curriculum in the workplace in the early 1990s. The project demonstrated that learning was organised and built upon the activities and relationships at work (Portwood 2000). Workers had to demonstrate learning in order to be appointed to a particular job, but then had to improve their proficiency and knowledge in order to remain in post. This perspective became the basis from which the Middlesex WBL studies curriculum developed, starting from undergraduate certificate level, through post graduate, and eventually doctorate level study. The concurrent introduction of modularised and credit based university wide academic frameworks contributed to the solidarity of the programme as these provided a framework in which programmes could be structured using a straightforward but innovative approach of four main curriculum components, which build upon the learner's experience and are guided by the learner's professional and personal learning needs. These programmes have been running successfully within a niche, non traditional student market since their inception in 1993, supplemented by the introduction of the Doctoral programme in 1997. The development of the programme and underlying philosophies and methodologies are explored fully in Portwood & Costley (2000), but we are aware that as time moves on, perspectives change and grow in order to respond to internal and external drivers, some of which, like Leitch (DfES 2006) have had significant influences on the uptake and interpretation of WBL approaches across higher education.

The distinctive approach that Middlesex has taken to WBL is rooted in the notion that WBL is a 'field of study' in its own right, rather than just a 'mode' of study (Portwood 2000, Gibbs & Garnett 2007). This allows each individual to create their own individually negotiated programme starting with accreditation of their learning from work, where work itself becomes the subject discipline, rather than traditional subject disciplines. Portwood (2000) makes the case for WBL as a subject of study wherein learning from the work perspective means it is a social activity within a specific context. Additionally it draws on some of the adult learning theories, for example, (Knowles 2005) and humanistic theory (Rogers 1983), and includes aspects such as communities of practice (Lave & Wenger 1991) and multi-faceted contexts of learning such as social, economic and psychological factors, thus focusing on work itself as the main learning activity rather than being just a training experience or a placement activity. It includes learning from voluntary, domestic and unpaid activity too which distinguishes it from other WBL programmes elsewhere that focus on the application of subject discipline knowledge and professional development per se. Another

3

distinctive characteristic is the impact of the WBL project and the contribution that WBL projects make in relation to both individual and organisational change and development. The knowledge that is generated through the WBL project rarely lies in any one academic discipline thus challenging traditional epistemologies of subject disciplines within academia.

The current definition of WBL as understood and used by Middlesex is:

> "A learning process which focuses University level critical thinking upon work, (paid or unpaid) in order to facilitate the recognition, acquisition and application of individual and collective knowledge, skills and abilities, to achieve specific outcomes of significance to the learner, their work and the University"
>
> (Garnett 2004, Inaugural lecture)

This definition has considerably developed the notion of WBL since Boud & Solomon (2001:4) stated:

> "WBL is the term being used to describe a class of university programmes that bring together universities and work organisations to create new learning opportunities in work places".

Learning opportunities have always been available at work; perhaps the difference is that now, more areas are recognising the potential within these learning activities and are aiming to exploit and capitalise upon them.

The simplest definition usually links learning to the work role, and identifies three strands; learning for, through and at work (Seagraves et al 1996) indicating a variety of learning activities which can be linked to work based learning. Different distinguishing features of each strand range from vocational training or in-house training which reflect the learning acquired through doing the job, i.e. being 'at' work, whereas learning 'for' work is more closely related to the concept of initial professional education, or development of specific management or subject specific skills, now often provided by Higher Education. 'Through' work utilises the HE perspective of developing intellectual skills, analysis of knowledge and application of learning which can be fostered within HE (Brennan & Little 1996), and which Garnett (2004) identifies as being the critical thinking skills that contribute to significant outcomes for both learner and organisation.

The Institute for Work Based Learning

WBL at Middlesex developed from a project located within a central service unit. In 1993 the university established the National Centre for Work Based Learning Partnerships (NCWBLP) which functioned as a department within a school structure of the university. From 1997 it worked closely with the WBL and Accreditation unit of the School of Health and

4

Social Sciences (HSSc). In 2005 the university was awarded a Centre for Excellence in Teaching and Learning in Work Based Learning (CEWBL). Part of the remit of the CEWBL was to further develop WBL on a pan university basis. Building upon the success of CEWBL the university created the Institute for WBL (IWBL) in August 2007. The aim is to be 'an internationally recognised centre for excellence in the use of work based learning to create innovation and achieve the development objectives of organisations and individuals'. This builds on the CEWBL aims which are to enhance, extend and customise WBL into each school and across the university, and to maximise the impact of excellent practice in WBL pan university by building upon previous award winning work. Additionally we aim to provide a catalyst for dissemination of good practice in WBL in partnerships with other CETLs and the Higher Education Academy. With this in mind the IWBL was separated from the School of Arts and Education where it had resided for a number of years and became independent so that it was equally accessible and available to all departments of the university as a resource for WBL programmes, accreditation and consultancy services and WBL research. While the IWBL advocates the 'field' of study approach to WBL, the sharing of good practice is not limited to this and includes aspects of teaching and learning that contribute to a wide variety of 'modes' of WBL, many of which will become apparent as each school featured within this book tells its story.

The Core Curriculum

The WBL curriculum at Middlesex University has four core components. The starting point is a personal review of work experience to identify the knowledge and skills the individual brings to the programme. This can lead to accreditation of experiential learning (APEL). Accreditation may be awarded for an individual's experiential learning or formal learning that is validated or accredited organisational training or similar. The underlying assumption is that the individual may have learnt valuable, university level learning elsewhere and does not need to repeat it through formal HE routes to prove it, but instead can demonstrate it through various sources of evidence which may be certificates of training or other evidence from work. For many learners, this process is highly significant, as it enables recognition of their personal and professional development, often achieved over an adult lifetime, and enables them to take stock of and appreciate their achievements.

Having established their individual starting point to the programme, the learner plans future steps by determining what s/he requires both personally and professionally. This leads to a tripartite learning agreement with their sponsor or employer and the university. A research and development module that enables the learner to develop skills of critical appraisal,

5

project planning and development follow, with particular emphases upon aspects of WBL learning that are crucial within the projects. These include aspects such as the role of the worker/researcher; the significance of the context in which the project is being undertaken; critical appraisal of the research together with organisational or national policy literature that influences current practice, combined with a suitable research approach that reflects work environment discipline, culture and areas of inquiry. These considerations are explored more fully within this book (see Gibbs & Costley, chapter 18). Having successfully completed these components, the learner then progresses to projects, which enable exploration of specific areas of interest and relevance to the workplace and award title. WBL projects are aimed to facilitate the acquisition of new knowledge from academic, policy and work sources to contribute to the area of work expertise as well as making up credit deficit towards the final intended award, so there may be several projects within an award, especially within the undergraduate programme. Figure 1.1 gives a diagrammatic representation of the core curriculum and indicates how each stage builds on the previous learning.

Figure 1.1 Demonstration of the development of a WBL programme with the APEL module forming the basis of the claimants learning

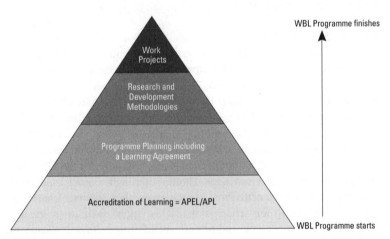

(From Doncaster 2000)

Introduction to the book
The book is divided into three sections. The award of CEWBL provided the opportunity to take a strategic initiative in spreading WBL across subject areas previously untouched by WBL within Middlesex University. The book captures the progress of WBL since 2000 and presents a range of case

studies of the application of WBL from relative maturity to infancy across the university, which demonstrate a variety of WBL approaches and practices in different subject disciplines and highlights some of the key issues that have arisen during this expansion. The case studies illustrate a range of factors that have encouraged or hindered the development of WBL with the intention for other practitioners to benefit from the collective experience that this book represents.

Section A discusses the Middlesex approach to WBL, its origins and development and its growth to this point in its development. It has been going for fifteen years in its current form and like all true teenagers is increasingly flexing its muscles and pushing the boundaries of what has been known and practiced to this point. Section B discusses the variety of forms that WBL has taken across the university and with partner organisations. While the core of the WBL programme remains the same, the interpretations and developments that each subject area has made provide examples of the infinite possibilities that a flexible curriculum in WBL can offer. This section shows how WBL has started at different points within the schools and curriculum, but has then responded to varying demands and styles of subject areas and adjusted within each academic area to make its own mark upon curriculum developments. Within this section there are also contributions from practitioners who have used WBL within specialist areas, such as the Doctoral programme, and professional developments. Section C explores themes of WBL in more depth and reflects issues raised by many enquirers about WBL. Quality and assessment issues, international developments and some of the core research themes that underpin the work are found in this section.

Section B Case studies of the Middlesex approach to WBL

The section starts with Durrant discussing the development of a WBL programme at Masters Level within an Arts discipline. He explores the challenges this presents to a practice based education, and how the programme provided the unique opportunity for HE to recognise and accredit practice based knowledge. Durrant considers the WBL approach taken here offers a valuable route for the established art practitioner, and using illustrations from actual students' experience with insights and perceptions of the programme, describes the consequential impact on lifelong learning both for the student and for the school. Durrant makes some useful observations about the supporting mechanisms within the school that contributed to the success of the programme. These include commitment from senior staff in recognising work programme allowances and the consequent impact that that has on the uptake and engagement with WBL by academics. Factors relating to WBL that have contributed to the teaching and learning practices within the arts discipline are identified and their contribution to the lifelong learning approach within an arts tradition are explored.

The next chapter (Critten) discusses how the Business school is involved in a range of WBL modes, from placements through to modules which enable the acquisition of WBL skills as required by employers. The school has adopted the fourfold WBL curriculum but has used it within a different terminology of 'practice'. This in itself reflects the range of understanding of what constitutes WBL and how it can be described within different paradigms of work and is also reflected in the formal assessment requirements of professional bodies. Critten uses three case studies to illustrate the range of opportunities that WBL has provided for the school, particularly in partnerships with employers, and suggests that such partnerships can make a significant contribution to the development of new subjects within the business curricula. He comments too, on the use of ICT as a learning tool and the piloting and contribution of new technologies to WBL programmes.

Jabbar in chapter 4 describes the current position that WBL holds within the Computing Science School. He lays out the agenda of the school within the current contexts of lifelong learning, multi-disciplinary and trans-disciplinary concepts which support the science of computing, and identifies the many facets of related subjects that buttress computing and the technological challenges that face today's students and practitioners. As an area within the university that has come to WBL somewhat late in its development, he recognises the increasing attractiveness of WBL to computing science as a means of acknowledging the diverse and interconnecting knowledge and skills that computing practitioners must be acquainted with. He considers the CEWBL targets during its five years in relation to the experience and needs in Computing Science, particularly the role that ICT takes in shaping the delivery of WBL programmes and the change of emphasis from theoretical to practice based learning, as filtered through the powerful lens of reflective learning. WBL is a new venture for Computing Science and while the potential benefits can be invoked, in reality things take longer to prove themselves and therefore this is a tentative acknowledgement of the introduction of WBL in computing, but one which recognises the immense possibilities that lie open before the field of computing science.

The School of Health and Social Sciences has been involved with WBL from early in its dissemination across the university, and has benefited from the opportunity to test its potential in a wide variety of situations and curricula. In chapter 5 Workman & Rounce identify a number of activities and features that have enabled integration of the WBL approaches into a broad based curriculum ranging from foundation to Doctoral level, and across a number of social science related subject areas. This chapter

8

discusses the circumstances that have conspired together to enable innovative programmes to be developed and contribute to a wide range of subject areas, but also how the flexibility of WBL modes of learning have enabled responsive creation of a wide range of programmes. However, they also identify some of the constraints which may emerge and which may hinder its developmental flow. They introduce the concept of a WBL continuum (Workman 2003, Costley 2006) which reflects the wide spectrum of WBL modes of delivery and application. It also discusses the usefulness of accreditation of organisational training programmes in their contribution to the success of WBL programmes within the School.

Frame in chapter 6, focuses on a smaller dimension of WBL within the full time Business student's undergraduate programme. He describes the use of a module to facilitate learning from work, with specific reflective processes to assist students in learning from the routine and mundane activities of part-time work. This module reflects the concept of WBL as a 'mode' of learning, rather than a 'field', and presents strategies to facilitate all learners in developing skills of articulating and evaluating learning from informal sources in the light of experience. Students are encouraged to discover a variety of sources of learning from work and to be proactive in seeking support and direction in their careers. Frame uses some case study illustrations to make this process become powerfully alive.

Foundation degrees are the recent qualification most closely associated with WBL and in some HEIs are considered to be the only form of WBL. Hilton, in chapter 7, describes the development of a Foundation Degree (FD) in Early Childhood Studies that was created to raise the status of those working in the sector, who are often poorly paid and rewarded for their skills and knowledge. Drawing on her experience as a QAA reviewer of FDs, the programme design incorporated factors that had been seen to be effective in other FDs. The complexities of delivery in either HE or FE are considered, as well as the needs of different students and education providers. The issues related to WBL and the inclusion of employers within the programme development are explored bearing in mind the difficulties that face a service industry which is restrained by government legislation, but is not fully recognised for its skills and level of service requirements within its pay and career structures. Financial issues including sponsorships and student support are included as well as the implications for delivery of curriculum for those who are working and learning simultaneously outside the traditional HE structures and academic timescales.

The undergraduate curriculum is also discussed by Bellamy in chapter 8, but here she explores the full time worker's experience of being a student as described in reflective writings generated from and running concurrently with their WBL programme activities. These are some significant insights into the power of WBL on an individual's learning, especially the impact upon the self that is engendered through the educational process. The students represented on this programme are often those who do not have the traditional forms of entry into higher education and this chapter demonstrates clearly the potential that WBL offers to non traditional students, as well as raising a number of issues in relation to accessibility of the curriculum and drivers for individual learning and professional development.

Costley and Armsby (chapter 9) consider WBL at the other end of the award spectrum as in the Doctorate in Professional Studies (DProf). They consider factors that have encouraged the growth of the programme, both nationally and internationally as well as some of the challenges presented to the DProf team that are essential to enable high level professional learning and development. They explore the pedagogy and philosophy underpinning the generic approach to doctorate study, and discuss key differences between the PhD and DProf approaches which have significant implications for both universities and Doctoral students. The role of PhD supervisor as compared with that of a DProf academic adviser is considered together with the resultant challenges that this brings in finding academics and high level professionals with appropriate skills and knowledge to act as advisers and consultants to DProf participants.

Portwood (chapter 10) describes the development of a sister programme to the generic DProf – that of the Doctorate in Psychotherapy developed by the Metanoia Institute of Psychotherapy and counselling and validated by Middlesex University. He discusses its development within the context of a community of scholarly practitioners who are contributing to their community of practice in the field of psychotherapy. A core element within this programme is that of the research approaches available to psychotherapy practitioners and he describes the development of critical research thinking and practice within this relatively new discipline, as it is influenced by the psychotherapeutic context, not least by the reflective components of the programme which link WBL learning approaches to the professional practices and beliefs of the practitioners. This chapter also reinforces some of the issues of academic support to the Doctoral candidates that Costley and Armsby have highlighted, not least the collegiality of the programme. The benefits of the programme in terms of the outcomes of Doctoral research and output is noted as having an impact upon therapeutic approaches and models of practice, thus making a significant contribution to the wider profession.

Chapter 11 presents the development of a post graduate programme for General Practice Vets emerging from within their profession facilitated by Fillery-Travis and Lane. As part of a research project to explore the Continuous Profession Development (CPD) needs of Vets, the Professional Development Foundation entered into a three way partnership with the veterinary professional body and Middlesex University. Using the WBL programme framework, a vehicle to explore the professions post graduate needs was enabled and the resultant programme included recognition of the role of reflective practice as crucial in the professional development for practitioners. Self awareness and reflection upon professional and personal practice was identified as key to the development of the profession as a whole. This has now been taken up by the professional body and used within the community of practice.

Chapter 12 by Nick and Andrew Hodgers draws on their experience of using management science within the WBL framework, thus providing a route for managers to develop new insights, make sense of their experience and contribute to the world of management science by learning through their own role. They argue that using the specific management framework of ISO 9000 to frame their programmes enables their clients to identify and articulate innovative and dynamic business practices which are not normally identified by academia until they become mainstream, by which time the industry has moved on, allowing theory to lag behind practice. This provides an interesting challenge to academia and supports Garnett's (2005) notion of positioning university WBL in relation to intellectual capital (Stewart 1997).

Light (chapter 13) discusses a management development programme which was designed and developed to meet the needs of small and medium enterprises. She recounts the significant shift required for HE to accommodate some of the learning generated through this programme, both as a facilitator and for the university. She highlights the differences between recognition of learning that is generated from work as opposed to that generated from the academy and considers some of the implications this has for participants on such a programme.

Section C   Themes in WBL development

A key focus of WBL at Middlesex is the use of accreditation of learning, both at individual and organisational levels, as being the foundation of the building of individualised programmes. The following chapter by Rounce demonstrates the potential for both individuals and organisations to gain through accredited learning. Rounce (chapter 14) discusses the role of partnership between the university and the organisation and identifies issues which may challenge or undermine strong partnerships. This is set within a case study which illustrates some of the complexities to be found when working in partnership, and which accompany the developmental thinking and actions that may be required by both parties to achieve a successful outcome. Both this and the previous chapter consider the issue of alternative sources of knowledge production external to HE and raise important questions as to what the consequences may be for higher education, as well as demonstrating the additional complexities of programme delivery faced by WBL facilitators outside the comfort zone of the HEI.

The widening horizons of WBL and its spread outside the UK is represented by Barbara Light in chapter 15 detailing the 'quiet revolution' currently occurring in the EU as a result of funding from the European Union Socrates Grundtvig fund. Light describes the development of a WBL platform across several European countries through the DEWBLAM project (Developing European Work Based Learning Approaches and Methods) and the gradual awakening of some academies to the possibilities that WBL offers, albeit challenging the traditional academic views of HE during the process.

Workman in chapter 16 considers aspects of teaching, learning and assessment within the WBL curriculum. She positions these within adult learning theory and applies them to the practice of WBL through the use of case studies to illustrate the diversity of application. Of interest to those who are considering the creation of WBL programmes or who are concerned with the coherence of the programme through the full range of higher education academic levels, is the use of level descriptors as designed by MU for the WBL programme and the application to individual components of the programme. Illustrations of application to specific students needs demonstrate the flexibility of the core curriculum.

As long term proponents of WBL, one of the first questions that any other HEI usually raises relates to quality issues and how the WBL programme satisfies the quality assurance mechanisms of Higher Education. Garnett (chapter 17) draws on a number of internal and external review processes successfully achieved in the WBL programmes, to demonstrate quality assurance activities already more than meet the QAA and HEFCE standards and provide a quality assured process and programme. However, he also raises the important question as to whether these external standards are the appropriate tools for quality enhancement of programmes that are designed to be work based with significance beyond the individual learner. These questions highlight that many routine quality assurance mechanisms are more akin to control measures, designed to get a uniform and guaranteed outcome, rather than tailored to assure organisational as well as individual development. He posits that the current concepts of quality assurance need to be broadened to take into consideration the needs of workers and employers, rather than that of the student experience within an HEI. In the current climate of employer engagement and employability skills, these questions are very relevant for those designing WBL programmes to meet the needs of employers. Garnett also considers the recent QAA (2007) Code of Practice for the assurance of academic quality and standards in HE, Section 9: Work-based and placement learning, as he had been involved in its development.

Costley and Gibbs in chapter 18 focus on the research undertaken by CEWBL academics in the broad area of WBL and reflect upon a wide range of issues in an emerging field of enquiry. They identify the themes of research that are currently prevalent within the WBL domain and that are emerging from the CEWBL research centre and consider some of the underlying themes, theories and related fields of enquiry. They raise questions related to issues of recognition and funding of a research area that is not yet mainstream but which challenges traditional academic thinking and practice. The key themes that are currently being explored in WBL research are those of reflexivity, insider worker/researcher and ethical issues as well as the transformation of a practitioner from non-researcher to researcher.

The final chapter draws the book to a conclusion, by considering the potential contribution of WBL to the HEI, the employer and the learner. Garnett draws on the concept of intellectual capital (Stewart 1997) as being of significance to WBL within organisations and HEIs. He suggests that the role of the university should move from one of knowledge transfer and development of individuals for employment to one of capturing the intellectual capital of organisations, and enhancing the human and structural capital within them. He considers key factors for enhancing intellectual capital, such as recognition of performative knowledge and shared and tacit knowledge of individuals through APEL and projects. This is often held within a community of practice, and is rarely captured and codified, even though it is essential to organisational performance. He argues that these factors take WBL beyond the employability and training agenda and into HEIs as part of the intellectual capital of the university, through harnessing the higher level critical thinking skills that are essential in recognising and capturing intellectual capital and enhancing enquiry into the performative and pragmatic nature of work.

Conclusion

This book aims to offer various ways of applying WBL within modules, programme short courses and subject disciplines and within the generic fields of work based learning and professional studies. We invite you to engage with our ideas and challenges, and hope that this book offers some ways forward, both practically and in theory, and that it will provoke discussion and further exploration of WBL. We are interested in your responses and questions and invite you to contact us through the Middlesex University website: http://www.mdx.ac.uk/wbl/index.asp .

References

Boud D & Solomon N (2001) (Eds) *Work based Learning: A new Higher Education?* Buckingham SRHE & Open University Press

Brennan J, & Little B (1996) *A review of Work Based Learning in Higher Education* London DFEE

Costley, C and Armsby, P (2006) 'Work Based Learning Assessed as a Field or a Mode of Study' *Assessment and Evaluation in Higher Education* Vol 31 no 4

Garnett J (2004) Inaugural lecture, Middlesex University

Garnett J (2005) University Work-based learning and the knowledge driven project in Rounce K, Workman B (Eds) (2005) *Work Based Learning in Health Care: Innovations and Applications* Chichester: Kingsham Press

Gibbs P & Garnett J (2007) Work Based Learning as a Field of Study, *Journal of Research in Post Compulsory Education* vol 12, (6) 409–421

Lave J, & Wenger E (1991) *Situated Learning: Legitimate Peripheral Participation* Cambridge: Cambridge University Press

Seagraves L, Osbourne M, Neal P, Dockrell R, Hartshorn C, & Boyd A (1996) *Learning in Smaller Companies* (LISC), *Final Report* University of Stirling, Educational Policy and Development

Stewart T (1997) *Intellectual Capital*, London: Nicholas Brearley.

Workman B. A. (2003) Methodologies in practice based projects as used by Work Based Learning students in the former School of Health, Biological and Environmental Sciences *Journal of Health, Science and Environmental Issues* Vol 4, 2, pp23–26

Case Studies of the Middlesex Approach to Work Based Learning

2

Developments
in Practice-based Arts Education

Alan Durrant

***

Introduction

This chapter covers the development of postgraduate work based learning (WBL) in the School of Arts at Middlesex University, with a particular focus on the practice-based 'creative' disciplines within art, design and performing arts. This chapter may be of interest to anyone concerned with knowledge generated within practice and how this can be recognised within a higher education arts programme. It will be of special interest to curriculum developers who are thinking about the potential of WBL to increase their capability to move beyond traditional entry level undergraduate training for practice into postgraduate provision for emerging and established professionals in the creative and cultural sectors.

This chapter will cover the development of a Masters level WBL programme within the Arts and how implementing the Middlesex WBL approach has created both challenges to the traditions of practice-based arts education and new opportunities for higher education to recognise and accredit practice based knowledge.

The underlying message within this chapter is that WBL can be a powerful tool for the development of emerging and experienced practitioners in the arts and worthy of consideration, provided curriculum developers are able to address the main disciplinary conventions that would otherwise find colleagues in teaching departments rejecting the approach. The key to developing WBL in a practice-based arts context is to engage the interest of the practitioner-teachers who populate the practice-based teaching departments. The major focus of this chapter is the consideration to how WBL relates to the conventions of practice-based arts education.

Masters Programme for Arts-based Practitioners

In 2000 the School of Arts at Middlesex University made the decision to use the generic Middlesex University WBL scheme to run a Masters programme for experienced professionals from a broad range of disciplinary areas across art and design. This programme became 'MA Professional Practice' ('MAPP'). It was thought that the main recruitment area for MAPP would be from the design disciplines, so the generic WBL structure was altered to include a major project module from the design group. The concern that colleagues in art and design might be resistant to the idea of explicitly addressing research methodologies resulted in the deletion of the WBL generic research methods module.

The programme was attractive to design professionals and recruited well both from home students and overseas, and built to an intake of around 25 students per year. The majority of applicants were in their forties with established and often complex careers encompassing disciplinary practice, management and teaching.

The quality of student work has been of a noticeably higher standard compared to that of postgraduate design students who have progressed directly from undergraduate study. Of our 14 latest finalists, four gained distinctions, six gained merits, and four gained ordinary passes. These excellent levels of achievement are not surprising considering that WBL students are experienced with well developed careers, giving them the opportunity to undertake significant projects drawing upon professional networks and senior positions within their disciplines. Some students undertook work of the highest importance, for example, drawing up national guidelines and working to influence government policy.

Following three years of running the programme, it was decided to make changes. Firstly, we decided to include a research methods module primarily to equip students with the research frameworks and planning tools that many practitioners lack and which are necessary for effective study at postgraduate level. It was clear from feedback from students and standards of research planning that a more explicit focus on research and project preparation was necessary. The effect of including research methods has been to enhance the coherency of research and has helped students to think through what it means to research into practice.

Secondly, we substituted the design project module with the generic WBL project module because the design project was not appropriate for the growing number of practitioners from performing arts, and the design project module allowed for a dissertation style output which was at odds with the WBL ethos of a project that provided a tangible and meaningful outcome 'in practice'. However, the benefit of using a subject specific module had been to give a clear comparison between WBL and more traditionally taught design postgraduates, and had built confidence from within art and design in the calibre of WBL students.

The emergence of MAPP and its WBL pedigree signalled a shift from the disciplinary, entry-level, undergraduate education that had dominated the practice-based arts school to the recognition of experiential, continuing education for established professionals. This values disciplinary skills at a high level of competency (expertise), and recognises the transdisciplinary skills and knowledge vital to a successful career in the arts.

Elitism and Access

The massification of higher education and its harnessing to provide for the needs of the economy are well documented in the literature (Scott, 1997, Henkel, 2000, Coffield and Williamson, 1997). A feature of this growth in student numbers has been a change in the character of the student population (Nicholls, 2001). This is seen by many as 'dumbing down' of standards. It may also be seen as a tension between maintaining disciplinary values and standards and greater access to higher education. Traditionally, arts based education has offered opportunities for young people who would not excel in a traditional academic setting, but who had other talents that might be developed. It is a well worn caricature that arts schools in the sixties and seventies were full of 'misfits' and 'creatives' and indeed they were exciting times. But 'who' received a place in art school was and arguably is still strongly controlled by practitioner-teachers. The argument here is that access to arts-based education has been, and is, limited to candidates who exhibit appropriate 'ability', 'talent' or 'fit'. Students are selected on a judgment as to their suitability and this judgment is made normally at interview, a portfolio of work, or demonstration of performance skills in the case of dance. It is clear that this places control in the hands of the practitioner-teachers to make judgments about the suitability of an applicant to their programme, and the potential of the programme to support the creative development of the applicant. Of course, the practitioner-teacher is well placed to make these judgements but the point is that authority resides with the practitioner-teacher and not the applicant. This exclusivity conflicts with the concurrent ethos in education through the latter end of the twentieth century where notions of equality and access have come to the fore (Morley, 1997).

WBL is not concerned with talent as a feature of practice but has been conceived as providing higher education opportunities to practitioners (Boud *et al*, 2001). WBL places value on the reflections of practitioners (Schön, 1983, Schön, 1976, Moon, 1999) and emphasises learning situated in a work or professional context (Lave and Wenger, 1991). These are primarily concerns that have emerged from within the field of education and the teacher researchers of the seventies and are not generally of significance to practitioner-teachers in arts-based higher education.

It would have been comforting and easy to have applied the same selective process to applicants to MAPP. However, the decision was made to value a non-selective admissions procedure. For MAPP this means any practitioner may come onto the programme. The only requirement is that applicants have a minimum of five years or equivalent professional full time professional experience upon which to base an APEL claim. While the programme attracts applications from highly regarded practitioners from across the disciplines, its underlying ethos is not to exclusively select these candidates.

Professional Practice

Professional practice is a theme that has emerged more recently in higher education, and is generally meant to define a set of values and competencies applicable in a work setting. Within practice-based arts education however, professional practice is most often interpreted as disciplinary skills practiced at a higher level of competency and artistry. The reputation of the practitioner, their contacts and networks, their portfolio of completed works or performances – these are the features of practice that are valued by practice-based arts education. This interpretation however, tends to pay little attention to the transdisciplinary skills and professional values that are foregrounded in WBL and evident in the literature on professionalism (Friedson, 2001). The transdisciplinary skills of leadership, management and communication and professional ethics are not central to practice-based arts education, yet interestingly, experienced practitioners themselves are drawn to the discourse on transdisciplinary skills and professional values as these are often expressed by experienced practitioners engaged in WBL:

> 'With regards to my freelancing career my investigations have had a profound impact on how I wish to be perceived as a professional designer, or more so heightened and reiterated my need to remain aware of issues of professionalism and how these issues will affect the outcomes and success of my ventures' (MAPP student feedback)'.

The meeting of these disciplinary values and education values provides the opportunity to question and reconfigure both. Entry level, undergraduate training for practice clearly needs to place emphasis on the acquisition of disciplinary skills. It is upon these capabilities that emerging practitioners will be judged. However, WBL has a valuable role to play for the established practitioner where experience replaces training as the basis of meaningful knowledge and where 'how to do' knowledge is surpassed by a sense of the professional self (Barnett, 1994 , Barnett and Coate, 2005):

> 'While assembling my (APEL) claim, I could most evidently see how deep and interlaced are the interactions between my professional curriculum, personal history and the way I operate – my modus operandi' (MAPP student feedback).

Student Perspectives

The following three short statements from graduates of MAPP serve to illustrate the nature of WBL students and their reflections on WBL.

Graduate A – Graphic Design Lecturer and Freelance Graphic Designer (age 37)

'On entering the MA Professional Practice programme I was delivering

FE design courses and working as a freelance graphic designer. My primary reason for choosing the programme was to further my professional development as both a design practitioner and educator. The programme enabled me to develop my understanding of research methodologies; a skill that I am now able to utilise in facilitating the learning and research of my own students. Also, I now have a far deeper understanding and practical application of instructional theory and its relevant technologies. My study helped me to initiate positive change to my team's working practice, which, in turn, benefits my students. I have now progressed to teaching within higher education and I am currently writing our faculty's new graphic design degree course'.

Graduate B – Visual Arts Practitioner / Consultant (age 54)

'I entered the Professional Practice Programme after 24 years as an informally trained Visual Arts Practitioner. I chose a work based study course because it is designed in such a way that would allow me to continue with my work while at the same time gaining more skills through studying. The programme enhanced my ability to extrapolate and interrelate practice and theory as well as understanding how to balance my research approaches and context of the subject under study. It also greatly increased my ability to analyse my material and synthesise concepts. Two of my works of art grace covers of two internationally distributed books, namely; 'Woman Work and Domestic Virtue in Uganda' by Grace Bantebya Kyomuhendo and Marjorie Keniston McIntosh. 'Africa: A continent of Economic Opportunities' by David Fick. I have also designed a course for design students entitled; 'Batik as a resource for design solution'.

Graduate C – Senior Fashion Designer (age 30)

'I am a fashion designer in Hong Kong and have been working in the mass market for about nine years. WBL is quite a new way of studying for me when I first engaged into the programme. The course in Middlesex is a flexible, distance learning programme, with the option of campus based tutorials. I can study at my own pace anywhere in the world. WBL is a very structured and useful studying model. In the working context, what I have learnt are the methods on how to effectively turn my experience into learning and knowledge and how to work through problems encountered in work. These two things enable me to learn continuously even after the end of the programme'.

The Academic School Context

Anyone involved in curriculum development will understand the evolutions and convolutions any new programme must pass through to become a reality. Bringing a programme to validation is an act of will and a test of the developers' belief in the academic veracity of the proposed programme. With the development of MAPP this was complicated by its transdisciplinary features. As WBL did not emerge from a disciplinary interest, it therefore did not carry the support of colleagues from the disciplines. Conversely, its lack of specific disciplinary focus meant few paid it any attention on its journey to validation as it did not appear to challenge any particular disciplinary territory.

The lack of specific disciplinary focus did bring the major drawback in that the teaching team would not emerge naturally from within a discipline but would have to be drawn out of their disciplinary work and into a new interdisciplinary team. The way this was achieved was to engage the support of senior management of the School. The broad market potential of WBL and its ability to employ academics from across the School for their supervisory skills rather than their disciplinary knowledge made clear economic sense. With budgets severely strained throughout the nineties and into the new millennium, all university schools have looked for ways to exploit markets and to utilise existing staff more 'profitably'. MAPP needed highly experienced academics who would have the confidence to act as academic advisers for students from across the practice-based arts disciplines. The programme was able to negotiate a small work programme allowance from each academic group in the School. This development was highly significant. Firstly, it meant that the needs of developing professionals were not limited to disciplinary knowledge held by university departments. Experienced academics who were willing and able to understand WBL could provide meaningful and credible support to practitioners undertaking WBL. Secondly, the development placed together academics from a range of disciplines to act as staff tutors and coordinators for the development of MAPP within their academic groups from: design, cultural and media studies, film, and performing arts. These co-ordinators have spread the word and recruited individuals to act as academic advisers for projects within their disciplines.

The key to this growing network has been twofold. The engagement and support of senior management is essential. Developers need to understand and work with the budgetary and managerial tensions all schools and faculties are working with. Additionally, the developers themselves need to hold, and communicate a passion for WBL, and an understanding of its place in practice-based education in the arts.

Disciplinary Cultures in Practice-Based Arts Education and WBL

Universities exist in part to transmit culture. Disciplinary boundaries exist to distinguish between cultures of practice and provide way signs that guide practice (Becher and Trowler, 2001). The guidelines can be formally codified and exemplified within the chartered professions, or be formulated and transmitted through behaviours and values that are not codified but transmitted by example. Practice-based arts education is a clear example of the latter. This has two underscoring features.

Firstly, these disciplines lack a codified, convergent body of knowledge on which to base practice. Practice is a 'self-construct' rather than a set of explicit and convergent principles applied in practice. This approach is the powerhouse that drives the creativity, novelty and individuality of the United Kingdom creative sector. Through this process, teachers respond to students in terms of the acceptability of ideas to a set of ever changing, unwritten codes. Students are trained to engage in this process through group crits and peer assessment. Teaching and learning is formulated around this principle, in that, study through 'projects' and 'performances' are intended to help students to acquire both the creative technical skills and to develop a sense of what it is to be a practitioner. This is quite different from other forms of higher education (Madge and Weinberger, 1973).

Secondly, the nature of the creative and cultural sectors in the United Kingdom are not structured in the same way as are public industries (e.g. NHS) or manufacturing, service and business sectors. Students do not undertake their first degree with the type of certainties of progression routes to employment that this brings in other types of work (Guile, 2006). Practitioner teachers know this well, many of whom are teaching precisely because it offered the opportunity for regular paid work in an otherwise fickle world of practice. Teachers in art, design and performing arts departments transmit the nature of the practice contexts students will progress to, and therefore, transmit cultural insights about what it will be to be a practitioner. This is social knowledge, and plays a vital part in arts based undergraduate higher education.

The development of WBL in arts based higher education at Middlesex University has placed a strong emphasis on transdisciplinary knowledge including the capability to manage complex careers and contribute to their professional communities of practice through a major project. Feedback from graduates indicates that this feature of WBL is a powerful tool for practitioners to further develop practice based on a transformative reflection on experiences. Where higher education has traditionally provided entry level, pre-service training for practice, WBL enables practitioners to consolidate and attribute values to practice that undergraduate study can not because of the focus on acquiring practice-based skills. Therefore WBL and practice-based arts education share a common interest in the development of practice individually constructed by the practitioner. However, these interests are engaged with quite differently and have quite different meanings.

It is still an accepted norm that teachers in arts based disciplines are employed by reputation and often by recommendation of existing staff. Few have extensive experience of curriculum design, or theoretical models underpinning such designs. Many are effective teachers, or become so, but the rationale is to employ good practitioners who can provide appropriate levels of technical and creative skills, while acting as exemplars upon which students can model practice. As Jenkins *et al* (2003) predict, there is a significant and growing movement towards more explicit standards in teaching and an understanding of how curriculum is informed by research. This is being realised by HEFCE's 'research informed teaching' development funding that universities are now receiving. However, many practitioner-teachers have received this development either as an infringement on disciplinary culture (Becher and Trowler, 2001) or have ignored its implications. For the most part, teaching and learning continues to be based on practice-informed judgments and an informality of relationships between teaching and learning.

The entry of WBL into practice-based arts education has brought a curriculum structure designed for quite different purposes and with a different history (Osborne *et al* 1998). While there is not the scope here to go into detail, it is clear WBL has been driven firstly by a response to government policy to guide higher education to support the economic needs of the country (Boud *et al.*, 2001). Pedagogically, WBL in higher education has made the accreditation of experiential learning a prime tool for configuring knowledge imported into the university by students, rather than knowledge held and disseminated to students by practitioner teachers.

Theory, Practice and the Practitioner-Teacher

It will be common knowledge to anyone in practice-based arts education that there exists a range of responses to pedagogical models of teaching and learning, and the extent to which disciplines are understood as either theoretical constructs or as 'lived' experiences. Fine Art rightly can argue it most wholly systemises the theory and practice of fine art, and its underlying educational purpose is to get students to develop their own theoretical models of practice. Somewhere mid-stream are design based disciplines, which mostly seek to integrate appropriate theories (e.g. sustainable design). At the least integrated end of the spectrum of disciplines are crafts and fashion, where theory is explored through art history modules, which are seen and felt as separate to the core of the disciplines. Crafts and fashion respond to materials, techniques and the momentary fads of the market. This range of separation between theory and practice in practice-based arts education is challenging for anyone seeking to develop WBL and argue for the relevance of theories about practice. Its specific implication for developing WBL is the need to be aware of the level of integration between theory and practice within a particular discipline. If a teaching department is comfortable with the idea of modelling theoretical models of practice, they will be less likely to find the strong theoretical underpinning of WBL alien or challenging.

Practitioner-teachers unused to an explicit and theoretically modelled curriculum design find the idea of the formal curriculum design of WBL challenging. Teachers are training students for entry level creative work informed by technological and creative developments. Education theory and the curriculum concepts of WBL are an alien way of thinking about teaching and learning. The Accreditation of Prior Experiential Learning (APEL) and the shift of learning and teaching from a master student or atelier relationship to one of programme adviser in WBL is a difficult cultural jump to make and colleagues need support in making this transition.

The most significant challenge has been to help colleagues see that WBL is an epistemological scheme rather than a procedural scheme. Its procedures are there to make real the principles that underlie WBL (APEL as a mechanism to establish the student as the originator of knowledge rather than the academy; programme planning as a tool for making the curriculum responsive to the work based or professional needs of the student; the learning agreement as a contract that shifts control to a wider group of stakeholders; the work based project being meaningful in the work based or professional context as well as in the university).

Valuing Practice

At first glance, practice-based arts education and WBL both seem to value practice. However this apparent convergence is perhaps limited to an interest in practice rather than a shared methodological approach to conceptualising practice. How these two interests are pursued is really quite different. Practice-based arts education focuses on entry level preparation for practice where practitioner-teachers pass on the cultural signifiers through teaching and learning activities that are informal in nature and passed on through the generations. It is fundamentally transmissive in nature because its purpose is to provide entry level training for practitioners. The primary value of WBL is felt at postgraduate level, accrediting experiential learning and work based projects and giving due interest to employers, professional bodies and other stakeholders. It is fundamentally contractual in nature, where the programme is subject to negotiation between practitioner, the university and employer. Its purpose is to accredit existing practice and provide a means to pursue a significant practice related project.

The two models of practitioner education are clearly not mutually exclusive, and faculties could relate the two together to provide practitioners with the opportunity for lifelong education from entry level undergraduate training to continuing professional development. This offers a new and exciting opportunity and purpose for higher education, and might go someway to providing a greater lifelong relationship between higher education and the establishing practitioner. The challenge comes in seeking to make this link in a faculty context where many practitioner teachers draw their identities from their disciplinary practice rather than seeing themselves as educators in a broader sense (Becher and Trowler, 2001).

Conclusion

This chapter has focused on the development of WBL in practice-based arts education. In order to best portray the development of WBL for developers, the chapter has problematised the issues in relation to practice-based arts education and in particular the practitioner-teachers in the traditional practice-based departments. This is because the key to the development so far, and its future, is most strongly influenced by the level of integrity it is able to muster. This integrity needs to compete with disciplinary subcultures within a fragmented academic community (Barnett, 1988). This means influencing colleagues and management and establishing confidence in both the initiative and the individuals associated with it.

Being passionate yourself or finding those who have passion for supporting established professionals is a good start. Building collegiality and showing selected examples of good work can influence the practitioner-teachers. Management is impressed by WBL's cross disciplinary potential and its ability to 'soak up' work programmes. For Middlesex, it has brought a distinctiveness which all HEIs are increasingly seeking.

A Trojan horse has been wheeled out into an indifferent fortress. What emerges may well change the academy and this may be of passing interest to academics. The real goal however will be how it impacts on conceptions of practice. It is clear that practitioners are looking for postgraduate study in increasing numbers and they are seeking out programmes that recognise and accredit practice-based knowledge and characterise the practitioner not as 'learner' but 'researching professionals' (Bourner et al., 2000). Whether this builds sufficient momentum across enough institutions to contribute to the shaping of practitioner education is the question remains, as yet, unanswered.

References

Barnett, R. (1988) Limits to academic freedom. In Tight, M. (Ed.) *Academic freedom and responsibility*. Milton Keynes: Open University Press.

Barnett, R. (1994) *The limits of competence*, Buckingham Society for Research into Higher Education/Open University Press.

Barnett, R. & Coate, K. (2005) *Engaging the curriculum in higher education*, Maidenhead, SRHE and Open University Press.

Becher, T. & Trowler, P. (2001) *Academic tribes and territories*, Buckingham and Bristol, SRHE and Open University Press.

Boud, D., Solomon, N. & Symes, C. (2001) New practices for new times. In *Work-based learning: A new higher education?* Buckingham Society for Research into Higher Education/Open University Press.

Bourner, T., Bowden, R. & Laing, S. (2000) Professional doctorates: The development of researching professionals. In Bourner, T., Katz, T. & Watson, D. (Eds.) *New directions in professional education*. Buckingham, Society for Research in Higher Education/Open University Press.

Coffield, F. & Williamson, B. (1997) Repositioning higher education. In Coffield, F. & Williamson, B. (Eds.) *Repositioning higher education*. Buckingham, SRHE and Open University Press.

Friedson, E. S. (2001) *Professionalism, the third logic: On the practice of knowledge.*, Chicago: Polity Press.

Guile, D. (2006) Access, learning and development in the creative and cultural sectors: From 'creative apprenticeship' to 'being apprenticed'. *Journal of education and work*, 19, 433–453.

Henkel, M. (2000) *Academic identities and policy change in higher education*, London: JKP.

Jenkins, A. Breen, R. & Lindsay, R. (2003) *Teaching in Higher Education: Linking Teaching with Research* London: Kogan Page.

Lave, J. & Wenger, E. (1991) *Situated learning: Legitimate peripheral participation*, Cambridge: Cambridge University Press.

Madge, C. & Weinberger, B. (1973) *Art students observed*, London: Faber and Faber.

Moon, J. A. (1999) *Reflection in learning & professional development*, London: Kogan Page.

Morley, L. (1997) Change and equity in higher education. *British Journal of Sociology of Education*, 18, 229–240.

Nicholls, G. (2001) *Professional development in higher education*, London: Kogan Page.

Osborne, C. Davies, J. and Garnett, J. (1998) Guiding the student to the centre of the stakeholder curriculum. Independent and work-based learning at Middlesex University In Stephenson, R. and Yorke, M. (Eds.) *Capability and Quality in Higher Education*. London: Kogan Page.

Schön, D. (1976) *Educating the reflective practitioner*, London: Jossey-Bass.

Schön, D. (1983) *The reflective practitioner*, New York: Basic Books.

Scott, P. (1997) The crisis of knowledge & the massification of higher education. In Barnett, R. & Griffin, A. (Eds.) *The end of knowledge in higher education.*

3

Middlesex University Business School: Returning to Vocational 'Routes'

Peter Critten

***

Introduction

Middlesex University Business School provides management education to around 5,500 undergraduate and postgraduate full and part-time students who can study a range of business disciplines: Marketing, Business and Management, Human Resource Management, Accounting and Finance, Law, Economics and Maths and Statistics. A high proportion of our students come from abroad from over 120 countries.

Middlesex has always had a strong vocational orientation and was the first Polytechnic Business School to offer an MBA, that is a multi disciplinary approach which involved the application of academic knowledge to the world of work with the aim of improving performance at the place of work. At the undergraduate level, work placements have been a compulsory element of our BA in Business Studies for many years, as they were for our BA in European Business. Students on the latter programme were able to take advantage of its exchange element, thereby gaining work experience in a European country other than the one in which they were born.

As a result of this work, we were one of the first HEIs to receive an Enterprise in Higher Education Award from the then Department of Education in 1989. This encouraged a number of further innovations which linked learning to the world of employment. One involved a small business start up simulation for first year students; another engaged second year students as consulting teams to a range of public, private and voluntary organisations (Frame, 1992). In both instances, the content and process utilised the world of work as a source of inspiration. Thus students worked in teams; activity based workshops replaced lectures and workshops, and oral presentations and peer assessment replaced three hour unseen examination.

The Business School has enjoyed a long relationship with a range of professional bodies such as Chartered Institute of Personnel and Development, Chartered Institute of Management, Chartered Marketing Institute, Institute Direct Marketing, Association of Chartered and Certified Accountants, Chartered Institute of Management Accountants, and Association of MBA and it considers such accreditation as an essential independent quality check and kite mark.

The overall mission of our programmes is to develop professionals who can manage ethically, sensitively and holistically in a range of organisations in an increasingly global and rapidly changing environment. Our aim is for the students to experience a wide range of learning, teaching and assessment methods. Students come from public, private and voluntary sectors and from the professions and from diverse national and cultural backgrounds.

The Business School has a track record of working in partnership with public and private organisations in designing and delivering tailored management and organisational learning development programmes. Companies in the private sector include Ford, Chesterton, Bovis, Lloyds TSB Asset Finance Division and Hewlett Packard. Organisations in the public domain include London Boroughs of Brent, Islington, Newham and Hackney. It has also validated two postgraduate programmes at Ashridge: The MBA and the Ashridge Masters in Organisational Consultancy. The university provides link tutors for both programmes.

Overall Ethos for Work Based Learning

Given its strong links with business, industry and professional bodies, the Business School would seem to be well positioned for WBL. For many years it has offered undergraduate students the facilities of an industry placement in the year before their final year. Three months into the placement they have to submit what is called a 'Learning Objectives Profile' in which they position themselves in their working context and identify learning objectives to be met over the course of the placement which the employer has to sign to signify their agreement as well as committing themselves to supporting a programme of development. At the end of their placement they have a choice of undertaking a work based project on their experience which is presented as a business report describing aims and objectives, methods by which they collected data in support of their aims and the outcome. Alternatively based on their initial 'Learning Objectives Profile', they can carry out an indepth reflection on their experience and learning from the placement, drawing on the same kind of methods described by Frame (Chapter 6).

A range of modules has also been designed aimed at developing the kind of skills required by employers, for example, presentation, communication and interpersonal skills. These modules are not subject specific and have been designated as 'Middlesex Business Studies'(MBS) modules. One particular module gives students opportunities to undertake a consultancy project in a local organisation and as a team present their findings. Another example of an MBS module is described by Frame (Chapter 6) who influenced the development of these modules back in the

1990s when, as now, (DfES 2006) FE and HE were being asked to address the issue of 'enterprise'. All of these programmes are examples of WBL but it has been only comparatively recently (2005) that the Business School, following the example of the NCWBLP, has decided to offer a whole range of modules that allow programmes to be created and accredited for all levels from foundation degree to a Doctorate in all aspects of Business and Management practice. These provide new opportunities for students to work through a systematic cycle of reviewing past learning and gaining accreditation, carrying out research in a work context leading to a WBL project. The keyword for the Business School is 'Practice' which is why all our WBL qualifications are to do in some way with Business 'Practice', such as in the Postgraduate Certificate in Marketing Practice (WBL) or MA in Leadership and Management Practice (WBL).

This chapter reviews the background out of which this approach has developed and gives examples of current practice and future opportunities.

Espoused theory and challenges

The 'Theory/ Practice' divide
Despite the market for practical 'business skills' the focus has tended to be on academic disciplines such as Marketing, Human Resource Management (HRM), Economics etc; each of which is led by subject driven theories and knowledge and often assessed by the traditional 'examination'. As previously indicated the Business School prides itself in offering a range of assessment methods so that both individual and group course work around case studies and/or practical applications, provide students with opportunities for reflection on practice. The challenge and opportunity is to reframe a mindset that practical skills are 'vocational' and therefore have a secondary place within an 'academic' institution into a mindset that recognises the wealth of knowledge that underpins good practice. Use of assessment methods as discussed in Chapter 16 can provide opportunities for students to obtain such practice and learn from it as well as encourage those in employment to use their practice to gain academic credit.

Academic requirements prescribed by Professional bodies
Professional bodies inevitably have had a big impact on the kind of subjects taught in disciplines like Law, HR, Marketing and Accountancy, for example. The traditional way students are expected to demonstrate their 'knowledge' of subjects dictated by the professions is usually by examination. However professions like the Chartered Institute of Personnel and Development (CIPD) are now becoming more flexible and are recognising the value of learning from experience for managers with five or more years practice as an HR professional. They offer 'Professional Assessment of Competence' (PAC) which, their website says 'will

recognise your existing experience, skills and competences and fit alongside your busy work schedule providing you with a seamless route to becoming a chartered member of the CIPD' (www.cipd.co.uk).

Recruitment of new tutors for their 'research' capability in preference to practical experience

WBL provides the scope for a wide range of approaches to research for the 'practitioner researcher', which in the Business School was initially an 'action research' approach; an underpinning premise of which is to encourage improvement in collaborative practice. It is hoped that more experienced professional practitioners will be encouraged to join HE using their practice as an opportunity both to develop themselves and others as well as build up core knowledge that will impact on their profession. This would apply to tutors and students alike. In particular the Doctorate in Professional Practice started with an action research approach, although later diversified, but has a key role to play here in making academic study more accessible and attractive to those working and also pursuing a Doctorate level of study in the workplace.

Improving Professional Practice

Examples of how the Business School uses a combinations of WBL modules to meet the needs of different professional groups.

Example 1:

Supporting professional accreditation in the 'Recruitment and Employment Confederation' industry

This £26 billion private recruitment industry is one of the fastest growing sectors today. Critical to its success is the development of its people. In collaboration with the Recruitment and Employment Confederation (REC) the Business School has designed a Foundation Degree in Recruitment Practice which combines taught modules with validated WBL modules.

In the beginning the students are introduced to the recruitment process and issues in employment (taught modules) as well as enabled to use WBL modules that help them review their existing learning (for which they can claim credit) and draw up a plan for a project. They then complete further projects which test their analytical and evaluative approach to issues within the workplace. This leads to the level of the foundation award after which they are eligible to progress to the final year of a BA(Hons) in Recruitment Practice where they are introduced to research methods which prepares them to undertake their final WBL project.

Those working in the Recruitment Industry who can draw on years of experience can also use combinations of modules to gain a university award in Recruitment Practice. In all cases they work through the same cycle of WBL modules leading to accreditation, research and planning of a project and the completion of a project at appropriate academic level.

The Director of Professional Development at the Recruitment and Employment Confederation, Judith Armatage sees this flexible way of blending taught and WBL modules as playing an important role in improving industry standards:

'The Recruitment and Employment Confederation has been working closely with Middlesex University Business School for the past two years. Their flexible and adaptable approach to learning in the work environment has resulted in a portfolio of relevant and realistic qualifications for recruiters and I am in no doubt of the benefit this has had on attracting, retaining and improving standards in the industry'

What are the lessons for the Business School? At one level the provision of a WBL route to accreditation as described above is a blueprint that any professional body can use to reward and accredit professional practice. The particular model for REC is a blended model of taught modules, provided by HR group and WBL. The same model may be used by other academic programmes in discussions with their respective professional bodies. Discussions are currently taking place with the Accounting and Finance group to look at how similar partnerships could be established with professional bodies in the fields of Accountancy and Finance. It is our belief that such 'partnerships' encourage flexibility, and that staff within the Business School, who might otherwise have favoured a more subject led syllabus, will be encouraged to explore alternative ways of engaging with and assessing their subject matter.

Example 2:

The Masters in Leadership and Management Practice (WBL) for senior managers in Lloyds TSB Asset Finance Division
Just over two years ago the Business School accredited an Action Learning leadership programme run by Value Projects Ltd (VPL) for senior managers in Asset Finance Division of Lloyds TSB. VPL, whose Chairman is Charles Margersion and is led operationally by Dr Richard Hale, specialise in running action learning leadership programmes. Tailor made to the needs of organisations the focus is on 'Action Learning Questions' (ALQs) each of which focuses on a particular leadership issue the manager wishes to address. The manager is helped to plan a project around the issue in question and gets support and challenge from colleagues in action learning sets facilitated by a member of VPL as well as workshops where all managers on the programme – 14 at the moment – are introduced to

31

various aspects of leadership run by VPL. The programme was designed to run over a period of eighteen months to cover eight ALQs, each of which is then written up and assessed against predetermined criteria.

The Business School assessed the programme against VPL's own assessment criteria which it considered to be at postgraduate HE Masters level and on the basis of content and learning methods employed agreed that the successful completion of each ALQ was equivalent to 15 credits at Masters level leading to a maximum award of 120 credits for the whole programme. In addition the Business School reached an agreement with VPL and Lloyds that 100 of the 120 credits could be used towards the newly validated MA in Leadership and Management Practice (WBL) requiring the managers to complete a combined 'Research and Planning Module' (20 credits) and a final WBL project (60 credits). Lloyds TSB Asset Finance Division gave each manager the opportunity to continue to complete the MA and all 14 managers have now taken up this opportunity.

This kind of partnership between outside provider of training/development, company and the university is seen as a model for recognising professional development particularly, as with the programme run by VPL, where the learning that is accredited is based around WBL principles. In fact the VPL programme of action learning questions facilitated through action learning sets prepared the students very well for our Masters award. The research methodology based around action research has a particular emphasis on 'Living Theory' (Whitehead and McNiff 2006). Action research, with its emphasis on collaboration to improve joint performance, was well suited to the kind of issues managers were having to address in Lloyds, and 'Living Theory' was particularly appropriate to the personal leadership issues each manager was having to wrestle with. Living Theory focuses on the beliefs and values of the individual in the context of achieving results in collaboration with others.

In line with previous emphasis on ALQ, each of the managers' dissertations focuses on an Action Research question. Examples include: 'How can I enable my team to create a coaching and performance culture?' and 'How can I improve my personal practice by becoming a more effective change agent?'

Bob Collingham, former Training Manager for Lloyds TSB Asset Finance Division has this to say about the future of such programmes:

'WBL, like this, we believe, prepares managers and leaders to deal with the relentlessly increasing pace of change far more effectively than taught programmes. In addition, the more traditional approaches to leadership development are less effective in developing the collaborative style of leadership that can deal effectively with increasingly complex and ambiguous challenges. We are delighted with the results so far which clearly show how both the managers themselves and the business have benefited'

What are the lessons for the Business School? The kind of model that applies to Lloyds TSB Asset Finance is being used, successfully, to attract other companies to such a partnership with the Business School. Additionally from our experience of working with a professional association like REC, as staff in the Business School work with managers from Lloyds and supervise their projects, they see new ways of working with existing students.

Working with companies in this way provides another pathway to be explored. This relates to our role not just accrediting WBL but helping the company as a whole articulate and recognise the human capital that is being added to its body of knowledge (Harrison and Jessel 2004). This is further explored in the last section when the opportunities for the future are considered.

Example 3:

The Doctorate in Professional Practice (DProf)
The opportunity for experienced professional practitioners to get recognition at Doctorate level for their achievements and learning that can benefit others has been available for over six years from NCWBLP. At the same time as the Business School validated its own framework for recognising WBL from foundation level to Masters it proposed a separate Doctorate pathway open to practitioners in the Management and Business world which had the Designation Doctorate in Professional Practice to emphasise the 'practitioner' theme that underpins its WBL pedagogy. The other distinguishing feature is the research methodology which embraces Action Research as Living Theory – see above. This is the view of one of the seven professional practitioners on our first cohort. Philip Squire is CEO of Consalia which provides consultancy services on Global Account Selling to companies worldwide:

> 'For me, the Middlesex programme combined a lot of things that felt right. One was that, unlike a more generic MBA type programme, the objective of the Middlesex programme was to examine ways of improving your own practice, and in that sense it made a huge amount of practical sense. Here you have the opportunity of reflecting on your own profession and in an academic sense, articulating what it is your 'learnings' have been. In the case of the doctorial project, looking for ways of helping your own profession to move onto a place that it's not at currently.
>
> It's had some surprising benefits ... this whole process of noticing, of

33

becoming more aware of what you do has been hugely beneficial for me, I think, at a number of levels. At a personal level it has given me further insights into what I do in my profession and it has, without question, helped in my personal development. I think outside of the personal development side, it has also helped through the networking opportunities that I've had, not just with academics, but also with other business colleagues who are going through a kind of similar process. So whilst it's been quite a challenge to do, it's also been hugely rewarding and inspirational'.

What lessons can the Business School Learn? At the heart of the DProf is bringing about change either to a profession or organisation. Working with professionals at the leading edge of their practice in Business, we have the opportunity of seeing new professions emerge with new underpinning knowledge that is likely to be transdisciplinary, (see Jabbar chapter 4). In the Business School where the traditional 'business' subjects of Marketing, Economics, HRM are taught there is opportunity to expand the curriculum to embrace new knowledge that is helping students bring into the light literally 'evidence' from their varied professional workplaces. For example a topic that Philip Squire is exploring in his DProf is 'Global Account Selling'. He is proposing it as the subject of a new discipline that the Business School might run as a validated programme. He notes that, as far as he can see, this is not offered anywhere as a postgraduate programme, but it could be run in partnership with Philip's company and would have at its heart 'living theory' and be 'grounded in the workplace using live data and enquiry with clients and co-workers at its heart'. How many more such subjects could be discovered? As programme leader of the DProf, a vision I had at the outset was that our DProf students would enter into a longer learning partnership with us whereby the output of their study would be an input to our professional development as well as theirs. At this level of learning the 'workplace' is a community of practitioner researchers which both student and Business School share and whose output allows both to improve their practice.

Future Developments

Technological support for WBL
One of the university's goals as a Centre of Excellence is to 'Extend access to and enhance effectiveness of WBL through the use of ICT'. We have used funds from HEFCE to achieve this by entering into a business arrangement with a supplier who specialises in creation of elearning portfolios and learning platforms to work with us in customising its software to the needs of our WBL students.

There are three levels of learning support we will be evaluating:

Firstly, support for the individual learner to collect evidence and codify for presentation in the form of an e-portfolio for assessment. This could be of particular use to placement students. Whilst learning from placements is by definition WBL, the link needs to be made more explicit so that the student is better equipped with a framework for learning from their placement, that can be translated into 'knowledge' that can be recognised and accredited leading to alternative pathways for study and development. It is hoped that provision of new e-portfolio facilities will facilitate this process.

For example, some programmes, such as the Masters in HRM, require students to complete a learning log to reflect on learning covering all modules on their programme in line with the CIPD focus on members becoming 'thinking performers'. While this is not assessed it is a prerequisite for successful completion of the programme. It also prepares students for CIPD membership. However, for many students the completion of such a document is a chore and, as it is not directly assessed it is seen as a peripheral rather than central activity.

With the introduction of user friendly ICT and in particular the facility of creating an e-portfolio it is hoped that the creation of a portfolio of learning will play a much more central role. There are two ways in which such an initiative can be seen to have an influential impact. First, the creation of an e-portfolio enables core knowledge to be created which can be easily assessed for use in assignments. Secondly, it provides a platform for lifelong learning and a readily available source for reflection and evidence of learning should the student want to go on to take higher level WBL qualifications.

The second level of support is for sharing of learning and knowledge within a community of practitioners. In the past, WBL has more often been associated with the accreditation of individual learning but it is the 'social context' of knowledge which will lead to knowledge creation. Wenger (1998) has popularised the concept of a 'community of practice' and shown how we come to know what we know through 'engagement' in a rich mix of social contexts. The current focus for ICT development is also within a social context although virtual, and the facilities of a 'learning platform' to link together groups of professionals and encourage them to share their learning by building a core body of knowledge and good practice. For example this could apply to tutors of work based learners ranging from the placement supervisor in industry to Business School staff advising students following a WBL pathway.

Finally, there is support to an organisation in codifying and disseminating learning and the creation of knowledge as evidence of its intellectual capital. This is a more ambitious target; to help an organisation capitalise on knowledge emerging out of the kinds of communities of practice described above. We are already working with our MA Students in Leadership and Management Development Practice to use ICT to pool the collective wisdom emerging out of their reflections on their individual practice so that it can inform future company policy making.

Link with CPD

The Business School runs a number of one-off programmes for companies and local authorities in a range of management and business areas. Some are accredited, some are not. Support by this kind of technology offers scope in the future to provide additional support facilities for individuals undertaking CPD to create e-portfolios for assessment. Equally there are opportunities for ensuring individuals undertaking a CPD programme can remain in contact with colleagues to create communities of practice both virtual and actual.

Promote links with business community and creation of learning partnerships

The kind of links we are establishing with companies like Lloyds TSB Asset Finance Division and local authorities will serve as a precedent for many more learning partnership agreements with organisations to support them to become 'learning organisations' and codify and disseminate the knowledge that emerges from increasing growth of local communities of practice. In our view this will encourage a more strategic use of WBL beyond individual accreditation towards adding value to an organisation's intellectual capital (Garnett, Comerford & Webb 2001).

Promote Links with Small Business Development

Finally, at the other end of the business spectrum we have close links with the university's Centre for Enterprise and Economic Development Research(CEEDR) who work with SMEs. They recognise the benefits of WBL for small businesses for whom the traditional programmes offered by Business Schools do not meet their specific needs. One example is in the area of 'strategic' decision making which for small businesses involves a more emergent and intuitive approach than that advocated in the standard text books. We will be cooperating with CEEDR to explore the creation of a package involving reflection on good practice in this area and the dissemination of such knowledge across a community of practitioners

Conclusions

The National Centre for WBL Partnerships has done much to demonstrate that WBL is academically respectable (chapter 1). Recognition for the whole University as a 'Centre for Excellence' requires all schools to demonstrate that WBL has an equal part to play alongside subject driven syllabi. The big opportunity for the Business School is to draw on its 'practitioner' credentials which played a key role in its success as a Polytechnic and subsequent achievements around supporting the enterprise driven initiatives as described, thereby building a future around providing students with a learning environment where practitioner skills and learning are recognised alongside academic learning. This is why students coming to the Business School now have an opportunity to study for a degree which recognises the subject (e.g. Masters in HRM) or the Practice; e.g. Masters HRM Practice (WBL) where the mode of study is recognised in the title.

By focusing on the central business discipline in our qualifications, e.g. HRM Practice, and putting WBL in brackets after the title, it might appear that for us WBL is at the 'mode' of study end of the WBL 'field to mode' continuum (chapter 1), but only one of the criteria characterising this end of the continuum is appropriate. This is the Award as a subject through WBL, because none of the other criteria apply. The criteria designated as 'field' of study, i.e. the workplace dictating the curriculum, and using the WBL assessment criteria, with the University as a knowledge catalyst and with work providing the knowledge, is most definitely perceived in the Business school as being 'Practice based'.

In conclusion, using WBL allows professional practitioners in the field of Business to reflect on and learn from their practice using the methodology and tools appropriate to WBL as a field of study but also recognising and giving expression to the professional context and community from within which the knowledge is emerging. So, for the Lloyds' students, having leadership at the heart of their practice and recognised in the title of their award reflects their professional learning. However, we do not see ourselves restricted by existing business disciplines, instead, as discussed, we expect to celebrate the creation of new disciplines and new bodies of knowledge.

References

DfES (2006) *FE Reform: Raising Skills, Improving Life Chances*

CIPD www.cipd.co.uk

Frame, P. 1992 'Students as Consultants: Proceedings of the International Colloquium on the Pedagogy of Decision-Making', pages 231–242, Nancy University Press, Nancy University, France

Garnett, Comerford & Webb (2001) Working with partners to promote intellectual capital in Boud D & Solomon N (2001) *Work Based Learning: A New Higher Education?* SRHE & OUP

Harrison R & Jessels J (2004) *Human Resource Development in a Knowledge Economy – an Organisational View* Palgrave Macmillan

Wenger E (1998) *Communities of Practice – Identity Learning and Meaning* Cambridge: Cambridge University Press

Whitehead J & McNiff J (2006) *Action Research – Living Theory* London: Sage

4

Work Based Learning in the School of Computing Science

Muthana Jabbar

***

Introduction

The global economy has witnessed a major transformation from one that is essentially concerned with and structured by wealth creation from the production of industrial artefacts to a post-industrial era in which the concept of wealth creation is associated with knowledge and learning. This transformation led to the emergence of life long learning as a philosophy, process and methodology essential for satisfying and maintaining economic viability and augmentation. The roots of this ideology can be traced to the recognition that the growth of advanced technological know-how in wealth creation should correspond to the development of an appropriately skilled workforce so as to engender a competitive advantage in developing and sustaining global markets.

The work place affords demands and significant opportunities for learning. Often this learning process takes place consequentially in the course of other activities; however, it can accumulate over time into a substantial body of tacit knowledge, know-how and skills. Prominently work based learning(WBL) is performance or task related, problem based, can be self-managed, often requires effective co-operation between people, is usually concerned with the constant upgrading and updating of skills, and, more often than not, is centred on new techniques or approaches.

This kind of problem focused learning at work differs from most mainstream university campus based programmes, many of which tend to be based on fields of knowledge or subjects, and are designed and delivered by scholars for students. Moreover, it is in contrast with the conventional learning sequence in academic institutions, whereby, typically, the underlying and governing concepts and theories are introduced first followed by their interpretation and manifestation in processes and applications.

Computing science as a profession plays an integral role in the process of wealth creation through the advance and production of hardware and software as end products, and through developing and managing the requisite infrastructures to support the different economic entities (e.g. service and manufacturing industries) via, for example, communications, multimedia and business information systems. Hence, the diversity of roles extends over a broad body of explicit knowledge. The experience gained from involvement in work based undertakings combined with the discipline specific scholarly knowledge enables the computer science professional to develop transdisciplinary tacit knowledge skills that are necessary for the contemporary knowledge dependent economy.

The proliferation of the Internet and the advent of the WorldWideWeb, eBusiness and related systems, and multimedia applications and integration has caused a paradigm shift in computing science. From a domain that is predominantly structured and informed by mathematics, physics and electronics to a transdisciplinary field that is affected and influenced by other fields, such as business, arts, design, humanities and social sciences. This paradigmatic change heightens the importance of the tacit knowledge and expertise accumulated at the workplace, which can be related to an academic level descriptor framework, and thus lends itself to APL.

The Computer Science Field

Computer science has changed dramatically over the last two decades in ways that have a profound effect on programme design and pedagogy. Moreover, the scope of what is referred to as computing has broadened to the point that it is difficult to define it as a single discipline. In the past scholarly attempts were made to combine computer science, computer engineering, and software engineering into a single autonomous academic discipline. While such an approach may have seemed reasonable ten years ago, there is no question that computing science in the twenty first century is informed, influenced and structured by a diversity of disciplines with their own principles and pedagogical traditions. In this respect computing science has become both a multidisciplinary and transdisciplinary field in concept and application.

The Council of Professors and Heads of Computing (CPHC) benchmarking document describes computing as 'the discipline associated with the structuring and organisation of information'. This broad description of the field outlines the defining principles of computing and, hence, assigns a varied range of facets that includes inter alia:

- Theoretical concerns, the purpose of which is to ensure a sound logical basis for the discipline; complexity issues which address feasibility and efficiency issues

- The concept of the algorithm, a logical step-by step procedure for solving a mathematical problem in a finite number of steps, often involving repetition of the same basic operation

- Distributed systems and pervasive computing including mobile computing systems

- Issue related to human computer interface (HCI), incorporating matters such as multimedia and usability in its broadest sense

- Information systems with its focus on problem identification and organisational issues, the purpose of which is to address the integration of processes, people and technology in contributing to effectiveness and efficiency within organisations. This encompasses technical, societal and technology management acceptance dimensions.

- Computer engineering, which includes the design and development of computers to serve a range of different purposes and the special needs of diverse environments, as well as embedded and real time systems whose operation may have safety or security implications

- Artificial intelligence (AI), which takes a holistic perspective in the development of computing systems, and includes computer science, neuroscience, philosophy, psychology, robotics, and linguistics, and is devoted to the reproduction of the methods or results of human reasoning and brain activity systems

- Professional, legal and ethical concerns as computing combines the traits and ethos of the scholar with that of the professional

As such, computer science draws its foundations from a wide variety of disciplines and computing is a broad field that extends well beyond the boundaries of computer science.

Computer Science: The professional context

A central disciplinary focus is on processes for handling and manipulating information. In this sense, the discipline covers both advancing the primary understanding of algorithms and information processes in general in addition to the practical design of efficient and reliable software and hardware to meet particular specifications.

Computer science spans theoretical studies, experimental methods, and engineering design all in a single disciplinary boundary. This differs radically from most physical sciences where the understanding and advancement of the science is distinctive from the applications of the science in fields of engineering design and implementation.

In computer science there is an inherent merger of the theoretical concepts of computability and algorithmic efficiency with the modern practical advancements in electronics that continue to inspire development in the discipline. It is this close interaction of the theoretical and design aspects of the field that fuse them together into a single discipline.

Hence, professionalism in computer science necessitates a sound base in the crucial areas, with a comprehensive knowledge in one or more of the other areas of the discipline. This entails that professionals should be able to apply the fundamental concepts and techniques of computation, algorithms, and computer design to a specific design problem. The function includes particularising of specifications, analysis of the problem, and provides a design that functions as expected, has satisfactory performance, is reliable and maintainable, and meets desired cost-effective criteria. Consequently, a computer science professional insight should transcend the scientific and technical to include liberal studies as a basis for understanding the societal implications of the task being executed. This shift to transdisciplinarity has consequential implications to the workplace as it shapes and constructs the accumulation of tacit knowledge and its application, and therefore to the WBL premise.

Disciplinary Transformation

Computer science is an evolving field. From its inception just half a century ago, computing has become the defining technology of the contemporary world. Computers and computer systems are central to modern society and are the primary vehicle behind much of the modern day economic growth. Moreover, the field continues to advance at a fast pace. New technologies are introduced continually, and existing ones become obsolete almost as soon as they appear.

Computer networks and the Internet have become the underpinning for much of the global economy. They have become critical foundations of computer science, and it is impossible to imagine that academic programmes would not devote significantly more time to this topic. At the same time, the existence of the web has changed the nature of the educational process itself. Modern networking technology enhances the ability to communicate and gives people throughout the world unprecedented access to information. Networking technology has become an essential pedagogical tool not only in computer science academic programmes, but in other fields such as business and commerce.

This rapid development of the discipline has a profound effect on computer science education, affecting both content and pedagogy.

Technological changes

Most of the change that affects computer science emanates from advances in electronics and telecommunication technology. Moreover, such advances are part of an ongoing evolutionary process that has continued for many years. Moore's Law – the 1965 prediction by Intel founder Gordon Moore that microprocessor chip density would double every eighteen months – continues to hold true. As a result, we have witnessed an evolutionary exponential increase in available computing power that has made it possible to solve problems that would have been out of reach just a few years ago. Other changes in the discipline, such as the rapid growth of networking following the emergence of the World Wide Web, are more remarkable, suggesting that change also occurs in a revolutionary manner.

Both evolutionary and revolutionary change affects the body of knowledge required for computer science and the related educational process.

Technical advances over the past decade have increased the importance of many curricular topics, such as:

- The World Wide Web and its applications
- Networking technologies, particularly those based on TCP/IP
- Graphics and multimedia
- Embedded systems
- Relational databases
- Interoperability
- Object oriented programming
- The use of sophisticated application programmer interfaces (APIs)
- Human computer interaction
- Software safety
- Security and cryptography

The diversity of the topics adds complexity to the ways in which *'practitioners'* acquire and apply knowledge and skills in the workplace and, thus to the WBL process.

Cultural changes

Computing education is also affected by changes in the cultural and sociological context in which it occurs. The following changes, for example, have all had an influence on the nature of the educational process:

- **Changes in pedagogy enabled by new technologies:** The technical changes that have driven the recent expansion of computing have direct implications for the culture of education. Computer networks, for example, make distance learning much more feasible, leading to enormous growth in this area. Networking also makes it much easier to share curricular resources among widely distributed institutions. Technology also affects the nature of pedagogy; simulation software, computer projection, and virtual laboratory stations have made a significant difference in the way computer science is taught.

- **The dramatic growth of computing throughout the world:** Computing has expanded enormously over the last decade. For example, at the beginning of the 1990s, very few households, including the US were connected to the Internet. However, a US Department of Commerce study shown that by 1999 over a third of all Americans had Internet access from some location. Similar growth patterns have also occurred in most other developed countries. The explosion in the access to computing brings with it many changes that affect education, including a general increase in the familiarity of students with computing and its applications along with a widening gap between the skill levels of those who have access and those who do not.

- **The growing economic influence of computing technology:** The dramatic enthusiasm surrounding high-tech industry, as evidenced by miniaturisation and the Internet proliferation, has significant effects on education and its available resources. The enormous demand for computing expertise across the economic spectrum has attracted many more students to the field, including some who have little intrinsic interest in the material. This paradigm shift makes WBL more attractive to CS as it significantly broadens and diversifies the learner population.

Computing Science (CS): The strategic response to WBL

Background

The rapid shifts in knowledge mean that institutions of higher learning should respond to adults who need continuing access to the latest developments in their areas, yet cannot leave their careers to study full time. Responding to these professionals will be an important role for CS.

The provision of access to learner focused and work related programmes not only offers flexibility in choice but, equally importantly, targets a decisive segment in the market, that is, mature students who historically constituted a significant proportion of the student intake. The school has been actively engaged in developing and delivering programmes that are geared to take higher, professional and vocational education into the workplace. At CS the diversification from conventional, native-oriented to customer responsive modes of delivery is effected via validating and franchising modules as well as undergraduate and postgraduate programmes (to partners in South East Asia and the Middle East for example) and by extending short inhouse professional qualifications by drawing on the 'Cisco' Local Academy, 'Microsoft' Certification in addition to the Foundation in Project Management (PRINCE2).

The shaping of the WBL rationale

To develop and formulate a response to WBL requisites, the opportunities it could afford and the required underpinning it is necessary to consider the aims and remit of CEWBL, which can be summarised by the following:

- Extending WBL to all Middlesex University Schools
- Embedding elements of WBL excellent practice within other university programmes
- Developing excellent pedagogical research

43

- Extending access and enhancing effectiveness through the use of information and communication technologies (ICT)
- Producing excellent teaching and learning resources
- Enhancing the expertise of the university staff in recognising, facilitating and assessing the use of transdisciplinary knowledge generated by APEL and real life work based projects
- Supporting knowledge creating partnerships between the university and external departments

1. Extending WBL to Computing Science

CS is considering a range of modules and programmes, which are appropriate to the needs and requirements of the workplace. These could be drawn from the existing pool in the three academic groups (computer communications, business information systems, computing and multimedia), deliberating the development and validation of a new range or a combination of both. These could include foundation, undergraduate and postgraduate (e.g. MProf and DProf). The MProf is of particular interest as it draws on the accumulated experience in delivering a number of Master's programmes via conventional and distance learning modalities. Parallel to this would be the creation of the necessary maintaining infrastructure in terms of academic and administrative staff to accredit and support the WBL initiatives.

2. Embedding elements of WBL excellent practice within other university programmes

This pivots on reflective practice, accreditation of prior experiential learning (APEL) and assessing work based projects. It entails assembling a pool of staff to access and accredit evidence of prior experiential and work based learning and develop CS related 'best practice'.

Reflective practice is an important premise of the embedding process via the promotion of autonomous learning that aims to develop students' understanding and critical thinking skills. Self and peer assessment, problem based learning, personal development planning and group work are typically used to support a reflective scheme. In this connection, CS related experience in both conventional and elearning modes of module and programme delivery is valuable.

The terms 'best practice' and 'lessons learned' are often used transposably. Lessons learned are usually best approaches and practices that have not been evaluated as rigorously as best practices, but that still offer ideas about what works best in a given situation. CS best practice approaches include, inter alia, active learning strategies, group discussion triggers, co-operative group assignments, reflective responses to learner contribution, rewarding learner participation and fostering learner responsibility

Although the supervision of undergraduate and postgraduate projects related to the workplace is already a common practice, such projects are presently exclusively assessed against module learning outcomes. These projects include, for example, the design and application of corporate network systems, multimedia applications and industrial databases. Diversifying into work related undertakings would require taking into account the level descriptors used by WBL.

3. Developing excellent pedagogical research

There is often a misleading dichotomy between 'traditional' and 'nontraditional' teaching and learning. Both have significant advantages and both have significant limitations. For most learners the issue is not 'how to learn?' but 'how motivating is the learning?'. Having a range of learning experiences – some online, some face to face, some tutor led and some independent – goes a long way to providing a stimulating and motivating learning environment.

CS has a heritage of conventional and non-conventional good practice approaches to pedagogy; the latter is exemplified by elearning via the Global Campus (GC). Such approaches constitute the requisite for WBL; this needs to be further explored and customised to address the requirements of the workplace.

A pivotal pedagogical premise in the WBL theme is 'practitioner research'. It has become a widely discussed issue in educational scholarship, and comes in a number of hybrid forms – local inquiry, industry focused research, action learning, problem based inquiry, etc. – but its predominant and most recognisable form is that of action research.

4. Extending access and enhancing effectiveness through the use of ICT

This is a determining factor in broadening the student capture area and would, therefore, need to be further exploited by utilising the tested GC facility and extending it to include other alternative ICT methodologies. 'Blended learning' is one such mode; it combines the best of traditional methods of learning and teaching with materials delivered via new media such as the Internet. Blended learning means that modules and programmes can be tailored much more precisely to the needs of individual participants on a particular course. This would require the development of a range of elearning programmes that allows CS to offer blended learning packages that meet workplace' needs and provide excellent value for money. One such programme could be a 'Virtual Learning Resource Centre (VLRC)', which provides a flexible just-in-time learner support that can be accessed via the web, thus making blended learning possible and accessible for customers whose network infrastructure is not adequate.

A major facet of the VLRC would be the provision of supporting learning material and guidelines that give work based students a prompt and concise overview of a programme, together with links to related articles and readings.

5. Producing excellent teaching and learning resources

This constitutes the core and essence of academic endeavours and what all academics seek and pursue. The changing economics of higher education require an ongoing innovative process in curriculum development, the provision of outcomes that satisfy customers and job markets. WBL and the diversification to practitioner based learning and research is an important ideology and vehicle in such an environment and, hence, needs to be adequately embraced and integrated into the learning resources that we develop for our modules and programmes. This is a necessary step for the provision of the required competencies for a new generation of work based, predominantly part time learners for whom ICT is a service provider and a learning tool; according to UCAS statistics this segment constitutes 40% of applicants to higher education.

6. Enhancing the expertise of the university staff in recognising, facilitating and assessing the use of transdisciplinary knowledge generated by APEL and real life work based projects

Experiential education is the process of actively engaging students in hands on experience that will have benefits and consequences. Students make discoveries and experiment with knowledge themselves instead of hearing or reading about the experiences of others. Students also reflect on their experiences, thus developing additional skills, new attitudes and alternative ways of thinking.

WBL is primarily about learning through direct experience, by action and reflection. This differs from traditional education where teachers begin by setting knowledge, including analysis and synthesis, beforehand with the object that students will later find ways to apply it in action. Moreover, WBL is associated with 'transdisciplinarity', which refers to development and application of a shared integrative conceptual framework based on non discipline specific theories, concepts, and methods. This constitutes a central approach change in that it is practice rather than subject based, and therefore, prescribes a different way of treating academic content through the combination of action and reflection. Consequently, transdisciplinarity would require a view across subject disciplines from a 'practice' perspective.

7. Supporting knowledge creating partnerships between the university and external departments

Competing in the contemporary global knowledge based economy involves extensive collaborations and partnership with other institutions of higher education, business, industry and international organisations that will respond to mutual needs in knowledge creation, transmission and application and to allow knowledge to flow freely to and from other sectors of the society. WBL frameworks can support these initiatives.

The School is endowed with a history of collaborative undertakings, and in fact many of the University's overseas initiatives were pioneered by CS. These include articulation, validation and franchising, and would be the foundation for accrediting practitioner based learning. The diversification of these partnerships would include consultancy and accreditation of practitioner based learning, and meshed with the school business development plans and its objectives, thus creating a strong framework that supports the use of WBL in CS programmes.

Computing Science contribution to the European Union design for all (DfA) project

The School is engaged in the 'FP6 funded collaborative action – DFA@eInclusion' project. This is an EU, elearning project for those with special needs, including those in the workplace; it covers eInclusion and Design for All (DfA) training across the EU and lends itself to WBL. It has 23 partners across the EU. The project start date was 1 January 2007 and the end date is 31 December 2009. CS at Middlesex is leading work package six on Training Activities. This work package will produce guidelines to implement DfA courses for a wide range of stakeholders, for example, designers, business executives, user groups, undergraduates (modules) and post graduates (MSc degree level) at the following four levels:

Table 4.1

LEVEL OF TRAINING	DESCRIPTION OF DfA TRAINING
Vocational e.g. person trained to ECDL level.	Design for All training at this level should consist of training in the use and setting up of accessible ICT products.
Undergraduate	Design for All training at this level should enable the student to appreciate the diversity of computer users, how their needs can be met and the legal basis of DfA in Europe.
Professional and Higher Degree Level e.g. European MSc in DfA.	Design for All training at this level should enable the student to demonstrate a commitment to incorporate Design for All into their daily work practice in addition to the knowledge and skills demonstrated at the lower levels.
Educator	Design for All training should enable the educator to teach Design for All using Design for All methods. This level will include support for cross disciplinary teaching

Table 4.2

PARTNER	TYPE OF LINK	LOCATION	PROGRAMMES
Ho Chi Minh City University of Technology [HCMUT]	Franchised partnership	Ho Chi Minh City – Vietnam	1. BSc Business Information Systems 2. MSc Business Information Technology
Hong Kong University of Science and Technology (HKUST) – College of Lifelong Learning (CL3)	Franchised Partnership	Hong Kong	1. BSc Business Information Systems – Global Campus 2. Certificate of Higher Education – Business Information Systems 3. BSc Business Informational Systems – Final Year
Intercollege [IGI]	Franchised Partnership	Cyprus	1. MSc Business Information Technology – Global Campus
Ningbo University [NIN]	Franchised Partnership	Zhejiang – People Republic of China	1. BSc Honours Business Information Systems – Global Campus 2. MSc Business Information Technology – Global Campus
October University for Modern Sciences and Arts (MSA)	Validated Partnership	Egypt	1. BSc Honours Computer Science 2. BSc Honours Computer Science (Software Engineering)
The Regional Information Technology Institution (RITI)	Franchised Partnership	Egypt	1. MSc Business Information Technology – Global Campus 2. MSc Electronic Commerce – Global Campus 3. MSc Computer Networks Management
The Regional Information Technology and Software Engineering Center	(RITSEC) Franchised Partnership	Egypt	1. Web Development for MSc Electronic Commerce
The Research Institute of Tsinghua University in Shenzhen (RITS)	Franchised Partnership	Guangdong Zhuhai – People Republic of China	1. RITS English Programme 2. BSc Business Information Systems 3. Joint Honours Programme BSc Information Technology (ITX) and/with Business Information Systems (BIS) 4. MSc Business Information Technology – Global Campus
The University of Hong Kong – School of Professional and Continuing Education (SPACE) [HKS]	Franchised Partnership	Hong Kong	1. MSc Business Information Technology – Global Campus 2. MSc Electronic Commerce – Global Campus 3. BSc Computer Networks

PARTNER	TYPE OF LINK	LOCATION	PROGRAMMES
The University of Hong Kong – School of Professional and Continuing Education (SPACE – Shanghai) [HKH]	Franchised Partnership	Shanghai – China	1. MSc Business Information Technology – Global Campus
Singapore Polytechnic Graduates Guild (SPGG)	Franchised Partnership	Republic of Singapore	1. MSc Business Information Technology – Global Campus 2. MSc Electronic Commerce – Global Campus
Middlesex University Dubai	Subsidiary	Dubai - United Arab Emirates	1. BSc Business Information Systems 2. BSc Computing Science 3. BSc Joint Honours Business Information Systems 4. BSc Joint Honours Information Technology

The proposed WBL MSc programme in computing

The rationale

Computing science as a discipline is related to the structuring, organisation and processing of information. In the contemporary digital global economy, information is both critical and decisive in corporate competitiveness, success and development. The programme will be designed and structured to provide a flexible, student-centered conduit to postgraduate learning for professionals and those in the workplace who aspire to advance their qualifications and career in the computing industries.

The programme seeks to recognise and accredit prior attainments and accumulated experience, and to provide opportunities for further directed learning through a major research project that originates from and closely relates to the workplace.

Computing science: the central learning philosophy

The learning process in computing science is typically characterised by:

- Knowledge and understanding of features of computer systems and their use
- The close integration of theories, concepts and practices
- Emphasis on applications and fitness for use
- The significance of specification, design, implementation, quality and maintenance as determining facets
- An understanding of related professional, social and ethical issues

The aims of the programme

The programme aims to:

- Offer a student centred learning provision
- Provide opportunities for students and employers to develop, together, research projects on subjects of their own choosing that are relevant to their professional and work requisites
- Provide Masters level study that recognises and accredits learning achieved through work experience
- Widens access and builds partnerships with employers and organisations which utilise accredited learning
- Develop transferable learning skills necessary for the workplace, including:

  o   research and analytical skills
  o   use of initiatives and personal responsibility
  o   decision making in complex situations
  o   independent learning ability essential for continuing professional development

Conclusion

In reviewing the above CEWBL targets vis-à-vis the possibilities they extend, individually and collectively to CS and what foundation already exists it is obvious that the school has in operation structures that reflect the kind of educational systems CEWBL is endeavouring to advance. What is, however, required is a scheme that integrates WBL with conventional approaches, utilises 'practice based learning' and related research in the design of modules as well as CPD, and ultimately disseminates the accumulated know-how.

The generic WBL Masters programme that is currently being developed would be attractive to professionals who would utilise their accumulated workplace experience for academic accreditation, and specialise via a supervised research project in different pathways, such as computer communications and networks, business information systems and multimedia technology. There is already quite an interest from our overseas collaborative and franchised partners as the majority of their student intakes are in employment.

The promulgation of the cyber net, the World Wide Web, online business and commerce and multimedia applications and integration has changed computing science from a multidisciplinary to a transdisciplinary field that is shaped by other fields, such as business, arts, design, humanities and social sciences. Moreover, this paradigmatic shift would mean that the workplace plays a very important role in the learning process. Hence, work related accumulation of both explicit and tacit knowledge and know-how can be academically accredited via descriptors that define the level of entry.

5

Using Work Based Learning in the School of Health and Social Science

Barbara Workman and Katherine Rounce

***

Learning through work has long been a central feature in the training and education of health care professionals, particularly nurses, so transferring principles of work based learning (WBL) to the School of Health and Social Sciences (HSSc) built effectively on previous structures and fundamental principles of learning in the workplace. HSSc is a large multi-vocational school of the university and the Work Based Learning and Accreditation Unit (WBLA) works across a wide spectrum of activity, offering modules and awards in WBL, from health care assistants at levels 0/1 (Workman 2004), to senior health managers working at board level within the NHS who are enrolled on the Doctorate in Professional Studies in Health (Rounce et al 2005). WBL programmes and components have become increasingly embedded into the HSSc curriculum at Middlesex University and have a wide appeal to both academics and practitioners alike. This chapter will review the variety of ways that aspects of the work based learning curriculum have been used within the school and some of the challenges and opportunities that WBL has presented to the school.

The school began its involvement with WBL firstly in 1996, initially as a means to confer academic credit to extremely knowledgeable and skilled nurses who were enrolling on the Diploma in Women's Health Care, enabling them to concentrate on gaining new knowledge, rather than revisiting previous learning. It was through this that the value of accreditation of prior learning was realised and henceforth the possibilities for using a whole range of WBL activities and approaches became apparent. Initially, it started in a small way, fulfilling the needs of a few individual students who had specific learning requirements that could not be easily accommodated within standard programme structures and who needed additional flexibility in order to meet their learning and work needs. This then grew into the use of whole academic WBL programmes which enabled students and their sponsors to negotiate their learning and development needs, timescale and focus of the programme, yet gain a Higher Education award which also recognised their previous learning, including organisational training. This latter being particularly pertinent to the NHS at the time, as it coincided with rapid changes and NHS modernisation, requiring much inhouse training to be undertaken by health service professionals, but which had no formal recognition by any educational bodies. The modernisation of the NHS and consequent demands for responsive and flexible academic programmes came at an opportune time for WBL in HSSc and several cohorts of postgraduate students were recruited to follow the standard WBL programme structure as described in chapter one.

Coincidently within the university a variety of changes and mergers resulted in two schools being merged into a larger school and an opportunity arose for a Work Based Learning and Accreditation (WBLA) unit to be formed as part of restructuring working groups and practices. Initially the unit was located within the Business Development Unit which had emerged from funding designed to exploit the business potential within schools to gain new markets from short courses, consultancy and research. This location was not without its tensions because the consequence was that the WBLA unit was perceived not to be academically credible by some people and by locating it within a business framework it was perceived to emphasise business rather than education. Staff were continually having to explain the purpose and function of the unit and eventually it was separated from the Business Development Unit and transformed into an academic group, which equated to other academic subject groupings within the schools. Currently, as befits an emergent discipline, both in terms of a new subject and introduction to a new school, the unit occupies a unique niche within the university, working in a matrix fashion across two schools, and thereby forming partnerships both within the university and increasingly with external organisations. The unit worked closely with the then NCWBLP and shared the award for the Centre for Excellence in Teaching and Learning in Work Based Learning in April 2005. The unit was expected to be financially viable and to work across the school in an encouraging and responsive manner and to develop structures and processes such as accreditation boards and programme approval panels that support school activities. It has also played a central role in the management and development of a Professional Doctorate in Health and Environmental Sciences, which includes accreditation of prior experiential learning as part of its programme (Rounce et al 2005).

Experiential or WBL within health care is not new, but is likely to have been termed clinical or practice experience or inservice training which differs significantly from the traditional apprenticeship learning associated with nurse training. These terms reflect the notion of WBL as a 'mode of study', where the practice experience is the source and intent of the learning activity with pre-determined learning goals. Alternatively, WBL can be confused with delivery of learning in the work place rather than taking place in an external academic environment. The WBL approach that we offer differs from these examples in that the presupposition is that valuable learning occurs not just at work but also through, from and in work, and therefore knowledge is situational rather than just discipline specific. It does not depend on the delivery of academic knowledge as a main factor in the learning process, but prefers a learner orientated focus of enquiry. As such it informs, empowers and enhances efficacy through the development of new insights and knowledge for the learner, and impacts upon the community of practice, generating new knowledge for the community or organisation (Garnett 2005). An example of this are the post graduate cohorts recruited to the HSSc WBL programmes who were often initiating new practices and knowledge within the health service as a result of them undertaking an academic programme where much of their new learning and knowledge was captured as part of their final WBL projects, rather than lost in the organisation.

The WBLA unit offers the whole range of WBL programmes as validated by MU and also works with over forty organisations from across the public, private and voluntary sectors including the Department of Health, by accrediting employer based training programmes. This accreditation has produced some surprising results, engaging and stimulating the participation of academics from different subject disciplines within the school. The accredited programmes represent diverse subject disciplines found within the School and include a range of activities varying from swimming teachers, organisational security, counselling, induction and orientation programmes in the health care sector, and in some instances includes service users together with inservice training for health care professionals.

An analysis of the use of WBL within the school can be seen as one which reflects a continuum (Workman 2003) within which WBL is facilitated. This continuum begins where the learning is prescribed, and is outcomes driven, usually by the organisation, profession or curriculum. This could be likened to the National Occupational Standards of specific competence which provide a minimum standard and aims to provide a consistent standard of competence; a process which the majority of healthcare organisations are currently familiar with. An example of a prescribed programme that was created and accredited by us in partnership with local Primary Care Trusts is that of an initial training and development programme for health care assistants in General Practice that was devised and to some extent delivered by the WBLA unit (Workman 2004). It provided a foundation for health care assistants to gain initial skills before progressing onto an NVQ programme or application to the pre qualification nurse education programme. Such programmes are examples of widening access to HE, as well as being an exemplar of the way the WBLA unit contributes to other programmes not only those of WBL, but also to the general provision within the school.

The WBL continuum extends towards autonomous practice where an individual's capabilities are developed through work as described by Stephenson (1998). This end of the continuum is characterised by individualised negotiated learning, emphasising the learning process rather than or in addition to, a specific product as defined by the learner, although may be influenced by organisational needs. The learning activity is negotiated by the learner who determines a path of study that reflects his/her organisation's requirements, personal learning needs and timetable, and its processes are framed by the WBL programme requirements. Examples of this are partnerships that have been made with the NHS Modernisation Agency and Cancer Services Collaborative to provide an opportunity for practitioners working on health service improvement projects to gain a Masters degree in WBL simultaneously. By focusing on work as the curriculum (Boud 2001), and by developing transferable skills of research and development within service improvement projects, learners were able to integrate much of the service improvement training into their individualised programmes as accredited learning, utilising and consolidating project management with critical appraisal and analytical skills to become, as a colleague aptly termed it; 'scholarly professionals'. These skills are then the abiding legacy of WBL as a 'field of study' (Costley & Armsby 2006).

The relationship that has been developed between the unit and the WBL students and organisations is based on partnership and negotiation, with the academic role being one of a facilitator and guide rather than subject expert. These are particular challenges for academia as the knowledge that is developed and used within programmes is owned not by the university, but by the practitioner and his or her community, particularly within the Doctorate programme, where the level of practitioner expertise may be greater than that of academic staff (Rounce et al 2005), thus presenting further challenges to academic culture and practice. These challenges to the academic world may result in insecurity and resistance behaviour by traditional academics towards WBL programmes. It tends to elicit responses that question the probity of the programmes, the value of the knowledge that is generated and the academic role in teaching, learning and quality assurance processes. Perhaps these same academics have forgotten how early professionalisation of subjects such as Medicine and Science started with practitioners observing their practice and then researching it within the academy in order to create a body of knowledge to pass onto the next generation of practitioners (Greenwood 1966). By this same token then, WBL has been used by those learning from their work practices and contexts for a number of centuries, although in many different forms.

There is a wealth of knowledge and research about work, although this has been identified by academics who act as outsiders looking in. WBL provides a rare opportunity for those inside to explore their own community and practice, to capture knowledge from inside whilst also reflecting upon the networking and organisational processes this involves. The epistemology of practice is rooted in the creation of use; of practical knowing through the identification of frameworks and maps, rather than by codification. It is contractual in nature and represents a true transfer of power. This power is concentrated on learning and change, and is ideally suited to professional practice and to the development of better skilled, more highly qualified and flexible workers that are responsive not only to the modernisation needs of the health service, but also of other emergent professions (as described by Fillery-Travis et al in chapter 11).

Positive outcomes of negotiated WBL pathways reflect learning that is responsive to adult learning theory (Knowles 2005), as it is relevant to the students readiness to learn, it builds on their life and work experience and enhances it. As the programmes progress participants are orientated towards learning by utilising problem solving approaches to work, thus allowing a reframing of the work situation. Health care practitioners find this particularly attractive as it is both work focused and dynamic with a pragmatic response to practice issues. The prescriptive end of the WBL continuum is left behind as it moves towards developing autonomous learning by using structured learning activities such as learning agreements, but which also require a degree of self direction, such as negotiation of personal goals. Progression through the programme extends independent learning thus moving an individual along the WBL continuum, although the degree to which this is accomplished depends upon the academic level and the quality of analysis and synthesis that is required. Altogether the path along the WBL continuum fosters internal motivation towards learning and promotes reflective learning as each stage in the curriculum encourages the learner to develop skills of reflection upon work, which results in recognition and articulation of new learning being incorporated into their WBL award. The concept of reflection upon practice as key to professional practice development (Schön 1987) is well known in nursing, and therefore nurses generally find it easy to respond to WBL learning strategies. However, some health care practitioners find reflection a challenging activity as their previous learning experiences tend towards scientific positivist approaches that exclude variables such as the unpredictable human element from research and critical inquiry, and as such are less comfortable with reflective learning, which involves challenging assumptions and behaviours. Some of these factors may account for the responsive and positive uptake of WBL approaches within nursing rather than in some other allied health areas, although anecdotal evidence within HSSc indicates that attitudes are changing, and other allied health care professionals are keen to explore the potential within reflection upon learning.

Subject areas within the school other than health which have worked with the WBLA unit include Environmental health, Criminology, Flood Hazard Centre and Sports Science. Several of these have become involved through the accreditation of organisational training programmes, but also the application and use of different teaching and learning approaches as used in WBL have made a contribution in these subject areas.

WBL programmes are mainly used by those students who choose WBL because it responds to the uniqueness of their learning environment, especially where a university programme may not be available due to a small market which cannot fulfil an HEI's recruitment and viability criteria for a validated programme. This is particularly pertinent for practitioners working in new roles such as service improvement facilitators or leaders, clinical matrons or nurse practitioners. There have been a few cohorts whose experience as work based learners arose from unique circumstances and whose programmes have been independently evaluated. One such was a cohort of experienced mental health nurses who had been maintaining a mental health service against a background of restructured services, funding cuts, and shortages of adequately trained staff. They had a number of student mental health nurses coming through their departments during their training, but had not had the opportunity themselves to be further developed by additional education. Consequently they were experiencing difficulties in gaining promotion as they did not have recognisable qualifications, and although they had undertaken major projects within the service, such as closing or opening new services, there was no mechanism for formally recognising this (Laycock & Coyne 2006). Undertaking a WBL first degree or Masters allowed them to gain recognition for their previous achievements, acquire new academic skills to complement their work based skills and promote career advancement (Beadsmoore et al 2001). An interesting factor relating to this cohort was that several of them deferred stages of their programme due to competing priorities of work and home life, but then much later, subsequently rejoined the programme and completed it, but within their own time frame. It would appear that the option to undertake it at their own pace was significant, in order that they as learners, could retain the locus of control over their learning.

The nursing programmes within the School have used components of the WBL curriculum to augment their curriculum content. The BSc (Hons) Nursing Studies uses three core components in a variety of ways. The review and accreditation of learning module provides a useful vehicle to enable experienced nurses to make a claim for experiential learning (APEL) and complete their degree programme more quickly. Typically nurses would have qualified prior to the introduction of the Diploma in Higher Education (Project 2000), and only had 120 CATS points at Certificate level for their registered Nurse training. They may have undertaken some additional modules, often at graduate level, to develop their clinical skills or teaching and mentoring skills, but these were often over five years old and therefore the credit rating on them was theoretically obsolete. These were often nurses in senior management, teaching or clinical positions where a degree is virtually mandatory, particularly if career progression was required. The use of accreditation enables claims not only for experiential learning from practice to gain valuable credits towards a degree, but also to recognise credits from modules over five years old. The accreditation process enables the use of evidence to demonstrate that certificated learning over five years old is still relevant and has been recently updated and contributes to current practice and clinical knowledge, thereby enabling the credits to become eligible to be recognised as part of the degree.

This is particularly important for nurses in London, who may move from one post to another within the capital, be sponsored by different NHS Trusts and therefore gain qualifications from different Higher Education Institutions for professional development courses, which are financed with public money through the NHS funding streams. As public services, both the NHS and Higher Education have a responsibility to recognise credit acquired from equivalent institutions and provide a vehicle for recognition of academic endeavour and public investment. Recognising the value of previous certificated learning towards an overall degree award is a cost effective way of acknowledging students academic endeavours and the investment of public funds into the national health care industry.

Another dimension to recognising prior learning can be found in community nursing. An ageing workforce, particularly of district nurses and health visitors means that their initial preparation for practice in the community did not carry degree level credits, but new staff that are now supervised and trained qualify with degrees, resulting in the experienced staff feeling inferior, undervalued and unappreciated. Being able to acknowledge their range of experiential learning and consolidate it towards a degree boosts morale and re-energises the workforce, which together with the opportunity to undertake a work based project, benefits the primary care team and gives added value to the academic award.

The BSc Nursing Studies programme uses the principles of a learning agreement from the WBL curriculum to ensure programme coherence, and provides students with the opportunity to make a case for an award title that recognises their area of expertise and draws their learning together. The validation of the programme expressly incorporated these features to enable a flexible approach to meet the educational and developmental needs of nurses.

The final WBL component that has been used within the nursing Degree framework is that of the WBL project. These are validated in 20, 30

40 and 60 credit formats at Degree level, which allow articulation with the rest of the university provision and can make up credit deficits that students may present with. The use of 20 credits is popular as part of a bigger award of an Advanced Diploma (60 credits at graduate level), which builds upon a clinical practice course such as Diabetes or Rehabilitation, and by undertaking a WBL project as the final component of this, it enables consolidation and application of new learning into clinical practice. A WBL project differs from a dissertation as it demonstrates a range of practical capabilities in the work place and focuses on activities within the workplace leading to a product. This product is a useful outcome of the learning activity, and often reflects a real need within clinical practice. The project process aims to develop the learner's personal and professional knowledge by using research techniques that can be applied to the work place, uncovering knowledge from the work activity, which is then embedded into work practices. This then contributes to the organisation's knowledge and contributes to the 'intellectual capital' (Garnett 2005) of the organisation. Typical examples of work based projects that contribute to clinical practice include a review and update of an immunisation policy within a Primary Care Trust (PCT), which also explored and catered for the policies of neighbouring PCTs so that movement of clients from one trust to another would not compromise the immunisation status of other clients. Another project reviewed the palliative care provision within the trust as a prelude to planning service development. Another popular approach is to undertake an audit of current practice; for example, the use of inhalers and nebulisers in a children's ward, as a prelude to developing training programmes and updates in a particular nursing intervention. These are not the traditional form of final dissertations, but give the learner experience in carrying out a real time project at work that uses research skills, and more importantly, provides the learner with transferable skills such as literature search and critique, data collection and analysis from a range of qualitative and quantitative sources which are applicable to every day work. The majority of the learners we work with do not consider themselves as researchers, but a number of them have had to undertake a project at work anyway so the WBL project process formalises and provides a vehicle for consolidating their project management and enquiry skills and demonstrates their practice capabilities.

An additional benefit for the learner from the WBL project includes a contribution to his or her personal career development as well as having practical outcomes for the organisation and academic recognition for the work. Work based learning projects tend to have an element of impact upon practice or a degree of change within them, which may be fully or partially explored in the project depending upon its size and scope. This can enable the learner to develop skills as a change agent within the organisation, together with associated skills such as enhanced communication and dissemination strategies.

Within the university procedures, a particular feature of the WBL project that is well used by learners, is that of automatic deferral of assignment submission without penalties. As these are real time projects, factors such as changes in funding or job role, workload pressures, relocation or redeployment are an ever present reality and the learner has the option of deferring submission of their project when "life gets in the way" of a study programme, as very often it does. This enables the programme to be responsive to work schedules without adding additional unnecessary pressure to the learner during a time of work difficulties. Surprisingly few learners fail to return to complete their studies, but many appreciate the flexibility that deferment brings.

During a recent revision of the academic framework of the university the WBLA unit were able to contribute to the development of a range of programmes that included some of the principles of WBL within them. These have included aspects such as negotiated learning agreements and the use of portfolios for assessment within some of the more unusual health care fields such as Herbal or Chinese medicine. Some of the postgraduate programmes have been designed to allow students to choose a work based route or a traditional dissertation route to complete the award to allow students to determine the most appropriate learning pathway for themselves. As the WBL route requires less attendance at university this often makes the decision for the student as there are increasing difficulties in getting funding or study time from practice areas, and therefore not having compulsory attendance times is a strong factor in its favour. A disadvantage of this is that the student may not be adequately prepared for being a self-directed learner as they have been used to formal taught sessions and the change in mode of programme delivery may be a challenge that can initially require a lot of academic support. The opportunity to use organisational training days as part of an accreditation claim has offered a model for continuous professional development (CPD) update days run by some health care programmes. The incorporation of such days into the academic calendar, with the option to turn these into WBL awards by accrediting them or including a WBL short project has been adopted by some subject areas within the school as a way of attracting prospective postgraduate students.

The WBLA unit has been able to offer valuable advice on accreditation for both individuals and organisations. The collective experience of the members of the unit, together with a full knowledge and understanding of the university regulations and permutations of the WBL curriculum allows staff to suggest ways in which programmes can be customised to meet purchasers requirements, resulting in a flexible, 'can do' response to most questions of programme design. Accreditation of external programmes has opened new market opportunities for example in nutrition, osteopathy and counselling. The opportunity to undertake accredited training programmes in the work place also encourages individuals to come to the university to formally complete their award by undertaking a proportion of Middlesex modules, the requirements usually being one third of the total programme being under the control of the university, thus allowing two thirds of accredited activity from a range of sources to be included within a programme. A recent revalidation of the social work programme was able to incorporate accredited training by one of our partnership boroughs to supplement the post qualifying social work courses in mental health, thereby involving a wide range of stakeholders in the validation process and incorporating valuable multi-disciplinary working practices and knowledge into the new programme. This has opened up new possibilities for the use of WBL within a subject area of the school where previously professional body requirements and traditional approaches to HE have placed constraints around the use of WBL activities.

The range of benefits from the relationship between the NCWBLP and WBLAU has been two way. The opportunity to use WBL practices and procedures has demonstrated the flexibility and potential of the WBL curriculum. The emphasis on evidence based practice within HSSc has influenced the WBL programme, and an increased awareness of ethical factors in practice has led to deeper consideration and understanding of ethical and confidentiality issues for all WBL learners who are learning and investigating inside their work. Experienced academics in HSSc are used to facilitating learning from practice due to personal experience of teaching in the practice areas and applying theory for and to practice, and as demonstrated from this discussion of the WBL curriculum, it does not take much ingenuity to progress along the WBL continuum towards increasingly negotiated learning, resulting in learners who are equipped with lifelong learning skills.

Additionally, using the WBL curriculum within the school programmes and learning activities includes learning that is clearly work focused with expected outputs which demonstrate evidence of new learning and application. Both the facilitator and student are aware that the requirements of the programme are pragmatic and can be responsive to work place developments and changes. Frequently trans-disciplinary interaction and learning at work are involved, especially within accredited programmes and the project element and activities. The design of the WBL framework, with negotiable content by an individual, provides a framework that can transfer to a wide variety of contexts and which is responsive to a number of customer demands. The use of accreditation for both individuals and organisations uses knowledge and training from the workplace without duplication of effort and resources, which, in this cost conscious age of public services, is crucial.

References

Beadsmoore A., Workman B. A., & Rounce K. (2001) *'Developing the Mental Health Workforce: A continuum of Work Based Learning'* Work Based Learning Network Conference – Models and Implementations of Work Based Learning UMIST

Boud D. (2001) in Boud D., Solomon N. (2001) *Work-based learning: A new higher education?* SRHE & OUP Buckingham

Costley C., & Armsby P. (2006) Work Based Learning Assessed as a Field or a Mode of Study. In *Assessment and Evaluation in Higher Education* Vol 31, no. 4

Garnett (2005) University and work based learning and the knowledge driven project in Rounce K. & Workman B. (2005) *Work-based Learning in health care: applications and innovations* Chichester: Kingsham Press

Greenwood E. (1966) in Vollmer H.M. & Mills, D.L., (Eds) (1966) *Professionalisation* London: Prentice Hall

Knowles M.S., Holton III E.F., & Aswansu R. (2005) 6th Ed. *The Adult Learner* London: Butterworth Heinemann

Laycock R. & Coyne P. (2006) Experienced Nurse Rotation Scheme, Phase two, final evaluation. Central & North West London Mental Health NHS Trust, www.nurserotation.com

Rogers C. (1983) *Freedom to learn in the 80's.* Columbus OH: Charles Merrill

Rounce K., Garelick H., Vernon L., & Portwood D. (2005) The Development of a Doctorate in professional Studies in Health in Rounce K. & Workman B. (2005) *Work-based Learning in health care: applications and innovations* Chichester: Kingsham Press

Schön D.A. (1987) *Educating the Reflective Practitioner: Towards a new design for Teaching and Learning in the Professions* San Francisco: Jossey-Bass

Stephenson J. & Yorke M. (1998) *Capability and Quality in Higher Education* London: Kogan Page

Workman B.A. (2003) Methodologies in practice based projects as used by Work Based Learning students in the former School of Health, Biological and Environmental Sciences *Journal of Health, Science and Environmental Issues* Vol 4, 2, pp23–26

Workman B.A. (2004) Growing our own: training health care assistants in general practice – a partnership between higher education and primary care trusts *Work Based Learning in Primary Care* (2) 220–9 Radcliffe Publ

6

Articulating the Learning
from Part Time Work

Philip Frame

***

Abstract

How we can help full time students identify and articulate their learning from part time work is the focus of this chapter. An outline of a level two undergraduate module, which was designed to support this learning development process, is provided, with an indication of the content of the topics covered and the methods of assessment. Five heuristics to aid the identification of learning are then provided: the articulation cycle, the ASKE typology, the learning analysis matrix, the external support matrix and the learning transferability matrix. All these have been developed specifically to aid students' reflective work, though they are, we believe, of relevance to other courses too. The description of these aids is then followed by three case examples of how students have used the module input on critical vignette analysis, organisational culture and SMART objectives in respect of their own jobs. A final case example outlines how students can manage their learning in circumstances of routine.

Introduction

The aim of this chapter is to describe the experience of running a module entitled 'Learning from Part Time Work' in order to share good practice and help colleagues consider the possibility of generating their own developments in this area.

The chapter is based on the experience of both the staff and the students who were involved. It will comprise of four elements:

- An outline of the module
- The identification of heuristics developed to aid the analysis of learning
- Case examples of analysis in practice
- Student strategies for learning from routine

Data presented here was collected via ongoing observations and discussions with participating students, an analysis of students individual learning reviews, the results of a module questionnaire and by extracting material from the module handbook.

The Module

This undergraduate level two module comprises of four compulsory developmental workshops (three hours) and four feedback surgeries (an hour and a half). It is assessed via a portfolio of evidence, which comprises of a learning review and evidence to support the claims to learning which appear in this review.

The workshops cover a range of topics in three broad areas:

- the process and foci of learning
- factors associated with being employed
- the collection and presentation of evidence.

Each is covered using a range of techniques, including tutor input, group discussion and feedback, individual activities and contributions, and whole group discussions. The aim is to provide a range of developmental activities that link the individual's ongoing employment experiences with the opportunities for learning that the module highlights, in a social and supportive setting.

Figure 6.1: Workshop Content

WORKSHOPS	TOPICS COVERED
1	**Introduction to module** - Introduction to reflective learning and learning styles - The importance of articulation - The practice of articulation **Collection of evidence**
2	**The context of work: job, organisation and sector** - Product and services, industry and environment **Skills and knowledge** - What are skills and knowledge? - How skills and knowledge can enhance graduate employability
3	**Content of work: duties, roles and relationships** - Job descriptions and personal specifications **Attitude and emotion** - What are attitude and emotions? - Critical incident exercise
4	**The organisation of work** - Organisational structure - Management styles - Organisational culture **Portfolio of evidence**

Feedback surgeries
These provide an opportunity for tutors to check on students development and progress in respect of identifying and recording their learning. They also provide an opportunity for social support as students meet and discuss experiences together. As the module questionnaire indicated, this is of great significance. Normally our students are the only people in their organisation who are pursuing such a course of study. It is therefore important that they meet with others who are similarly engaged, and at regular intervals. Finally they can ask questions of tutors and of each other, and, indeed, suggest solutions

Assessment
Assessment on this module is 100% coursework. It is based on a portfolio produced at the end of the module which includes a reflective learning review (50% of assessment mark) and a range of supporting evidence, including learning logs, testimonials, critical incident analyses and research on their employing organisation (40% of assessment mark). The final 10% of marks are based on quality of presentation.

Module handbook
A sizeable handbook that currently runs to 112 pages supports the module. The contents of the handbook are also available on the Middlesex University Business School's Intranet. Much of the handbook comprises advice on how learning can be identified, described, analysed and recorded. Set out below are five examples of how the module helps students articulate their learning. These aids to understanding, be they models, typologies or figures, provide a means for students to examine and translate messy working life into learningful experience.

Articulating Learning

1 The Articulation Cycle

The foundation for this module is the concept of articulation, that is, the ability to specify, describe and analyse an experience or concept and share the results with others. A number of commentators, including Harvey et al (1998) and employers have recommended the development of this facility. Thus, the then Human Resource Director of Sainsbury's (Earning and Learning Conference, 1997) noted that whilst students, as potential employees, laid claim to 'lots of experience' few were able to generalise as to what they had gained and what they could do, as a result of this experience.

The 'articulation cycle' was then developed as a means of helping students appreciate the meaning of, and benefits associated with, the articulation of their learning. The cycle is made up of four elements, which are now identified.

• **Self-awareness:** rather than being innocent of your capabilities you become aware and constantly review what your current skills, knowledge, attitudes and emotions are.

• **Self-development:** being self-aware will help you identify and focus upon those areas which you need to develop in respect of attitudes, skills, knowledge and emotions.

• **Self-actualisation:** being aware of your ambitions and what you want to achieve, and identifying and sharing your personal goals.

• **Self-promotion:** being clear about who you are, what you have to offer to an employer and what you want to achieve, and thereby presenting yourself honestly and clearly in the world of work.

These are combined in the figure set out below.

Figure 6.2: The Articulation Cycle

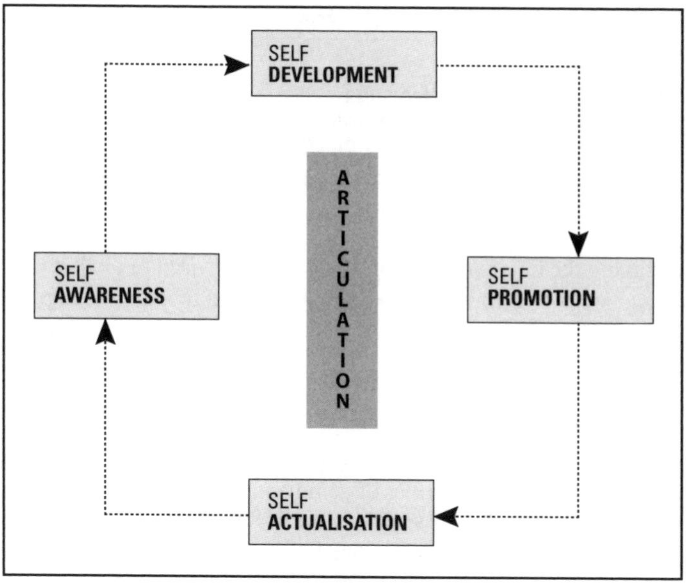

2 The ASKE Typology of Learning Domains

Traditionally, HE has concentrated on content knowledge as the focus of learning: 'the what'. Developments in the last decade have encouraged us all to widen our concerns to the area of 'the how' or skills development (for example: EHE, 1989–94; Dearing, 1997). These two foci are recognised by both Kolb (1984) and Honey and Mumford (1992), when they consider different learning styles. More recently, DfEE (1998) identified attitude as an area of learning and Heron (1999) included both attitudes and emotions as aspects of what he identified as 'whole person learning'.

In the light of these developments, a typology of learning was developed to help students differentiate between different domains of learning, and this is set out below.

Figure 6.3: The ASKE Typology

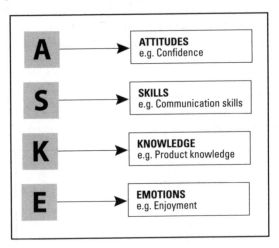

In examining the range of learning, students are advised to think about the following: areas of learning (see ASKE above) and foci of learning. These are combined to form a matrix to help identify the potential range of learning.

3 Foci of learning

There are four principal foci of learning students are advised to consider.

- Themselves: how they have developed as a result of work experience
- Their job: what have they developed as a result of doing the job for which they were employed.
- Their organisation, including for example its structure, culture, human resource management practices, marketing strategies and business.
- The external environment of their employer, such as the manufacturing or service sector within which it is located and its customers, suppliers and competitors.

Students are advised to examine their experience to determine what they have achieved in respect of these four areas. This may include the following:

- The development of something new, such as a new personal skill.

- The enhancement of a pre-existing capability, such as increasing their knowledge of the sector in which their employer is active, or their ability to control and utilise their emotions more effectively.

- Shedding 'student' attitudes, such as a lack of self-confidence and an attitude of passivity.

The matrix set out below encourages students to comprehensively review their learning both in respect of areas and foci, and, for example, can help them consider their attitudinal learning in respect of self, employing organisation and its external environment.

Table 6.1: Learning Analysis Matrix

FOCI / AREA	Yourself	Your job	Your Organisation	Your Organisation's External Environment
• Knowledge				
• Skills				
• Attitudes				
• Emotions				

4 Supporting Claims to Learning: Externally Referenced

Here we encourage students to consider the sources of support they can utilise to support their learning claims. We encourage them to be more than passive recipients of information, but rather to be proactive and seek the information they require. We identify two sources of support:

- People with whom they come into contact during the working day, both inside their organisation and within its external environment. They may include: their boss/supervisor, their fellow employees, senior managers, and customers.

- Documents, that is, anything in writing that includes a reference to the student and their work performance. This may include letters, memoranda, organisational newsletters, minutes, reports, appraisal forms, probationary reports and references.

In addition we identify two main forms of support.

- Formal, that is, where there is a public comment on their performance. This may include performance reviews, letters or emails of thanks and speeches of thanks

- Informal, that is, where there is private feedback on their performance. This may include telephone conversation, chats in the corridor and third party comments.

The matrix set out below combines source and forms of support in a useful aide memoire to help in identifying examples of external support.

Table 6.2: External Support Matrix

FORM SOURCE	Informal	Formal
People		
Documents		

5 Learning Transferability

The aim of this final piece of guidance is to encourage students to consider what learning is transferable and what is not. Again they use the areas of learning referred to above, together with categories that requires them to make a judgement on the degree to which their learning was specific or generic. Whilst there is little agreement amongst academics as to whether transferability is a reality, students are able to distinguish between specific and generic learning and appear to agree that transferability is most likely to occur in the case of the latter.

Table 6.3: Learning Transferability Matrix

SPECIFIC LEARNING	Job Specific	Organisation Specific	Sector/industry Specific	Generic/Non-Specific/Transferable
Knowledge				
Skills				
Attitudes				
Emotions				

Case examples of analysis in practice

The aim of this section is to provide examples of how the students used the module input to reflect on aspects of their working lives in order to develop their living wisdom, and to indicate techniques, other than those identified above, which were used by students to examine their working experience. These examples are presented in the 'voice' of the students concerned.

In the first example, and as a means of demonstrating the emergence of students' 'living wisdom' (Hartog and Frame, 2004), we have followed MacFarlane's (2003) example by encouraging the utilisation of 'critical incident vignettes'. He suggests that traditional case studies are limited, whereas, 'work related examples of learners ... can often provide a rich source of real life material' (p.57). They are, he suggests, 'raw, firsthand commentaries of real events affecting individuals' (p.58).

1 Critical Vignettes Analysis

'I'm Jerome, a business studies undergrad. I'm in my final year and I've always worked part-time. The West End is best, lots of shops, lots of demand for part-timers like me but lots of businesses coming and going. Like I used to work for 'Guess' in Bond Street, but they closed down. I'm working for 'Mulberry' now, at their concession in Harvey Nicks. I've been there eight months now and sometimes stand in for the manager, Shawn.

Mulberry sells clothes for men and women and leather goods like cases, bags, wallets and picture frames. They are very expensive and how the merchandise is displayed is very significant in attracting passing trade. One day Shawn asked me to re-do the display. We get a general outline of what should go with what from Head Office, but then it's down to us as to how we adapt the guidelines to our particular space. Anyway I spent about two hours or more re-doing the display space; its not big but it's complicated. I was pleased with the results and went off for my lunch. When I came back I was horrified to see the display had been dismantled and put back to where it was before I started. It turned out that another bloke who worked with me, Atif, decided there had been a mistake and decided to take action off his own bat.

I was well annoyed. I'd gone to so much time and effort; the boss had told me to do it and now along comes Atif and mucks it all up. When I tackled him about it, he said it was his job. Shawn was off for the day; what to do: I felt like punching him. But I walked away and thought about it.

So I talked to the boss about it next day. It turned out that Shawn had not told Atif anything, and Atif thought I was getting ideas above my station and he wanted to do the display job anyway and so on. I'm glad I didn't punch him one. It shows the need for effective communication, and how helpful to control your initial impulses before you act. Firstly I'm glad I didn't thump him: I'd have got the sack whatever the provocation. I'm glad

69

I could control my negative emotions. And I'm glad I talked about it and came to some agreement on talking to each other about who is going to do what. It showed me the good of communication between us. And the whole thing showed me how I'd developed too'.

The above demonstrates that the analysis of a critical incident can prove a useful source of reflection on the individual's behaviour and a means of helping decision making for future actions.

2 Organisational culture

'I'm a bit unsure what organisational culture is about but this is something we do at the Call Centre where I work.

I'm based in West London. We're all young, a lot of students and we answer calls for different sorts of organisations from their customers. We answer calls about banks, insurance companies, retail shop, transport, anything and everything. What you say is up on the screen, your script. My trainer said you had to stick to that, no deviations or you'd get the sack. The atmosphere is fairly relaxed though; the customer cannot see you and the dress code reflects this. People come along in what's most comfortable for them. And that's OK except when some clients, the companies, are coming to check out the call centre service.

It's a rule we dress in a way that reflects the companies whose calls we are answering. So if it's a fashion company we can come in dressed in our normal clothes but if it's a bank or insurance company we have to put a collar and tie on and a suit for those who have them: we are told to look smart and conventional. This is the way we do things around here, and we're just told to do it. If you don't, it's talked about and you're reminded of the rule. It seems funny to me but that's one of the things you need to do to keep your job here'.

Organisational culture is a difficult area to get to grips with. Here the student has made an attempt, as a means of explaining what, at first sight, appears to be unusual behaviour. It also provides a nice example of 'fitting in' to the work environment.

Smart Objectives

'Hello; I'm Jash. I'm at Uni doing a degree in HRM (that's human resource management to you mate) and I'm full time. This is my second year, second semester. I work in a shop selling white goods, you know fridges, washing machines, irons, stuff like that. I've been there for about eighteen months and it's a good laugh.

I do all right, no complaints, but the boss, Dean, picked me up last week about selling insurance. Had I forgotten, he said, about always trying to sell a warranty with everything the customer bought? Why wasn't I doing that?

We all had to try, and I wasn't. He seemed well p****d with me and shouted at me to make a bit more effort.

So I thought I'll use this insurance thing as a smart objective

- **Specific:** I need to sell warranties on all relevant purchases, like dishwashers and irons.

- **Measurable:** Well I can check what my warranty sales were at the start and end on the module.

- **Achievable:** Look my mates in the shop can do it so I should be able to.

- **Realistic:** it's part of the job, it's what we should all do. Company profits depend on selling these warranties.

- **Timebound:** I need to do this within the next four to six weeks or I might get the push.'

Here the student tackled a work-related problem (under-performance) by utilising the model of smart objectives to improve his performance.

The above case examples indicate how students have applied the module content to their jobs as a means of increasing their understanding of themselves and their circumstances, and as a vehicle for development.

Student strategies for learning from routine.

A major barrier to learning is presented by working with routine. Students expressed the view that if there were no critical incidents, what could be learned? What can the learner do in such situations to break out of the routine without endangering their employment status? An example of how one student coped with this situation is set out below.

Learning from routine

'Look I work in a very boring place; nothing much seems to change from day to day, week to week. There aren't any major disputes, upheaval, changes. We all get on well but it's not very stimulating. So what am I learning, or what can I learn?

I'm employed on a part-time basis for a hospital. I'm a receptionist in the X-ray section, so I take peoples cards from their GP and add them to the list of those waiting to be X-rayed. I sit in the reception area. That's what I do, three days a week for a four hour stint. Sometimes there are lots of people waiting and sometimes like the early evening, almost nobody.

So what I have is time. I decided to go for promotion. The hospital has fairly clear guidelines as to what you need to do to move up in this area so I got the details. I looked at what I needed to do so that the next time an opportunity came around, I could apply. I read various things and talked to my supervisor and so on. It gave me something to do when there were no patients. So instead of sitting there being bored I did something, I took the initiative. And it paid off. The next time a promotion came up I applied and at the interview showed them what I'd been doing. They were impressed by that said it showed initiative, an interest in the job, even though I was only part-time, and I got promoted.

So instead of sitting around being bored I did something about it and got a good result. So that's how I managed the mundane'.

In this example, the learner created his own opportunities by being proactive rather than passively awaiting a 'learning experience'.

Conclusion

This paper has provided an outline of a module entitled 'Learning from Part time Work' with the aim of spreading good practice and helping those who may be considering a similar development in their own institutions. To this end, it has described a number of techniques, models and matrices that were developed to help students think about their learning. It also provides some case example of how these aids to thinking have been used in practice. It concluded with an example of how learning in circumstances of routine is possible, if a proactive approach is adopted.

Key words:
Learning, part time work, work based learning(WBL), articulation.

References

Dearing, R. (1997) *National Committee of Enquiry into HE*. HMSO: London.

DfEE. (1998) *Skills Development in HE*. Sheffield: DfEE.

Frame, P and Dattani, A. (2000) What do Students Learn from Part time Work? in *Proceeding of the 8th Annual Teaching and Learning Conference*. Nottingham: Nottingham Business School, The Nottingham Trent University. 14–31.

Hartog, M., and Frame, P. (2004) 'Business Ethics in the Curriculum: Integrating Ethics through Work Experience'. In *Journal of Business Ethics*, Vol. 54, pages 399–409.

Harvey, L., Geall, V. and Moon, S. (1998) *Work Experience: expanding opportunities for graduates*. Birmingham: Centre for Research into Quality, University of Central England.

Heron, J. (1999) *The Complete Facilitators Handbook*. London: Kogan Page.

Honey, P and Mumford, A. (1992) cited in Reid, M. and Barrington, H. (1994), *Training interventions; managing employee development'*. 4th edition. London: CIPD.

Kolb, D. A. (1984) *Experiential learning – experience as the source of learning and development*. New Jersey: Prentice-Hall

MacFarlane, B. (2003) 'Tales from the Frontline: Examining the potential of critical incident vignettes'. In *Teaching Business Ethics*, 7, pp. 55–67.

7

Improved Qualifications and Career Opportunities of Early Years Practitioners
Gillian Hilton

***

Introduction
This chapter describes and evaluates the role of work based learning (WBL) in the introduction of a Sure Start endorsed foundation degree in early childhood studies at Middlesex University in 2003 and the experiences of students and staff during the period of its inception, development and consolidation. The degree developed initially from a part time BA Hons in childhood studies, run with partner colleges and three of the schools in the university. This initial experiment on working with Further Education (FE) led to a realisation that the management of such a complex award was better with one university school working with the colleges. After representations from the colleges the School of Lifelong Learning and Education's academic group, 'Education Policy and Practice' agreed to develop a new set of degrees in the area of Early Childhood, including a Foundation Degree (FD).

HE providers were encouraged to bid for the introduction of prototype foundation degrees by the Higher Education Funding Council for England (HEFCE, 2000) with the idea of raising the skills level of the workforce, particularly in 'new industries' (HEFCE, 2000:2). The degrees were to have a vocational focus and consortia of providers were encouraged; FE being deemed to have the vocational expertise and industrial links and HE the academic focus. HE was to provide validation and possibly delivery whilst FE were the deliverers and employers were to play a fundamental part in the design and implementation of the courses (QAA, 2002a). The numbers completing foundation degrees has grown considerably so that in 2007 28% of the 94,900 FE students following HE courses are studying for FDs (QAA, 2007). It was made mandatory from the outset that these degrees worth 240 credits and at levels 1 and 2 of HE were to have a strong work based element suited to the specific needs of a particular industry where "there is evidence of a demand for higher technical and associate professional skills" (HEFCE, 2000: 5). Whether in this description the early years workforce was specifically considered is unclear but the author when training as a foundation degree reviewer for the Quality Assurance Agency (QAA) was given examples from aerospace, accountancy and business rather than the care sector.

Government's intention, it appeared, was to phase out the existing two year HE programmes, such as higher national diplomas and over time see them replaced by the foundation degree, which would contribute to the intention to raise the numbers of students in HE, particularly from those sections of the community under-represented there (HEFCE, 2000). The characteristics of the foundation degrees offered were to include a set of 'core features' (HEFCE, 2000: 7)

- Employer involvement
- Development of skills and knowledge underpinned by academic learning
- Application of skills in the workplace
- Awarding bodies should allow for the accumulation of at least 240 credits some of which could be via accreditation of prior learning
- There must be a guaranteed progression route onto an honours degree or higher level NVQs.

Foundation Degrees for the Early Years Practitioner

For many years workers in early years settings have been low paid, with poor career prospects and the work is considered as being of low status. Hargreaves and Hopper (2006) point to similarities with the problems faced in the 1970s with the status of teachers and the condition of the early years workforce today. They refer to Banks' (1971 in Hargreaves and Hopper, 2006) ideas of a large workforce dominated by women with a generally low level of qualifications, poor training possibilities and the lack of an accepted body of knowledge and expertise. However, workers in this area have a wealth of experiential learning and had acquired valuable practical knowledge related to the needs of young children. Qualifications however, are often limited to the post school nursery nurse examinations board two year qualification or later national vocational qualifications, British Training and Enterprise Council or the Council for Awards in Children's Care and Education, diplomas or certificates. Many employed in this sector had previously worked in other areas and had gravitated towards early years as a result of having children and needing child friendly working hours. If Hoyle's (2001) suggestion that an occupation's status is determined by how others see it applies, then there is little hope in improving the standing of early years practitioners. However, as Brock (2001:2) has suggested, since the advent of the labour government in 1997 early years is "at the forefront of educational change in the United Kingdom". Despite this raising of the profile of the early years sector, the status of workers in this area is still in question Moylett and Abbott (1999) demonstrating the urgent need to raise the qualifications of those working in the sector and this effort is progressing under the present government's initiatives. The advent of the foundation stage (DFES/QCA, 2000) raised the profile of work in the sector though not at that point, the status of the workers. However, the introduction of foundation degrees gave Higher Education Institutions (HEI) and FE Colleges an opportunity to address this problem.

Further developments occurred with the advent of Sure Start endorsement of early years foundation degrees. These degrees 'were introduced to allow people in the Early Years sector to build on existing expertise and continue working at the same time as studying for a higher level qualification' (Taylor et al., 2006:1). To be endorsed and allow successful students to progress in their careers to Senior Practitioner Status in early years settings new criteria in the degree design had to be followed. Students had to have at least two years experience of working or volunteering in the sector and a level 3 qualification (DfES, no date). Work experience on a continuous basis was to be continued throughout the degree course (DfES, 2006) and accreditation of prior learning at HE level was to be built into the course design, whether formally assessed or work-based experience. This meant students who had followed FE level 4 qualifications could be admitted to year two of the degree. To gain endorsement HE institutions had to fulfil the list of criteria when planning modules and the organisation of the degree and the academic level had to follow the QAA intermediate guidelines (QAA, 2002).

Acting as a QAA reviewer for other early years FDs aided the process of designing and developing the Middlesex degree. Reviewing FDs already established in other consortia gave insight into the problems encountered and the 'emerging' nature of the expected standards (QAA, no date Session 2:2). The judgements of these standards were to be "Confidence or No Confidence" there was no section for limited confidence (QAA, no date Session 2:2). Reviewers considered five key questions 'teaching and learning, academic support, learning resources, employers/work placement providers, monitoring and enhancement of quality and standards' (QAA, no date Session 3:4). Awareness of the difficulties of embedding the work based element into the course, marrying theory and practice and the difficulties in working with employers from such a wide variety of early years settings was becoming evident from the reviews undertaken. This knowledge helped the Middlesex degree design team to attempt to overcome some of these problems in their original design.

The degree planned by Middlesex was audited against the Sure Start criteria to show where the proposed content met the Sure Start requirements and as a result of this endorsement of the degree was obtained. Initially forty places were granted by Sure Start but the initial recruitment for the first cohort was thirty three and we lost five of these students after a few weeks due to lack of support from the settings or financial concerns (settings would not give them paid day release). In the following year recruitment dipped and we struggled to recruit twenty but subsequently it has become more healthy with thirty five starting in 2006 and the possibility of a cohort of fifty for 2007. This increase may in some part be attributed to a further government initiative at increasing qualifications through WBL, that is, the new early years professional status and a recognition by local authority co-ordinators that there is a need for more advanced skills and underpinning knowledge in the workforce. Early years workers are also seeing the need to enhance their WBL with some academic study.

The Middlesex FD in early childhood studies was designed by staff from a consortium of six FE Colleges and the HEI team. QAA (2007) stresses the importance of this type of partnership; the way forward appearing to be the establishment of consortia of an HEI, FE colleges and employers. Subsequently three colleges have dropped out of the involvement as they do not provide courses at FE level 3 thereby not recruiting students to the FD. One more has joined the group, though we as yet have received no students from this college. It was decided in the first instance to concentrate delivery in the HEI rather than dispersing to colleges. Nationally 46% of students following FDs are taught in HEIs but when part time attendance is the pattern this figure rises to 56% (FDF, 2007). QAA reviews of FDs undertaken by the author had found a wide variety in provision between members of consortia and the Middlesex team therefore decided to keep control in-house initially, which would also ensure viable numbers of students. Teaching was to be undertaken by FE staff and the Programme Leader was also from one of the partner colleges. Staff from the colleges are paid through the university and their teaching time for the FD is counted in their hours in FE. This has proved a very successful model as the expertise across FE and HE sectors has been used and has been found to be complementary. Research conducted for Foundation Degree Forward has shown the need for what is described as "academic backbone" in "design and delivery" as this "adds status to the degree" but respondents felt that few organisations had the ability to train at this level (FDF, 2007: 5). Academic rigour equal to that of the Honours Degree level2 was at the heart of the planning for the Middlesex early years FD as the team believed that the status of the degree had to be equal standing to that of level2 of the BA. Students are made members of both the university and their local college, having access to both libraries and a personal tutor based in the college who visits their work setting. Bearing in mind the guidance of QAA and the increasing need for early years practitioners, a three year BA Hons, degree in early childhood studies was planned and validated at the same time as the FD though its start was delayed by one year to allow time for recruitment.

This was to enable progression from the FD (as required by HEFCE) as well as attracting the more traditional university student. Many modules were shared by the two degrees, but the profile of students was very different. The FD attracted experienced workers whilst the BA recruited mainly young people from school or college. An important difference therefore was the need to incorporate WBL into the FD and to introduce work placements into the BA.

Work Based Learning
To enable the work based element of the FD degree to become embedded into the course employers and local authority co-ordinators were contacted at the outset and asked to comment on the degree design. Employers were also asked to agree to support their worker's study, giving time for them to carry out work-based tasks and to provide mentoring. A contract was drawn up by the HEI and the employers asked to sign to agree to support their student and a booklet was issued to the employers explaining the nature of the FD and possible progression and career routes for successful candidates. Some problems arose as the small nature of many of the establishments sending students resulted in a lack of suitable mentors and an inability of workplaces to send representatives to planned meetings or mentor training. Taylor et al's (2006) review demonstrated that most mentors are nominated by the students and that there is some confusion about the demands of the mentors in this situation. There is great variability in the amount of support given to mentees and the amount of contact between mentors, mentees, employers and the course providers (Taylor et al., 2006). One of the main requirements of the FD as stated above is the involvement of employers, but possibly this was originally intended for larger employers rather than early years settings. Taylor et al's (2006) evaluation of the early years sector endorsed degrees showed that some employers struggled to support their employee as funding has been limited or non-existent and that in many cases there was insufficient contact between the education institution and the workplace. At Middlesex we encountered problems in getting employer involvement, trying different meeting times and offering training for mentors face to face or online, but attendance at these events was low. Lack of time and limited staff numbers are the main reasons given for non attendance. So, to maintain this contact we enlisted the help of the colleges who had established contacts with the employers and HE staff attend both college and local authority employer events to explain the nature of the qualification and the need for employer support. Creation of a local Centre for Vocational Excellence (COVE) in early years in two of our partner colleges helped greatly with this employer contact problem but it is still a cause for concern.

Problematic too was the possibility that the students under training would rapidly become better qualified than their managers in the work place with more up to date knowledge and a more substantial theoretical background in early years issues. In some cases this did lead to difficulties when students were asked to discuss settings' responses to government directives and report back to their study group. It became clear that in some settings there was a lack of a theoretical basis for decision making or policy implementation and students had to be counselled on how to raise these issues with work colleagues. However, students were also able to critique and question theories put forward in texts and research from a position of strength from their work-based experience.

Financial provision was made for the first cohorts of students from Sure Start, including a computer and printer on loan, finance for books, mentoring payments, cover for settings to allow students to be released and childcare payments. As the years progressed these incentives were steadily cut so that now students have to self-finance or apply to their local authority for payments from the transformation fund. The administration of the payments and computer loan was left to the HEIs and caused considerable problems particularly during the disbanding of the Sure Start team in the DfES. Programme leaders had a large variety of forms to complete and long delays occurred in payment to students causing real hardship. In recent years the advent of the transformation fund has also caused problems for the teaching team. One local authority decided to fund 75% of the students' £3000 year fee for the two or three years of study. Neighbouring authorities initially gave nothing, causing dissention amongst the student group. To compound this the partner college in the generous authority also gave a bursary to all their students following a FD with Middlesex, causing further resentment in the affected student cohort. For 2007 a second authority has also offered some support payments but not the other colleges.

Learning and Teaching

Learning and teaching strategies had to accommodate the needs of the students all of whom were in work or volunteer placement for at least twelve hours per week; many being in full time work. Day release was negotiated for the first four cohorts, but it has subsequently become obvious that this has prevented some potential applicants applying for the course. With the disappearance in funding for the early years settings and the needs of some workers in small organisations or those working as childminders, there is a growing need for twilight sessions. This idea has been discussed with local authority representatives and the local COVE and will be trialled next academic year with two evenings a week being offered as an alternative to day release. To accommodate the limited time the students had to attend classes it was decided to offer the FD over three terms rather than the two university semesters, working from September to July on the same weekday for two years (three if continuing to the BA) and allowing half term breaks. This caused considerable problems with room allocation and fitting into the university assessment, summer school and induction schedules, but these difficulties had to be overcome to meet the needs of work based learners. However, it allowed the potential three year part time FD (initially funded for only two of those years) to be studied in two. This was an important consideration as workers in this sector are poorly paid, most of our students earning well under £15,000 per annum and several coming from one parent households.

These students needed considerable amounts of support mainly in areas such as academic writing, English and in the raising in their self-confidence. Most had never previously considered themselves university material and were very unsure of their ability to be successful. HEFCE (2007) points out that FDs have increased the numbers of students from low participation neighbourhoods and the Middlesex degree is no exception here. To choose students who we thought stood a good chance of success all students are interviewed in small groups and then given a passage to read related to a child development topic and asked to provide written answers to questions about the passage. This allows tutors to judge if the students have the potential to meet the course requirements for writing in English. Some students, despite possessing level 3 FE qualifications do not appear to be able to comprehend the written task and some have very limited ideas on policies or regulations that are essential for early years settings such as equality or health and safety. We are in the process of discussing with our partner colleges the need for a pre–FD course to improve study skills and writing and to add an academic element to NVQs which do not seem to prepare students for the academic demands of the FD.

Areas covered in the degree range from child development and learning theories to history and policies on education and care and professional concerns such as law, health and safety, equality, child protection and first aid. The second year examines the curriculum for the foundation stage and for Key Stage 1 including the core subjects and the assessment of children. Students also study modules on special educational needs and management of early years settings.

Students on this programme demand a great deal from their tutors and the FE staff at times have to be reminded that in HE there is a greater expectation of learner autonomy than in the FE sector. The students are used to college courses where the tutor is always available for help and support. In feedback at Boards of Study students complain of too little help from tutors despite having personal tutors which are not normally provided for degree level students. These concerns are generally caused by a lack of self-confidence and worry that their commitment of time and work, which often causes family problems, meets with success.

With this in mind the study skills module used by the university as a whole is used to help prepare the students for note taking, essay and report writing and making presentations. ICT skills vary widely and some students had previously had no access to computers, but over the four years the course has run, more students have come to us with IT literacy and used to internet usage and email. ICT skills, such as the use of Power Point to make presentations and the need to use the interactive white board have grown and are regular parts of the present course. The university uses Oasis as a web based interface to aid student learning but it proved problematic to train all the tutors from FE colleges in the use of this particular medium, the main problem being our inability to gather all tutors together at the same time for training sessions. A similar problem occurred with the student computerised recording system; allowing remote access to FE based tutors proved an initial problem. However, these challenges are being gradually overcome by the continued use of a stable group of tutors and the added bonus of our own BA Hons students now working in the colleges and returning part time to teach on the FD. This is a plus we had not envisaged. There is a national shortage of well qualified teaching staff in the early years sector and this means colleges have problems in recruiting staff as tutors on courses in this area. We are now therefore growing our own and expect next year to have three mature ex students teaching on the FD. As these students are totally familiar with the university system, library and staff and have had years of experience in the early years sector, they are proving a tremendous asset to the course planning and provision.

The use of FE staff to teach modules also delivered by HE staff on the BA degree has meant that FE staff have had career progression opportunities from FE to HE. We now have three members of the HE department who have initially taught on our FD as college lecturers. This enables us to ensure that we can overcome problems noted by QAA where in some colleges staff and students lack a true understanding of the demands of HE study (QAA, 2007). Basing the work in HE has also prevented problems with the provision of HE resource materials. The author noted in FD reviews that some colleges did not have sufficient material at the right academic level for students to consult. There is a strong tendency for students to use books designed for level 3 (FE) study rather than more academic texts and it is therefore essential that good library provision at the right level is easily accessed. Our partner colleges have upgraded their book and journal stock but students still have the tendency to refer to texts familiar to them from previous FE courses.

As the FD is work-based, some tasks, to realise the Sure Start criteria, have to be completed in the work place and tutors are intent on expecting students to bring their practical experience into assignment responses. Indeed it has been found that FD students were better able to complete assignments where observations of children were required than were the BA students. In one first year module students are required to carry out observations of children in early years settings focussing on their cognitive development. This links to the university taught element on cognitive development theories for example those of Piaget, Vygotsky and Bruner. The FD students come with years of experience in carrying out observations and know how to structure, report on and evaluate their effectiveness. Many have level 3 FE qualifications in this form of assessing children. They understand how and what to observe and therefore find it easy to link theory and practice. BA students however, many coming to us at eighteen, have little or limited practical experience on which to base observations, so are tentative and unsure of what to look for and find linking theory to practice much more difficult. In effect we are asking these students with little WBL to understand and learn two different things at the same time and relate them to one another. By constantly demonstrating to our FD students that their WBL is a vital adjunct to their academic studies, we boost their self-confidence which enables them to develop and realise the worth of their practice based learning.

Our FD cohorts also have years of experience in this regard with the demands of the foundation stage curriculum and its assessment. Year two of the FD includes two modules which are entirely work based. It was decided to put these two, twenty credit modules at the end of the course as at this stage the students have the academic knowledge and sufficient confidence to apply that knowledge in the practice without direct supervision, but with the support of a mentor and personal tutor. These modules echo two theoretical modules on special needs education and management in early years settings taken in the previous term. The work based modules are designed to bring theory and practice together linking university learning with the study and analysis of actual work place practice. Assessment of these modules is in the form of a portfolio of completed tasks and students are visited during these modules by their personal tutor who carries out the final assessment. The tasks involve activities such as completing the professional development profile (a Sure Start requirement) which has to be workplace witnessed and evaluating the setting's special needs policy and then writing activity plans for children with special needs and carrying them out. Management and staff roles and teamwork facilitation in the setting are analysed and evidence collected from the setting on management as if for preparation for an inspection. This portfolio of tasks is then presented to the personal tutor for assessment. As with all assessment, tutors meet to ensure that marking criteria are applied consistently and where FD and BA share modules staff cross mark between the two degrees to ensure maintenance of standards.

Initially we considered the need to demand that students attended another setting during the course, to see how other organisations are run. There is such wide diversity between state and private provision in the sector coupled with the need to have an understanding of the needs of children from babyhood to school age and beyond and also the demands of *Every Child Matters* needs consideration. However, it was found that this ambition was not practicable and that students had to remain in the setting from which they came. This is to be regretted as this does narrow the possibility of students observing other work practices and gaining richer work based experience with a wide range of children aged from a few weeks to early school age.

At the outset of the degree students are asked about their career ambitions. In the first cohorts many had not considered this element but expressed the feelings that "I just want to do more than the old NNEB – think I am learning more" or "I can't think that far ahead, just want to see if I can do this". It became fairly clear however that some students in state settings such as special schools or state run nurseries had ambitions to join the teaching profession. We had to make it very clear the possible routes to achieve this aim, such as the PGCE, or work based routes such as registered teacher or graduate teacher schemes, but also had to point our strongly that none of these could be achieved without GCSE at level C or equivalent in maths and english and science for those born from 1979. This was a blow to some, particularly the maths requirement, as many students did not possess this qualification. Equivalency tests are available but many of our students are not able to meet the requirements without further input and practice.

Towards the end of the two years for the first cohort we began to explore how they could continue to BA Hons if they wished. QAA in their initial work on FDs had suggested that a bridging module to prepare students, who had been following a work based qualification, for critical analysis would be desirable. This fitted well with year three of the BA Hons to which the students would transfer, where a dissertation was required. We therefore used a level 2 HE module from the Hons degree as the bridge. It is a module on research methods, which allowed some practice of methods and techniques and analysis of research articles. This was a good choice as it prepares the students for the dissertation and also heightens their critical analysis abilities. It runs during the summer term of year two of the FD, when the timetabled modules are based in the workplace. Students are advised that they must pass this module as well as the FD to proceed to Honours. The result is students finally achieve 380 credits, not the normal 360, but this is allowable under QAA regulations. The 20 credits for the bridging module do not count as a mark on the students' academic record, being recorded as pass or fail only. This is to allow the university grading system to cope. These pan university electronic systems do seem to have problems with out of phase or unusual courses, being designed for undergraduates on traditional three year programmes.

Students were counselled and some were advised to leave with the FD and aim towards senior practitioner status but some, even two who initially failed the bridging module, wanted to progress against advice. Students were asked their preferred style of delivery, join existing groups of year three students, which would mean attending on different days in the week but having options or, being taught as a group on the same weekday but having to all choose the same modules to follow. The choice was to continue on the same weekday but module selection became difficult and had to be put to a vote. We therefore decided in the future to offer no choice in year three to prevent schism in the group. This is one of the drawbacks of student following what is in effect a full time degree whilst working but as the desire is to finish as soon as possible and proceed to other qualifications sacrifices have to be made. This successful transfer to BA Hons early childhood studies by the majority of our students (about 75%) is a bonus beyond that expected by the team and certainly by many of the students and is considerably more than the 54% given as the figure by Foundation Degree Forward for 2003/4 graduates of FDs who proceed to Honours. Domestic, financial and work related problems do not seem to deter these determined women (and the occasional man). To watch the first cohort traverse the graduation platform and see their smiling faces and the pride of their families was reward enough for the teaching team. Comments such as "I am four feet off the ground and don't know when I will come down" and "I never dreamt I could do this" were common. From this high reality had to set in and studies begun for the required maths and english for those lacking these qualifications, but some students supported by encouraging headteachers applied for and gained places on the graduate teacher scheme.

An example of this success in progression are two students, one a single parent, working in a special school with mainly younger children. Their practical abilities were excellent and the headteacher was eager to further their careers. He gladly supported these two teaching assistants in attending the degree course, though this caused great difficulties for himself and the rest of the staff who had to cover for two missing colleagues one day each week. The greatest support offered and the possibility of progression in careers was at its most successful in schools and larger private nurseries echoing the findings of the Taylor et al's. (2006) study of the sector endorsed FDs. The amount paid by Sure Start for cover to the above mentioned school was in no way realistic and in reality finding two such 'experts' in special needs work from the local community was almost impossible. Prior to the successful completion of their degree the author visited the head to discuss their possible progression to the BA and the graduate teacher scheme. Initially concerns were expressed about another year with two members of staff missing for one day a week but every effort was made by the school, the students and the head to ensure the development of these members of staff. They both successfully completed the BA and the graduate teacher scheme and have gained qualified teacher status.

Recently further movement in the sector means that students with the FD in Early Years can progress onto the new Early Years Professional Status (EYPS) courses overseen by children's workforce development council (CWDC). The long programme is designed to allow workers in early years with FDs and considerable practical experience to follow a course which will award the EYPS and a pass degree (300 credits). This is problematic, as all universities in England require students to have at least 100 credits studied at their institution before they will award a degree. Our EYPS course design therefore has borne in mind that we may recruit students with a FD from another institution which has not been awarded EYPS cohorts in the initial bidding round. It has been decided that all students on the CWDC long programme will progress to an Honours degree and EYPS at the same time. This development, involving four pathways to EYPS, is a new venture for the university and has had to be planned very quickly to meet government demands. We share the desire to offer early years practitioners the possibility to improve their status but would have wished for a longer planning time. However, this means our students graduating with FDs now have another work based route to a full degree and the possibility of being the person in a setting responsible for the early years curriculum. Students working in the integrated care sector in children's centres can also now apply for the National Qualification for Integrated Centre Leadership (NPQICL) which is at Masters level and at Middlesex forms part of the MA in Early Years. This is further evidence that the marrying of WBL with academic study is successful for employees and employer.

The success of the Middlesex FD in early childhood studies has delighted staff and added to the expansion of the HE sector bringing into the university students from non traditional backgrounds. Our success is measured by the numbers of students we successfully guide through the programme to the award of FD and also the numbers who progress onto other qualifications. The rich experiences of these students in the workplace has brought a range of practical understanding into their academic study and the whole degree has been focussed on the relationship between theory and practice. Academic study has enabled students to question work related practice and government policy from surer ground. Students have grown in confidence and are ready to be even more vociferous in their support for the needs of young children for access to good quality education and care. As yet we have not seen much movement in the pay scales of these workers which in the end is how their status is determined. Possibly attracting more men to the workforce would benefit the children and also the pay rates, as traditionally men are not content to work for the low wages which many women have to endure. However, until society see the importance of caring for the next generation the raising of the status and earnings of the early years workforce is unlikely to occur.

References

Brock, A. (2001) An enhanced understanding of early years educators. How do they sustain and redefine their professionalism and knowledge through the changing demands of education today? Paper presented at the *British Education Research Association Annual Conference* Leeds June
http://leeds.ac.uk/educaol/documents/ooool825.htm (accessed 04/04/2007).

DfES (no date) 'Statement of Requirement for Early Years Sector Endorsed Foundation Degrees' (accessed 30/03/07).

DfES/QCA (2000) *Curriculum guidance for the foundation stage*, London, QCA.

FDF (2007) Foundation Degrees: policy developments *forward*, 11, pp6.

Hargreaves, L. and Hopper, B. (2006) Early years, low status? Early years teachers' perceptions of their occupational status. In *Early Years*, 26, (1) 171–186

HEFCE (2000) *Foundation Degree Prospectus* Bristol, HECFE.

HEFCE (2007) Foundation degrees key statistics 2001–2 to 2006–7
www.hefce.ac.uk/pubs/hefce/2007/07–03 #9accessed 10.04.2007).

Hoyle, E. (2001) 'Teaching: prestige, status and esteem', *Educational Management and Administration*, 29(2), 139–152

Moylett, H. and Abbott, L. (1999) A vision for the future – reforming or transforming? In L. Abbott & H. Moylett (Eds.) *Early education transformed*, London: Falmer

QAA (no date) *Foundation Degrees Training Manual*, Gloucester, QAA.

QAA (2002a) *Foundation Degrees Training Manual*, Gloucester, QAA.

QAA (2002b) *Foundation degree qualification benchmark (final draft)*, Gloucester, QAA

QAA (2007) *Higher Quality Bulletin of the Quality Assurance Agency for Higher Education* No23 March

Taylor, J. Brown, R. Dikens, (2006) *Evaluating the Early Years Sector Endorsed Foundation Degree – Qualitative Study of Employers and Mentors* Research Brief RB752 National Centre for Social Research, London, DfES
http://www.dfes.gov.uk/research/data/uploadedfiles/RB752.pdf (accessed 31/03/07)

8

The Undergraduate Curriculum: Echoes and Traces of Contemporary Cultures of Work

Molly Bellamy

***

Introduction

In this chapter, I discuss how Work Based Learning (WBL) as a field and mode of study is structured on the undergraduate programme so as to combine the learning of the individual with organisational learning, and how that learning becomes negotiated by the student worker researcher in relation to contemporary discourses of work, and student narratives of self as a worker researcher.

Lifelong learning represents one of the major 'drivers' of the Dearing Report (1997) to have shifted the focus of learning away from a university subject discipline premise, to one of experiential learning; it may be said in this sense to have reconfigured the construction of knowledge as well as the relationship between tutor and student in higher education. WBL as a mode and field of study characterises this shift in several ways; not least through a 'reversal' of roles between tutor and student, wherein it is the student worker researcher who constructs the knowledge claim, in relation to a sphere that has hitherto been formally outside the university domain – work. This reversal has several implications, a discussion of which forms the basis of this chapter; in terms of what work means today, in a post-fordist economic paradigm that privileges knowledge (rather than industry) as its economic base; a notion implicit in such epochal terms as the knowledge based economy, the knowledge driven economy, and the learning age[1]; in terms of epistemology – or the way in which knowledge is being constructed in a knowledge based economy, by whom and in whose interests; and thirdly, in terms of worker researcher subjectivity, that is, what it means to be a worker, learner and citizen in the new twenty first century economy.

I shall begin with a discussion of WBL as a mode of study, and then as a field of study from the perspective of the undergraduate programme and the undergraduate student population.

Work Based Learning as a Mode of Study in a Knowledge Based Economy

As a mode of study, what is distinctive is the way in which the study is applied to the specific domain of 'work', a domain which is researched by the 'worker researcher', whose knowledge is therefore drawn from and put back into that domain of which she or he is a part, as an 'insider'. At a structural level this mode of study works on an individualised principle of customisation with an emphasis on the worker researcher in the first part of the programme, and organisational learning in the second part.

At the heart of WBL studies for many undergraduate students, whether UK students or international students, is a structure which acts as a vehicle for self-hood, for the achievement of those 'rites of passage' that study leading to a recognised qualification signifies, that for whatever reason may have been withheld from the individual previously, but which enables the student to become someone with rights and status in the public sphere, to be taken seriously as a person of worth with education, as a professional, and a citizen.

In this sense WBL may be said to embody a democratising ethic as a mode of study, in so far that it facilitates access to Higher Education both through the world of work and through a flexible range of pathways, for people who were formerly disenfranchised in relation to Higher Education study;[2]

In terms of credit transfer it is possible for students of WBL to gain entry onto other Higher Education programmes via the WBL 'RAL' module which is an (APEL) claim for prior/present learning that can award up to 240 credits, (the equivalent of two full years study in Higher Education); students may then progress onto sector specific programmes (such as the RTP- Recognised Teacher programme for example) to complete a degree. Other students arrive with 240 credit points which they have gained either from former certificated learning through a HND, or an overseas qualification (recognised by NARIC), or a Foundation Degree ; they come with a view to completing their Honours degree in WBL.

Typically, we have groups of teaching assistants or overseas trained teachers en route to Qualified Teacher Status (QTS). We have groups of driving instructors sponsored by the Driving Instructors' Association who want to 'top up' to a university certificate or a Foundation degree in Driver Education. We have groups of MOD personnel who are funded to undertake a degree in a sector which is professionalising its workforce, as well as individuals from across the public and private sector work domains. In certain sectors such as schooling, the qualifications gained often lead to salary increase and promotions, so that the benefits may be felt in real terms, frequently and tangibly across the undergraduate student population.

These are some examples of the flexible 'top and tail' routes that we offer pre and post degree, which appeal to a working population that cannot take time out of work to gain qualifications or study, or who do not wish to engage on a full degree course but wish to partake in short courses or programmes of Continuing Professional Development.

This recourse to 'flexibility' which characterises WBL is a key principle in most recent HEFCE and DIAS policy and government white papers which link education to the employer engagement agenda[3]; both SME employers and large corporate groups identify the importance of a field and mode of study that can facilitate the practice and culture of industry and commerce sector work values.

As a mode of study, it can be said in this sense that WBL fulfils the conceptions of how to achieve a 'high skill equilibrium' amongst the workforce. Its students are professional and mature and already in the workplace focussing on workplace development – they are not training to get work, so much as retraining as part of an 'economic imperative' that privileges continuing professional development. The framework uses a 'blended learning' approach to learning and teaching, and a flexible, distance learning mode, providing a vehicle for raising the levels of skills required for a 'high skill workforce' and 'high skill economy equilibrium' – by meeting the sectors' needs; in some cases employers want level 2 skills and in some cases they want higher level skills of management and leadership, and WBL can facilitate that complexity of demand.[4]

In this sense the beneficiary in the field is not only the worker researcher as an individual, developing skills and achieving personal and professional 'gains', but the organisation also, in terms of the 'tacit' knowledge gains that it benefits from, in the form of 'structural capital' (Garnett 2005).

WBL as a field of study and student narratives of self as a worker-researcher

Conceptually, for our undergraduate students the notion of 'work', as a complex practice and concept often provides a challenge in itself. We introduce it as a term of reference that is not a 'free-floating signifier' not that is 'value free', particularly as there is a common sense perception that 'work' is something we all 'just do'. The first task for the undergraduate student in this sense is to review this familiar and taken for granted activity, to stand back and re-think it as a key term of reference in a field and mode of study in which they are engaged, and reconsider this familiar activity as strange, by thinking about it in a 'big picture' context, that is, in terms which are historically contingent. In practical terms, 'work' signposts a domain across the public and private spheres of the world of work, such as health, education, local government, business, industry, the services, the arts, the paid and the voluntary sector and so on, from which employments and spheres students arrive to undertake a degree with us.

The undergraduate curriculum addresses the term of reference 'work' variously in different ways across the programme. In many cases this is with a claim for work based knowledge being made by the student, where in prior and present learning is accredited. This is called the RAL which stands for the 'recognition and accreditation of learning'. Students make the claim through "Areas of Learning" where they identify experiential learning in terms of knowledge, skills, competencies, insights, understanding and analysis. The search for a vocabulary that will articulate this hitherto unidentified and unwritten WBL is the main difficulty experienced by students at this stage.

Often students assume a 'personae' through which to write their claim. There are several 'persona' made available through the dominant pedagogical discourse of lifelong learning, with its wardrobe of diversified academic literacies and vocabularies which inscribe and reproduce certain worker-learner ethics – or ways of doing work and experiencing the self as a worker or learner. For example, 'professionalisation' is one of the imperatives that drive lifelong learning, which constructs learning and teaching within a capability and competency based paradigm of skills that is work oriented. Lifelong learning (as a discourse) aligns the project of Higher Education with the work place in many respects, and in this sense 'serves' the country's drive towards developing employment and training initiatives in industry and commerce, demanded, it is perceived, by global economic forces. Lifelong learning also contributes to inscribing the meaning that many students attribute to work, and it does this by aligning the activity of work with the researcher worker self, in a conflated self/work ethic[5]. In this sense the researcher worker is identified with the sphere of work, and experiences 'work' as an expression of or indication of self worth.

Self-management is a characteristic of this self/work ethic that informs many of the RAL claims of WBL students, across all domains of work. Students often draw on a managerial lexicon of entrepreneurialism, when writing their claim:

> 'During my role as Head Teaching Assistant, who is also undertaking a degree in WBL, I have gained an ability to organise my time and energy to optimum effect along the way. This time management skill is something which I have also been able to transfer over to my personal life, so I know how to spend quality time with my children and family, and I take a proactive role as a parent-governor, and overall ensure I achieve a good work life balance – which for a woman these days is crucial'.

This 'self as an entrepreneur'[6] has been a frequent persona that students adopt to express themselves as workers, drawing on prevailing work place cultures of managerialisation and audit[7], it produces an economistic effect.

However there are other 'personae' available to characterise the knowledge claims students make, that draw on different qualities to that of the 'professional' or 'entrepreneurial self ', requiring a different lexicon to express the learning. A more 'feminised' set of work place literacies have become established in the work place recently, as part of a 'cultural turn',[8] inscribing a new 'soft managerial' working culture, so that themes such as 'turn to life', 'life work balance', 'quality time', 'mentoring', 'life coaching' and so on, characterise a different work ethic and persona made available and framed by work place policy and strategies such as Workforce Development.

This 'soft' more pastoral ethic in work and learning is reinforced by the strong pedagogy of reflection inscribed through lifelong learning that places the self at the centre of knowledge-making. Reflection on practice is a derivative of Donald Schon's theory of 'The Reflective Practitioner' (1983); it provides the theme which coheres the WBL Programme and field of study; the pedagogical imperative is that the 'learning' comes from the reflection (on work based activity), in what Marx called a post-festum sense[9].

Epistemologically, the pedagogy may be said to be rooted in a British tradition of philosophy that places particular emphasis on the empirical (as in privileging 'sense data' in for example the tradition of Locke and Berkley)[10], and by the same token on the self as a site of knowledge making; in this sense 'experiential learning' provides the epistemological claim that underpins and legitimises lifelong learning, as something which is rooted in a tradition of empiricism, which in turn privileges an enlightenment notion of selfhood.

In this sense, it may be said that the academic and professional literacies of lifelong learning and workforce development, converge to reproduce and reinforce a particular personalised discourse of work and worker identity, making available a 'new' pastoral lexicon, where knowledge claims in the form of Areas of Learning may be constructed through several different, but joined-up 'personae'.

Accordingly, *we* ask the students to present a reflective essay with their Areas of Learning, as a vehicle for observation, the objective of which is to reflect on the experience of putting the claim together and it is this that constitutes the 'learning'. Both the Areas of Learning and the reflective essay are forms of self-narrative, 'cameos of self' as worker or learner. This turn to selfhood as the site of meaning making often ascribes a lyrical trope to the student 'narratives of self', a storytelling element that takes on an autobiographical style, with frequent recourse to 'epic' metaphors, such as: the arduous journey, the impossible mission to fulfil, or the heroic self pitted against adversity, in a 'holy grail quest' – symbolised by the end of programme award of a degree. In this trope, knowledge is linked to journeying in a classic mode so that exploring new pathways, coming to a crossroads, undertaking an uphill struggle, getting so far and then turning back, getting there in the end are common characteristics of the student narratives.

This notion of Bildgungsroman or 'narrative of experience' has been likened by philosopher Jonathan Ree to Homer's Odyssey, as a journey man, a universal individual, a hero's travelling through his life having experiences that lead him to a state of great wisdom or 'enlightenment' (Ree 1984). Perceived in this way it is easy to see the philosophical 'echoes and traces' that characterise the WBL narratives constructed during the initial RAL stage of the programme, where students recount a professional autobiographical adventure, through their claim and reflective essay, revealing 'echoes and traces' perhaps of a western philosophical tradition. Certainly these narratives of experience are part of a tradition of academic genres such as the auto/biography, professional biography or life history that have become much more established in mainstream university, particularly over the past ten years, as legitimate forms of knowledge-making; they sit within a social science or constructivist paradigm, one championed particularly by feminist theory in the twentieth century.[11] Philosopher Pierre Bourdieu comments on the 'life history' nature of this genre as being particularly empowering, by 'making oneself the ideologist of one's own life'. There is in this sense often an accompanying cathartic dimension to the writing of the Areas of Learning, as on one level students author their own life-stories past and present. This being the case, the evidence students use to support their knowledge claims may need to come in the form of analysis, or reflexivity, made within the body of the claim, as well as in the form of documentary evidence. In a sense we might say that this same 'spirit' of enlightenment, is to some significant degree reproduced, interpolated or inscribed by the very term learning.

Students 'choose' from this wardrobe of 'learning' languages and personae which habit to wear in the construction of their claims, the entrepreneurial self, the pastoral self, the journeyman self, are familiar ready made subject positions within discourses of learning that are known across different spheres to UK students, partly because they are part and parcel of the widespread discourse of lifelong learning that is prevalent throughout the work place, the public sphere of citizenship, schooling and higher education in the UK. In effect students with English as a second language and culture, be they UK based teachers working in the UK, but trained overseas, or students living abroad, need to acculturalise to these technologies of learning before being able to engage with this culture of study and write a 'good' claim.

The engagement with a 'culture of learning' is learned through doing the writing assignments, where-in the de-coding of these (historically and geographically contingent) academic literacies is in grand part the hidden task for all undergraduate students of WBL during the RAL module; it is also what characterises its undergraduateness.

The various 'personae' which are used by undergraduate students during the early part of the programme in the Areas of Learning, as points of entry into the knowledge claims they make, are 'cousins' to the 'subject positions' that student worker-researchers identify as points of entry into their final project at the end of the programme. In this sense, there is a continual negotiation of worker researcher subjectivity on the part of the student in relation to the knowledge produced.

Negotiating the Project: part two of the programme

Within the most recent set of degree awards were many different kinds of projects adopting different standpoints or positionalities and producing different kinds of organisational learning in relation to different work place themes. I present two sets below as contrasting cameos; the first set identifies two cameos from an emancipatory standpoint, and the second set identifies three cameos from a managerialist standpoint.

Set one: an emancipatory standpoint

The first cameo is an ethnography about black boys failing in mathematics in a London school as researched by a male Afro-Caribbean overseas trained teacher. The researcher-worker produced a 'model of good practice' for the school in relation to a school objective to develop access to the curriculum for this ethnic group. It was ethnography. The second of this set is a case study, wherein a white female teaching assistant undertook a project whose aim was to explore in depth the needs of one particularly 'gifted and talented' child, over two terms, in the form of a case study, with a view to putting into place mechanisms that could support this child, her family and the teachers working with the child in school, as well as informing (the OFSTED recommendation for) a school strategy on Gifted and Talented.

Both projects identified 'a gap between policy and practice', which the researchers used as leverage to argue for the necessary access and support for the target group or child within their work place. The 'positionality' of the worker-researcher in the first cameo was aligned with the ethnic group, hence his choice of ethnography as a research approach, and in the second cameo the researcher's positionality was aligned with her role as support staff as against mainstream teacher, hence her choice of case study as research approach. In both cases however there was a subject position or one might say a standpoint on the part of the worker-researchers, assumed in relation to the research project that included a personal interest dimension as well as a professional one. The literacy used in this set was one of social democracy, calling on themes of empowerment, disenfranchisement and advocacy. The research approach and data collection techniques were predominantly qualitative in character.

In these two cameos the worker-researcher deliberately identified with and 'did advocacy' for disenfranchised groups of young people and adopted an emancipatory standpoint or subject position. They could just as well have chosen a research focus and subject position which was managerialist as the second set of worker researchers do in the cameos below.

Set two: a managerialist standpoint.

Within the same group of degree awards were the following three research projects: a survey to determine the role and the work load of personnel in a small private sector SME undertaken by a senior manager of the organisation with a view to putting into place new management structures that would achieve a new 'economy of scale'; a London hospital recruitment and retention scheme for lab technicians based on a survey undertaken by an administrator in the Human Resource Management department; and an action research project on new management strategies for the achievement of literacy and numeracy performance targets across one inner city London school undertaken by a Head of Department .

The themes of these three projects – restructuralisation, recruitment and retention, and organisational targets, are of course very familiar workplace themes. The positionality of the worker-researchers in this set is aligned with managerial concerns; the work ethic is in this sense managerialist. Written partially within a discourse of audit, the projects in this set rationalise the research project in terms of 'more and better management' strategies[12], and use a literacy of measurement in the form of benchmarking, league tables, and performance indicators and scale to rationalise the projects' aims and objectives for efficient and effective work place practice. The research approach and data collection techniques used were predominantly quantitative.

These two sets serve to contrast (and not polarise) the kinds of organisational learning that is produced through the undergraduate programme, and to illustrate that learning it is not determined by the work place or sector, but negotiated by the worker-researcher in relation to the organisation.

Standpoint/positionality as a 'point of entry' into the knowledge claim.

It is the 'standpoint' that the worker-researcher assumes (whether to enfranchise the disenfranchised or implement managerialist practice to meet institutional targets) rather than the work domain or research area that determines the 'point of entry' into the knowledge claim; as, whilst the influence of the workplace has significant bearing on the knowledge claims constructed by students of WBL, in relation to the particular leadership of that institution for example, or the funding of the degree by the institution, and whilst there are multiple discursive practices that converge to prescribe specific sector ethics – as in imperatives, not least in the form of policies and strategies that inscribe normative ways of being and behaving as a worker, and whilst on the undergraduate programme many students come from the public sector and much of the public sphere such as schooling and health is a statutory sector where in these ethics are reinforced, and whilst the candidates on the undergraduate programme tend, generally speaking, to be in a position that is less powerful in the organisational hierarchy (than for example candidates on the D/Prof programme), then the question of individual agency and autonomy on the part of the insider worker-researcher in relation to the knowledge claim, may be legitimately raised. However, there remains a requirement that is built into the curricular design and facilitation of the programme, for the student to negotiate the ways of doing work and experiencing the self as a worker by navigating her way through these discursive practices and power dynamics in such a way as to arrive at an informed standpoint or positionality. It is this process that provides the 'point of entry' into the knowledge claim which ensures so far as possible, that the knowledge claim belongs to the individual worker-researcher as well as the organisation.

In this sense also the 'echoes and traces' of competing work ethics and worker identities, of a changing political hegemony, can be 'read off' from the undergraduate student corpus, rather than 'taught to' the student cohort. In this sense WBL may be said again to invert the teacher-pupil relationship and the traditional concept of holder/receiver of the knowledge. As one Cypriot student said recently:

> 'You come (onto the programme) expecting to learn, like from a course something new, to be fed with new knowledge, but what happens is you find out what you know already, and see what it is worth, and how to use it'.

The Learning Agreement

What links and coheres the first part of the programme which places a focus on the experiential learning of the worker learner as an individual, and the second part which places a focus on organisational learning – both structurally, and in terms of the knowledge claim being produced overall, is the Learning Agreement.

Structurally, it serves as a 'contract' between the organisation, the student worker researcher, and the university, which is ethically binding. This 'contract' represents the different interests of the three parties, as well as those of the 'stakeholders' implicated in the research projects undertaken by the worker-researchers.

The organisation signs the Learning Agreement and by doing so agrees to the worker-researcher undertaking research that will develop organisational learning. The worker researcher signs the Learning Agreement and by doing so agrees to undertake study that will develop work place practice. The university signs the Learning Agreement and in doing so agrees to approve the plan of study set out by the student according to university academic and ethical standards. The approval depends on several things: that all the assessment criteria informing the learning outcomes are met, that the ethical implications are addressed, that the programme coheres where in the title, the credit points and the modules taken are right and appropriate, and that the university academic standards and Learning Teaching and Assessment Strategy is informing the plan.

The learning outcomes are in effect linked to assessment criteria through a range of twelve generic level descriptors. This also ensures that different academics within the Institute, which include also its international centres, as well as the university school based co-ordinators, work to the same generic criteria. The Programme Plan of the student identifies the pathway the student has taken, which is a customised one. There is an ethics release form which must be 'signed off' by the academic adviser, and the programme plan itself is 'signed off' by the chair of the Approval Panel in successful cases. These various procedures of quality assurance and approval serve to ensure that the standards of the programme are in keeping with university regulations. The implications of this are significant, as for example if a project is felt to have unethical components, the approval panel will not approve it. The signatory of the university signifies an academic and ethical approval of a programme of study.

On another level, these rituals of verification (Power 1997) that characterise WBL and the 'modernised' university, signify also a convergence of work place discourses, wherein economic efficiency (audit) and ethics (morality) are aligned through a notion of 'good' or ' best' practice (Strathern 2005). These discourses 'cluster around a nodal discourse'[13] of selfhood, that is at the centre of lifelong learning. We see the 'effect' of this convergence in the student corpus, particularly in the (self regulatory) narratives of self that students construct both during the RAL stage and the project stage of their programme.

The extent to which government initiatives rationalise and operationalise the discourse of ethics to effect a regulatory practice and a form of neo-liberal governance, and the extent to which the presence of accountability in contemporary higher education is felt to undermine the very mechanisms of trust, collegiality and professionalism amongst the academic community, are subjects of debate within our own academic community (Bellamy 2006, Costley and Gibbs 2006). The contested area of the role of ethics in the work place and in research is in this sense a through line which we address as facilitators and through the curricular design of the undergraduate programme, most especially (as discussed above) in relation to the insider positionality of the worker researcher.

Necessarily, students coming from different workplace domains will work to different codes of ethics, both on a formal institutionalised level as well as on a cultural level as different work domains inscribe different values. However for all students the need to comb through the ethical implications of their project from a research practice perspective that goes beyond anonymity and confidentiality, accountability and corporate transparency, and addresses the well-being of the research participants, is what brings the critical distance needed for a successful project.

Conclusion

In conclusion I would say that as a field and mode of study this 'assemblage' is notable for its diversity of pedagogical, epistemological and research paradigms, but is recognisable also in terms of a 'set of family resemblances'[14]. It has both a more or less social science character, and a humanist premise, in so far that it privileges a sociological perspective which places the human subject at the centre of the knowledge frame, and privileges the self as the site of the knowledge making claim. Overall as a field of study, WBL draws on notions of the social construction of knowledge as a legitimate knowledge form. In this sense a 'social construction of knowledge' strain may also be admitted (more readily by some than others) into the family frame.

As a mode of study, what remains most distinctive about WBL perhaps, is the way in which experiential and organisational knowledge is made possible not through a content based curriculum, but through a carefully designed structure that produces a framework approach to learning: generic assessment criteria, diverse techniques for identifying experiential learning, a range of pedagogical tool-kits through which to rationalise the learning, and quality assurance procedures through which to legitimise and formally acknowledge the hitherto tacit learning of the individual or the organisation. This framework is the 'grammar' of WBL as a field and mode of study; it serves not only to articulate (experiential and organisational) learning already out there so to speak, but also and precisely to not impose a content or academic account of work based knowledge by prescribing any one specific discipline based theory, according to the 'academy'. As a field and mode, it is in this sense necessarily 'pluralist', as is the domain of work. Just as it attempts to not impose a preconceived content through its structural approach, it actively attempts to inscribe a critical awareness dimension in the knowledge claims produced by work based learners, through its curricular design and facilitation. What is of value in WBL is the way in which its elements combine, in what is essentially a ' framework' approach to knowledge making, that enables tacit learning to emerge in a system that is supported by a critical thinking design built into the curricular programme in order to facilitate a reflexive knowledge-claim.[15] In this sense the undergraduate programme is structured so as to encourage maximum autonomy on the part of the worker researcher, who takes up an informed 'positionality' (standpoint) in relation to the project, and facilitates maximum learning in relation to the tacit knowledge of the organisation – precisely by structuring itself as a system of frameworks, rather than a content based programme.

And it is perhaps the framework-like character of WBL that best enables the student an agency which, combined with a genuine opportunity to access university qualifications through a work based route for people who have to work to live – produces a strong sense of personal achievement – as though the real search all along were one of selfhood.

Finally, I have indicated that as academics in WBL we act as 'facilitators' – whose role is to safeguard the 'quality' of the knowledge claims, from an epistemological, practical and ethical perspective; a role which however requires an academic's expertise – but that the relationship with the student is primarily a reversal of the traditional teacher student one which privileges the teacher as knowledge maker, as in effect we receive the WBL rather than produce it; that is, we are in the peculiar position of 'witnessing' the echoes and traces of both former and contemporary cultures of work; the shifting and converging trends in work ethics and worker subjectivities that are taking place as our society responds to a new post-fordist economic paradigm, one however in which we operate as workers ourselves, be it as 'knowledge workers' according to some discourses of work, or 'ethnographers' according to others. We are in a unique position to 'read off' the trends and narratives of contemporary work culture from the student knowledge claims; we are therefore less the authors of a twenty-first century sociology, genealogy or single unifying theory of WBL, in the traditional academic mode, than spectators – whereby the meaning of ways of doing work and experiencing the self as a worker and researcher is played out in front of us – by undergraduate students, who come onto the programme like so many Pirandellian characters in search of an author …and leave as scribes.

Notes

1. The following three terms are used to characterise a 'new economy' in the twenty-first century. They do however have different meanings and come from different sources;

a) Knowledge based economy or KBE is a term used by Professor of Sociology at Lancaster University, Bob Jessop, to identify a new economic paradigm which 'reflects the general importance attributed rightly or wrongly to knowledge as a 'factor of production' in the post fordist era. The paradigm acts as a strategic guide for economic, political and social restructuring.

Jessop discusses the role of states being involved in the promotion and production of diffusion of knowledge, and an increased emphasis on the training of 'knowledge workers' to mean skilled manual and intellectual workers.

Jessop talks (critically) about the KBE as an emerging post-fordist model for a new economy.

Jessop, B (2003) *The Future of the Capitalist State* p 96 Polity.

NB The strategy for the knowledge based economy has received backing from International institutions such as the organisation for Economic Cooperation and Development (OECD) and the World Trade Organisation (WTO)

b) Knowledge driven economy is a term of reference in many New Labour documents and policies; originally used in the Department of Trade and Industry, London 1998, White Paper, *Our Competitive Future : Building the Knowledge Driven Economy*

http://www.dti.gov.uk/comp.competitive/wh¬_int1.htm

c) 'The learning age' is a term used in policy documents on Higher Education. Originally used in the DfEE (1998a) The Learning Age: A renaissance for a New Britain, London: HMSO (Cm3270) as well as National Committee of Inquiry into Higher Education (NICHE) (1997)

Higher Education in the Learning Society (the Dearing Report) London: HMSO

2) By 'formerly disenfranchised' I am referring to the role of higher education under New Labour. WBL has been very much a part of the transformation of higher education that has taken place over the past ten years alongside and in relation to the terms of office in government by New Labour, and the Dearing Report, both of which came into being in 1997, and have provided the horse and cart that has driven transformational strategies such as: lifelong learning, continuing professional development, widening participation and more recently workforce development; strategies that have brought about a very different higher education in England to that of 1997, a different student population and a very different workforce ; this is not to say that access to Higher Education in general is not still problematic, it remains uneven, as many social groups remain significantly marginalised.

3) 'Workforce development' HEFCE and DIAS (which is the former DOES) policy and government white papers link education to the employer engagement agenda. This refers to a shift in emphasis in HEFCE policy which formerly privileged lifelong learning as a discourse to align the project of higher education with the economy in an agenda that is neo-liberal in character, the focus of which was on the individual learner. HEFCE is now prioritising a different discourse called workforce development: 'Workforce development is economic development; it raises the overall capability of all organisations. It is particularly vital for the UK's international competitiveness that we invest in increasing the level of knowledge skills and capability across the whole workforce.' (CIHE 2005)

Workforce development as a discourse is characterised by an aim to create a 'whole workplace ethos' wherein it is the organisation rather than the 'learner' (of lifelong learning) that becomes the new site of learning. Moreover, the organisation as a unit is conceived in relation to a national workforce where in the signifiers point to a global conception of the role of work and worker.

To compete successfully in this fast moving global arena, a constant flow of ideas and skills experience is essential. People have to be motivated to change...motivated to learn...motivated to act. And that is true for a country...a company or you and me as individuals.

4. Themes taken from the LEITCH Review of Skills (2006) Prosperity for all in a Global Economy – world class skills. London HM Treasury.

5. Self/work ethic – this concept is taken from an essay by Paul Heelas called Work ethics, soft capitalism and turn-to-life, in *Cultural Economy*, edited by Paul du Gay and Michael Pryke. Sage publications 2002

6. 'Self as an entrepreneur' or the 'entrepreneurial self' is a term and concept used by Foucaldian scholars based on Foucault's notion of subjectivity and technologies of the self; see Paul du Gay *Consumption and Identity at work* 1996 London Sage, and Nikolas Rose *Inventing the Self* 1998 Sage, London.

7. Managerialisation and audit. These two terms are often linked as contemporary discourses of organisational and public sector change. Please see:
The Audit Society rituals of verification by Michael Power 1997 Oxford
Audit Cultures edited by Marilyn Strathern 2005 Routledge London and New York and *The Managerial State* John Clarke and Janet Newman Sage Publications 2001

8. The cultural turn, is a term used in much post modernist literature to indicate the increasing culturalisation of modernity; originally used in *The Cultural Turn*: the cultural turn of contemporary capitalism. Frederick Jameson 1983 – 1998 published by Verso 1998. See also an introduction to this notion in Hall, S *Critical Dialogues in Cultural Studies* London Routledge 1996.

9. Post festum is a term used by Karl Marx when talking about reflection: "Reflection begins post festum – after the feast i.e. after the events reflected on have taken place....and therefore with the results of the process of development ready to hand." Marx, K *Capital Volume 1: The Commodity*, pg 168, Penguin classics 1990.

10. Experiential learning

See Locke and Berkley for a discussion of the ways in which a British tradition of philosophy has provided a legacy for a twenty first century Anglo/American discourse of experiential learning that informs European Union policy (UNESCO) and serves to legitimise the pedagogical premise of Lifelong Learning. Also see Bellamy, M. *Positionality and the Insider Researcher in WBL* in Universities Association for Lifelong Learning (UK) WBL network annual Conference Proceedings, November 2003, Nicosia.

See also Norman Fairclough's chapter *Re-scaling the nation-state* in *Language and Globalisation* (2006) Routledge, for a case–study perspective on Romanian higher education changes in relation to EU directives.

11. Feminist theory in the twentieth century. The feminist slogan the personal is political was part of a movement which saw feminist theory blossom in the academy during the late 1970s and 1980s. Auto/Biography was one genre amongst others that privileged the experiential and the emotions as valid sites for knowledge construction. In many ways the feminisms were in the vanguard of challenging the legacy of sciencism in the academy. Please also see Bellamy, M. *Tidy in the Self* given at Gendered Choices and Transitions: part time pathways

and, full time lives; Women in Lifelong Learning network conference Birkbeck College London University, 18 May 2005. See also Stephanie Taylor's *Ethnographic Research: A reader*. Sage 2006

12. More and better management as a strategy for organisational change with roots in Taylorism. See discussion in *The Managerial State* John Clarke and Janet Newman Sage Publications 2001

13. Discourses which 'cluster around a nodal discourse' this is a notion of Norman Fairclough, used in his theory of 'Cultural Political Economy' (CPE) wherein he contends that different discourses converge around one nodal one much like a magnet and that this one nodal discourse such as for example the knowledge based economy articulates many others. This kind of discursive practice is a characteristic of cultural political hegemony. Please see N, Fairclough *Language and Globalisation* (2006) Routledge.

14. A set of family resemblances this is a phrase used by many social theorists and linguists and ethnographers to try to articulate the way in which a phenomenon is made up of different but related features. For an introduction to this notion please see Vivian Burr's introduction in her book *The Social Construction of Knowledge* The phrase was used originally by Wittgenstein.

15. I am claiming that a reflexive knowledge claim is possible with recourse to learning materials that inscribe a critical thinking awareness and set of skills as a pedagogical tenet; a module on critical research methodologies WBS3835, which inscribe awareness of worker researcher positionality and highlights the power dynamics involved in any knowledge making claim, and again through a literature search and review module which 'teaches' critical reading skills to analyse policy and sector specific literatures and review theory, as well as developing a through-line attention to the ethical implications of research related to quality assurance practice in other modules. The curricular design also embraces the tenet of reflection on learning which provides the pedagogical perspective to experiential learning, and which when properly accessed induces a post-festum focus on work based activity, that may achieve reflexivity.

References

Armsby, P, Costley, C and Garnett, J (2006) The legitimisation of knowledge: a work based learning perspective of APE. In *International Journal of Lifelong Learning and Education*, 25 (4) pp 369–383.

Bellamy, M (2007) *The Learning Agreement; Contracting in…* conference paper published in Proceedings of A Multidimensional approach to knowledge. Universities Association for Lifelong Learning Conference Middlesex University. http://www.middlesex.ac.uk/wbl/research/uall07.asp

Bellamy, M (2005) *Assessment as Audit* paper given at conference and published in the conference Proceedings of Assessment and Evaluation in Higher Education, Work Based Learning network conference Edinburgh University, 21–22 March

Bordieu, P (1986) *The biological illusion* Originally published as *L'illusion biographique Actes de la recherché en sciences sociales* –62/3, pp69–72, is taken from Working Papers and Proceedings of the Centre for Psychological Studies, ed RJ Paramentier and G Urban (1987)

Clarke, J and Newman, J (2001) *The Managerial State* London: Sage Publications

Costley, C. and Gibbs, P. (2006) Researching Others: Care as an ethic for

Practitioner Researchers, *Studies in Higher Education*, 31 (1) pp21–33

Du Gay, P (1996) *Consumption and Identity at work* London: Sage

Fairclough, N (2006) *Language and Globalisation* London: Routledge

Garnett, J (2007) Challenging the Structural Capital of the University to support Work Based learning In *Work Based Learning Futures* (eds) David Young and Jonathan Garnett, pp21–27 Bolton: UVAC

Hall, S (1996) *Critical Dialogues in Cultural Studies* London: Routledge

Jameson, F (1998) *The Cultural Turn* Verso

Jessop, B (2003) *The Future of the Capitalist State* p96, Polity

Marx, K *Capital* Volume 1: The Commodity, p168, Penguin classics 1990

Power, M (1997) *The Audit Society rituals of verification* Oxford: Oxford Universoty Press

Rose, N (1998) *Inventing the Self* London: Sage

Taylor, S (2006) *Ethnographic Research: A reader* London: Sage

Workman, B (2007) Casing the joint: explorations by the insider-researcher preparing for work-based projects. In *Journal of Workplace Learning*, 19 (3) pp146–160.

9

Developing Work Based Learning at Doctoral Level

Pauline Armsby and Carol Costley

***

Introduction

As reported in Portwood and Thorne (2000), developing the Masters/Doctorate in Professional Studies was a significant challenge for work based learning (WBL) studies in 1997 at Middlesex University. After three years research and discussion the university was prepared to be innovatory and approved it as an important alternative pathway at doctoral level for professional learning. The main reasons at that time were that it would explore new opportunities from emerging professions, national and international reports advocated this kind of development and there was institutional commitment for access to higher education at the highest (doctoral) level. The fact that these things remain true may account for the subsequent flourishing success of the programme and its dissemination across the university. Although ten years on, following a range of research into its inception, pedagogy and influence, as outlined in brief in this chapter, it is timely to review the context of the development; its teaching, learning and assessment issues and contemplate our possible future challenges.

Our aim in developing the programme was to enable high level professional learning and continued professional development. The experiences outlined here will illustrate the context in which this has taken place including; globalisation, the growing prominence of the knowledge economy, the professionalisation of work roles and changes in higher education. It will also explore its pedagogy including; the transdisciplinary nature of WBL, learner centred learning, reflexivity, praxis, the place of methodology in practice based learning and the importance of impact. Finally, developments such as the birth of another innovatory programme, the M/DProf by Public Works will be presented as an example of our continuing focus on providing higher education academic provision for high level professionals.

Overview of the M/DProf Programme

The Doctorate in Professional Studies (DProf), approaches learning from a transdisciplinary perspective. Students are known as candidates on the programme, have an average age of 43 and are usually in middle or senior management positions from varied professions and backgrounds. The structure of the programme was modelled on the existing WBL Bachelors and Masters programmes that holds a position relating to knowledge which is practice based and draws on practitioner led enquiry as a principle for research. It has not emerged from an existing academic department that had operated within a particular paradigm with an existing pedagogy. The DProf doctoral project was designed to be equal in level and rigor to a doctoral thesis (Thorne 2001) and develop the practice of people at work. It did not borrow from existing subject based curricula within the university. The doctorate was developed during a time when new programmes have had to subscribe to programme outcomes, level descriptors, inbuilt evaluation strategies, student progression and monitoring through modular frameworks, quality control and audit structures. Outcomes based programmes have received considerable criticism for their highly behaviourist and sometimes, shallow presumptions about learning development (Ecclestone 1998) with which we have some agreement. This programme is designed to support a reflexive approach to learning which does not separate academic subjects from practice but construes the knowledge wholistically (Costley 2000) and, if anything, prioritises horizontally relevant knowledge produced from informal learning (Guile and Fonda 1999). The programme supports the greater emphasis that doctoral learning is required to place on the immediate practical skills that better prepare students for and in work as described in the Roberts report (HM Treasury 2002), the QAA revised Code of Practice (QAA 2004) and the skills training requirements for research students: joint statement by the (UK Research Councils 2001).

At the time of writing there are over 300 candidates on all variants of the doctoral programme, roughly equally split between men and women. In the past ten years there have been over 100 graduates at DProf level and a similar amount at MProf level. The vast majority of these have been individuals undertaking their own professional development for their organisation and/or profession. The range of professional groups is enormous, with pockets of specific groups according to partnerships the Centre has developed. The vision of collaborative doctorates has not yet come to fruition. Possible reasons for this are the individual nature of doctoral level study and the lack of organisational partnerships the Centre has that wish to pursue learning at doctoral level. Organisational partnerships such as the City of London Corporation have been the most likely to produce collaborative doctoral work .

Perhaps the biggest development has happened in our international activities. There are significant groups of candidates located with our overseas offices in Greece, Cyprus and Ireland and we are now beginning to see candidates apply to our Hong Kong offices. In addition, we have candidates from other countries that are managed from our London office. The overseas operations have been differently affected by local attitudes and educational policy in relation to what is seen as 'distance learning', 'work based learning' and professional doctorates (as opposed to PhDs). British awards are usually respected overseas, however, when delivery takes place in these countries, territorial issues can emerge. What seems clear is the demand by individuals for the doctorate. This, together with taking a flexible and responsive approach to local conditions has meant that numbers have steadily grown leading to the resultant issue of staffing. Local Advisers are needed and this requires substantial staff development as, in our experience, advising on the DProf requires a good understanding of practice based research, which is not necessarily present in those who have worked as tutors, for example, with PhD candidates. One solution to this issue has been in the use of a cascade model in which previous successful candidates take on the role of Adviser to new candidates. All new Advisers are mentored by a core team member. Thus personal experience of undertaking the programme, together with mentoring, (when fully engaged in) has been found to work effectively.

Other increases in demand have arisen from partnerships with organisations who have wanted to work with our programme because they believe it captures the spirit of professional learning whilst retaining the more 'academic' elements grounded in research. These partnerships have taken the generic field of WBL to specific professional groups (sustainable development- Forum for the Future; psychotherapy- Metanoia Institute; organisational consultancy- Ashridge Management College). Combined with specialist pathways of the DProf that have been developed in other parts of the University (health and environment- Health and Social Science School; business- Business School), a more diverse picture of professional studies emerges, with more contained epistemological and pedagogical boundaries than the initial generic framework. And yet, the generic framework is still popular with professionals from the groups that could be served by these specialist pathways. Our experience suggests that some candidates prefer to engage with a generic programme as it may offer opportunities to conceptualise ideas and develop practices more widely and enable them to recognise and honour the extent of the transdisciplinarity of their work practices.

The rapid increase in candidates working at the highest level of programmes offered in Higher Education has proved challenging to manage. Administrative processes developed to mirror those of the PhD, for example internal and external examiner processes, and of WBL in general, for example Programme Approval Panels, Accreditation Boards, have had to be set in place and then mirrored by the specialist pathways. A range of academic and administration staff development has been required by a small core team. A challenge for each member of this core team has been balancing the range of responsibilities within the normal expectations of an academic or administrator in a university. Without blanket understanding across the university of what a WBL professional doctorate is and is not, and hence what is involved in managing it successfully, there has often been an element of winning hearts and minds, and 'educating' colleagues.

To address colleagues' natural concerns over the level of this new type of doctorate it has been important to pay particular attention to quality assurance and enhancement processes. Marking, second marking and moderation to ensure parity across markers including those from international centres and specialist pathways is routine for non project work. For projects, very similar processes and procedures to the Middlesex PhD are used, in particular in relation to internal and external examiners. All internal and external audits undertaken on the DProf have noted our exemplary attention to process. In terms of research degrees, the DProf has representation at the highest level of the university at the Research and Research Degrees Committee. This is entirely fitting as DProf related candidates now make up over one third of those undertaking doctoral level work.

A tool we are developing to help unify the whole range of practitioners involved in the DProf and its specialist pathways is a Virtual Learning Environment. Apart from offering a place for resources for all learners and an opportunity to provide some parity of experience for the diverse groups, one of the main advantages is in enabling communication between the community of practitioners and learners involved in our programmes. A natural extension of this for current learners and learning facilitators (advisers and consultants) would be to enable communication with the alumni.

The doctorate began by setting out the standards required for successful completion and further detailed this with a generic set of level descriptors. During the normal review processes of university programmes we have taken the opportunity to revisit and review these, aligning them carefully with our lower level programmes. Table 9.1 shows the criteria currently used which are defined further for HE levels 4 and 5. These have proven to give assessors a useful range of criteria by which to assess the learning and developments made as a result of undertaking the DProf.

Table 9.1: Doctorate in Professional Studies Assessment Criteria

A Knowledge and Understanding	
A1	Knowledge
A2	Research and Development Capability
A3	Ethical Understanding
B Cognitive Skills	
B1	Analysis and Synthesis
B2	Self Appraisal/Reflection on Practice
B3	Planning/Management of Learning
B4	Evaluation
C Practical Skills	
C1	Awareness of Operational Context +application of learning
C2	Use of resources
C3	Communication/ Presentation Skills
C4	Responsibility and Leadership

The programme has a simple credit based structure with the programme including 180 credits at HE level 4 and 360 credits at level 5. An important and innovatory facet of the programme is in enabling the recognition and accreditation of learning (APEL). Experienced practitioners usually have relevant master's degrees that they can provide a rationale for as underpinning their doctoral programme. In addition, they often have high level experiential learning arising from their professional work such as reports, inventions, artefacts, manuals that have prefaced their doctoral project. The accreditation process is undertaken with a review of learning in part one of the programme at the same time as planning the practitioner research project that will be undertaken in part two of the programme. The structure is designed around the candidates' own individual experience and required development. The relevant knowledge the candidate has is accredited and the future project they need to undertake is planned and then undertaken. Each part of the programme is assessed against the criteria in Table 9.1.

An important aspect of the DProf presented here is the learners' situatedness outside the academic sphere (Lave and Wenger 1991). The candidates, already 'experts' within their own working environment through their doctoral study, can make significant high level innovations in their organisations or professional spheres and this is commensurate with a high level contribution to knowledge.

Its generic form has application to any field and is predicated on a form of transdisciplinarity that has been evolved and researched within the community of WBL academics in recent years. The diversity of specialisms within the different professions represented by the cohort of learners in our study, does not allow an imposition by academics based on pre-defined contexts or methodologies. For example, there are no special modules containing what academics believe to be important information about Engineering, Education, or whatever field the candidate's doctoral project may be considered to be about. Candidates on the DProf are usually at senior level or equivalent, have high level professional expertise and usually hold a master's degree. They cannot enter the programme if they are not in a position to introduce the possibility of appropriate change in their organisation or professional area. They have sufficient authority and leadership in their work to undertake doctoral level research and development projects that can have a wide-ranging effect on their organisation, community or professional field (Portwood and Thorne 2000).

Instead of the conventional supervisory team, support for candidates is provided by an academic programme adviser who guides and works alongside the candidate throughout their programme, ensuring both academic standards and practical effectiveness (Boud and Costley 2007). The candidate also draws on expertise from across the university and from senior professionals outside the university in its provision of subject specific and real world consultancy to candidates. By this means, the programme is able to accommodate candidates from a wide range of professional areas in the public, private and voluntary sectors. As described above, a challenge has sometimes been in pinpointing staff across the university who have an understanding and inclination to work with candidates engaged on organisational and or professional development projects

The programme is able to provide formal recognition of, and academic credit for, the candidates' critical reviews of their existing professional experience (Doncaster and Lester 2002) and any achievements they may already have at doctoral level (Chisholm and Davis 2006) before they plan the next stage of their development (Doncaster and Thorne 2000). The credit based and modular structure of the programme allows candidates to negotiate their preferred balance of weighting between credits for the recognition of their current professional learning and credit for their final doctoral projects. A review of their learning which is used to enable the recognition and accreditation of their relevant certificated and experiential learning forms the initial element of part one of the programme. Part one also includes a substantial programme project planning and development element. In part two, which forms the project work, there is also acceptance of a wide variety of final outcomes proposed by the candidates themselves as the basis for final assessment; such as professional project reports, book, policy documents, sets of guidelines and regulations describing programmes of action designed to achieve significant impact in the professional context. There is a critical commentary embracing candidates' professional achievements as a whole, the methodology and the specifics of the final outcomes that defines how candidates have played a unique role in implementing change, developing innovative approaches and creating sustainable solutions to complex issues (Doncaster 2000, Lester 2004).

The programme includes involvement of representatives of the candidates' professional fields in the university's decision to approve the proposed final projects for assessment. Assessment criteria provide generic descriptors rather than prescriptive outcomes and are applicable to contexts appropriate to the candidates' distinctive programmes. The learning outcomes and assessment criteria relate specifically to work based practice.

The contexts of our developments

At a global and societal level, states and politicians, institutional leaders, students, business leaders and consultants are forming knowledge interests, alliances and regimes that define new kinds of knowledge (Bleiklie and Byrkjeflot 2002). At the same time Professional Doctorates (PDs) and some PhDs are becoming a means by which mid to late career learners can become accepted in professional communities as leading thinkers in their fields. Science/ research used to 'speak' to society now it is integrated into society, embedded in a context that speaks back to science. Most knowledge production is increasingly based on its communities. For these reasons, research education needs to expand the kinds and types of knowledge that are recognised and diversify the criteria by which it is judged.

The purposes and products of the DProf are often determined by the knowledge interests and alliances of the candidates, and of other stakeholders, in relation to their professional communities. In contrast to the university determining the knowledge content and purpose of doctorate learning, practitioners who undertake the DProf make a personal and professional difference to a specific community (Bourner et al 2001) resulting in the major products of DProf projects thus providing useful and innovative contributions to professional work. The DProf is able to link the theory and scholarship of higher education with practitioners' professional knowledge arising from specific communities of practice to both produce and apply knowledge. A balance of scientific authority in relation to these different, more professionally focused interests and values; at how practitioners form alliances through partnerships, strong personal and professional relationships, economic imperatives and other reasons that are based on common knowledge conceptions. This 'professional view' which is seen to prioritise the question of purpose and consequences of knowledge also involves values because there is always an immediate engagement with the views and needs of others. We consider a wider concept of the knowledge sphere that may reflexively engage with academic and socially responsible principles.

The Middlesex University DProf is a PD where knowledge application means real time projects undertaken by candidates on the programme in their places of work and the learning of the successful candidates that results in a higher level approach to future project research and development. PDs appear to be engaging within their focus on professional knowledge, pedagogical issues relating to the support of mid-late career professionals with considerable expertise. There is a repositioning of social, individual, professional and market forces so that universities are changing their role in their approach to knowledge creation, generation and use, and this may involve a fresh look at knowledge regimes, and at how and why they are changing. The complexities of knowledge interests and alliances for doctorates may be leading to a changing pedagogical role for universities that requires them to engage more closely with communities outside academe. A better understanding is needed of the situatedness of professional doctorate candidates within their communities of work, and the contexts within which they work and undertake their doctoral work. Whereas a PhD holder typically enters the professional community of the people who have taught him or her to PhD level, the holder of a PD has typically remained within the professional community in which his or her new knowledge and understanding is intended to be (and may already have begun to be) put to use throughout their period of study. For this reason, it is reasonable to expect that the concept of 'becoming peer', which Boud and Lee (2005) understand as a typical PhD holder's entry into academia, must be reconceptualised for holders of the PD; for them, becoming peer means becoming regarded as an active, acknowledged contributor to the development of a professional area which is not in itself primarily concerned with knowledge generation as academia is, but with knowledge application to the improved production and other, usually more concrete, goods and services.

In about the last 15 years, the number of people undertaking Professional Doctoral (PD) study in UK universities has been increasing by 20% per annum (Bourner et al 2001). In 2005 a UKCGE report recorded that in 1998 there were 12 different kinds of professional doctorate and in 2005 there were 51 with an approximate total of 6633 graduates with the new degree nationally. This illustrates the steady professionalisation of many work roles. To date, relatively little research has focused on this new set of stakeholders in higher education.

As noted earlier, in the UK doctoral learning is required to place greater emphasis on the immediate practical skills that better prepare students for, and in, work and are the fastest growing area of research degrees. A new generation of PDs that have a clear focus on practice based professional knowledge open up new areas of inquiry (Bourner et al 2000) and suggest that control of content and methodology is referred to the candidate within a generic framework of standards, regulations and support offered by the university. Maxwell (2003) demonstrates how PDs have developed to become more involved with professional knowledge and how one curriculum model in Australia places mode two knowledge (Gibbons et al 1994, Nowotny et al 2001) at the centre of learning. Bourner et al (2001), in a survey of English universities identify twenty distinctive features of PDs

Whereas the conventional PhD degree continues to be primarily a pathway into the academic profession of university teaching for people in the relatively early stages of their lives and careers, the DProf functions primarily as a means of professional and personal development for mid to senior professionals. It is to be expected that these two student populations differ widely not only with respect to the background knowledge and understanding that they bring to their studies, but also with respect to the their hopes and aspirations for life beyond the study period, and the role that they expect the degree to play later in their careers. It is acknowledged that many PhDs are also engaging with mid to late career professionals and that many of the ways used for categorising knowledge are complex and overlap. In these circumstances of radically altering knowledge regimes (Bleiklie and Byrkjeflot 2002) there is little clear identity for a PD and a PhD. The conventional PhD has always maintained an open structure and a knowledge content based on peer review that has the capacity to change and be reinterpreted. Some universities have developed their doctorate provision in this way; for example the University of Bath PhD in Education has very similar content and structure to many PDs. We still have diverse approaches to doctorate education in the UK and elsewhere, that range from the conventional thesis that contributes to theoretical knowledge, to professional, real time project work (in some cases a series of related projects) that contributes to high level practice. The DProf can be thought of as being positioned at neither end of this range of approaches as it culminates in a large scale project that has the propensity to make a significant contribution to practice that is also underpinned by theory.

Teaching, learning and assessment

WBL requires a pedagogical understanding that relates not only to the teaching of adults but also to the acknowledgement of the existing experience and positionality of the student. It offers students the opportunity to develop themselves further because it is project based, grounded in practice and tailored to the requirements of people at work. From current research, based on student interviews, we have found that an important reason why many practitioners select WBL is that it offers them a new and challenging transdisciplinary learning opportunity that will develop them further and provide a new challenge (Stephenson et al 2006). Students are also particularly attracted to the way work based projects are conceptualised in that it is usually, directly related to their real time work activities. WBL is necessarily focused on the learners themselves within their particular organisation or professional area; not within the university, but informed by the university. It formulates the possibility in which control of content, research method, context, assessment, and partnership between university and the profession lies with the participant within a generic framework of procedures and support offered by the university.

Professional doctorate learning demands the knowledge of professional contexts informed by a more wide ranging knowledge of the area. Many issues arise from the growing number of doctoral projects using enquiry techniques to meet a particular object of investigation in a working context (Costley and Gibbs 2006). Research undertaken as part of the DProf has become a way to enhance practice and develop benefit to particular professional groups and organisations (Scott et al 2004). Engaging with research methods requires, we argue, not only adherence to ethical codes of conduct but caring for the researched. Researchers who are also workers in the same organisation or community where the research will take place, have a particular ethic of care because the subjects of the research are already known to them and will continue to be colleagues when the research has been completed. This concern can be progressed in a research methods course that uses reflective diary writing as a way for researchers to reflect and articulate the complexities of their approach to ethical considerations in their planned research (Gibbs and Costley 2006; Gibbs et al 2007). Although reflection does not necessarily lead to action, reflective diaries are useful in capturing a period of personal transition. This is demonstrated through the diaries of a candidate and worker

The place of literature in the DProf can be challenging due to the transdisciplinary nature of work and WBL. Projects can include a more diverse set of 'literature' both in terms of the 'subjects' covered and the types of literature of relevance for example, reports, websites, minutes of meetings. Some projects have more focus on theory and some on practice. Candidates, as actors within their professional contexts, often have a rich underpinning knowledge which they need to present to justify their arguments for project focus. This can sometimes be theoretical knowledge but more often it relates to current practice. Where PhDs are criticised for having little practical value, some DProfs have been criticised for lacking theory. As with most research there is often a difficulty in staying focussed and the real world contextual issues can exacerbate this. Bounded rationality needs to be used to enable effective management of the project work which must lead to development. Appropriate recognition of theory is important but as a programme that primarily aims to develop practitioners and, not develop theories, it often takes a secondary role.

Work based doctoral projects have been around in HE for a long time but it seems extraordinary now that the issues around them have been so little explored. What has been named as practitioner research, insider research or the worker as researcher has been mostly explored by colleagues in education and specifically those educationalists who support Action Research. Some other approaches to investigation that can inform work based projects can be found in the work of, for example, ethnographers and in case study and collaborative enquiry whilst some particular research techniques such as participant observation, interview and questionnaire often enable work based learners to conduct theoretically informed projects. There is also the growing literature on reflective and reflexive practice that theoretically informs the work based researcher who is usually researching and developing a work based issue or innovation in order to enhance or create new processes and practices in the context of a particular work environment.

Products such as manuals or exhibitions and evidence of new working processes are important in showing professional impact. Solving real world problems often requires tangible outcomes. Avenues for disseminating these developments are also important. As indicated in Table 9.1 the DProf requires a range of capabilities to be evident and arising from project work that leads to a major organisational and/or professional development.

As well as being dependent on context the field is concerned with the generic area of work and transdisciplinary knowledge. Learning gained in, through and for work represents a significant proportion of what is counted as 'important knowledge' according to contemporary discourses concerning the knowledge society. Multinational corporations, the education sector, professional bodies, government departments and other agencies and communities are redefining their roles regarding access to, and ownership of, knowledge. Drawing on the spheres of the professional, the academic and the experiential, WBL can use instruments that approach knowledge that is not confined to discrete disciplines but focuses on the multi–dimensional nature of knowledge needed for understanding differing contexts of work. Scott et al (2004) present five modes of knowledge (disciplinary knowledge, technical rationality, dispositional and transdisciplinary knowledge, critical knowledge and 'hybridity'). The transdisciplinary model, is 'essentially concerned with the individual and their own practice' (p51) and each student's programme is distinctive in field and method (p48).

Research and development projects are real world, real time in the work place and use practitioner led approaches for small scale pieces of development work which can be undertaken collaboratively and have a useful and 'real' outcome. The process can be revealing and expose a repository of knowledge previously unexplored by the student. This is because knowledge is usually bounded between experiential knowledge and formally taught knowledge; formal learning in education institutions and experiential learning through work experience being the traditionally acknowledged ways of assessing current standing. Knowledge is bounded again by different kinds of experience (workplace, community, domestic etc.) and in formal learning, between disciplines. When these sets of entities are broken down and explored in synthesis according to their application, new transdisciplinary work based knowledge can be revealed.

Following this approach to knowledge creation our pedagogy has necessarily shifted towards facilitative styles. Our candidates are often highly successful professionals in their field who seek personal and professional development for their own and/or their organisations', communities' or public benefit. The personal adviser role alluded to above enables this kind of development through encouraging reflexivity and vision, and assisting with project planning and implementation. In most ways 'adviser' is probably a misnomer as the skills required to work effectively with DProf candidate require more of a mentoring or coaching style. Individuals' needs vary but in essence advising enables the candidate to define their professional role and extend it through a significant project.

Challenges and Developments

This section briefly draws together some of the challenges confronting us that we have touched upon in this chapter and outlines some of the recent and planned developments that have emerged from our experiences and practice.

Power, control and vested interests

WBL, as a field, follows criteria that conform to a generic, higher education level but not necessarily to other conventions of more traditional subject disciplines. We define the field of WBL as a 'subject' area because that is an accepted term in universities, and moving away from established perspectives and practices can be risky in times of uncertainty in the HE sector. Bleiklie and Byrkjeflot (2002) use the term 'utility oriented knowledge' to mean more 'social', vocationally oriented knowledge that has utilitarian demands within its research focus. This concept has become a cause for concern in universities and has come about because of new actors such as Professional Doctorate candidates with new interests and ideas about knowledge. The value of 'social ability' held within the utility oriented view is seen as in opposition to the cultural value of academic autonomy which is to seek truth for its own sake. New knowledge alliances with differing interests often connected to Professional Doctorates' professional affiliations has implications for the power balance, with values that change the rank order of established values. Alliances are formed through partnerships, strong personal and professional relationships, economic imperatives and other reasons that are based on common knowledge conceptions. The utility view which is seen to prioritise the question of purpose and consequences of knowledge also involves an ethics oriented approach because there is always an immediate engagement with the views and needs of others. However, whilst knowledge production can be argued as being led by a relationship between the utility and truth perspectives, knowledge application is around ethics and utility. A wider concept of the knowledge sphere in Professional Doctorate learning may reflexively engage with scientific (truth and merit) and socially responsible (ethical and utility) principles.

Expansion

Societal shifts are bringing about the gradual changes alluded to above and the DProf is meeting the needs of actors in this knowledge society. This has resulted in rapid expansion of the programme locally and globally. Many of our pragmatic challenges result from operationalising this expansion within the HE culture that prioritises theoretical knowledge developed for its own sake. As a new field, there are limited numbers of people with knowledge and skill in facilitating WBL, particularly at HE's highest level. The average academic does not always make a good WBL doctoral adviser and alumni are often deeply imbedded in their own profession. Hence staffing rapid developments has been problematic. Staff development into the adviser role has worked best with mentoring, with mentors assisting and checking mentee's facilitation and assessments throughout at least one candidate's programme. This lack of expertise in WBL professional doctorates also affects quality at assessment in the dearth of people experienced and highly qualified enough to act as external examiners for our finalists. Parallel to the academic staffing issues are those related to administrating the programme. All WBL is administratively intensive by virtue of the individualised nature of the programmes. Administrators need to manage complex procedures and be highly skilled in making university systems, designed for standard undergraduate students, meet their different needs.

Developments

WBL is topical in the present climate which is encouraging HE to prepare people effectively for work. Yet at the moment we see the focus of this at undergraduate level. At doctoral level a WBL professional doctorate is not preparing people for work, it is often a means of continuing professional development. Our experience has shown us that high level work, comparable to that undertaken within traditional university programmes is being practiced by a range of workers in the knowledge society. The DProf has enabled these people to focus and extend this work into a doctoral level programme. But there are others that have already undertaken such an extensive range of developments that it was felt that their accomplishments already mirrored those of the DProf. For this reason we have recently developed the DProf by Public Works (Armsby 2007), which is a sister doctorate to the PhD by published works, to enable CPD for this new group of practitioners. High level professionals may expect and achieve challenge and progression from their work roles but our conclusion is that HE can facilitate or add value to these endeavours. To develop this we plan to facilitate an alumni network that could provide postdoctoral opportunities and assist in the networking and partnership development that lies beneath the knowledge economy. With alumni across the globe this network development will inevitably, for the most part, be virtual. Social networking has always had an important part in developments. Software that is enabling more and wider, but focussed opportunities should help support the forward thinking individuals we call our alumni.

References

Armsby, P. (2007) Doctorate in Professional Studies by Public Works in DEWBLAM

Bleiklie, I. and Byrkjeflot, H. (2002) Changing Knowledge Regimes: Universities in a new research environment. In *Higher Education* 44 pp. 519–532

Boud, D. and Costley, C. (2007) From project supervision to advising: new conceptions of the practice. In *Innovations in Education and Teaching International*, 44 (2) pp 119–130

Boud, D. and Lee, A. (2005) 'Peer learning' as pedagogic discourse for research education. In *Studies in Higher Education*, 30 (5) pp. 501–516

Bourner, T., Bowden, R., and Laing, S. (2000) 'Professional doctorates: the development of researching professionals', in T Bourner, Katz, T. and Watson, D. *New Directions in Professional Education* Buckingham: Society for Research in Higher Education / Open University Press

Bourner, T., Bowden, R., & Laing, S. (2001) 'Professional Doctorates in England'. In *Studies in Higher Education* 26(1): 65–83

Chisholm, C. and Davis, M. (2006) 'Analysis and evaluation of factors relating to accrediting 100% of prior experiential learning in UK work-based awards'. In

Assessment and Evaluation in Higher Education vol32 no 1 pp125–137

Costley, C. (2000) 'Work Based Learning: an accessible curriculum' In *Widening Participation and Lifelong Learning Journal* vol 1 no 5 20–27

Costley, C. and Gibbs, P. (2006) 'Researching Others: Care as an Ethic for Practitioner Researchers'. In *Studies in Higher Education* vol. 31 no.1 pp 89–98

Costley, C. and Stephenson, J. (2008) 'Building doctorates around individual candidates' professional experience'. In *Changing Practices of Doctoral Education* Eds. David Boud and Alison Lee, London: Routledge

Doncaster, K. (2000) The Middlesex University professional doctorate: a case study. In *Continuing Professional Development* 3 pp1–6

Doncaster, K. & Lester, S. (2002) Capability and its development: experiences from a work-based doctorate. In *Studies in Higher Education* 27 (1), 91–101

Doncaster, K. & Thorne L. (2000) Reflection and planning: essential elements of professional doctorates. In *Reflective Practice* 1 pp391–399

Ecclestone, K. (1998) 'Empowering or ensnaring? The implications for outcomes based assessment'. In *Higher Education Quarterly* vol. 52 no 1 pp29–49

Gibbons, M., Limoges, C., Nowotny, H., Schwartzman, S., Scott, P., and Trow, M. (1994) *The New Production of Knowledge: The Dynamics of Science and Research in Contemporary Societies* London: Sage

Gibbs, P., Costley, C., Armsby, P. and Trakakis, A. (2007) Developing the Ethics of worker-researchers through phronesis. In *Teaching in Higher Education* vol 12 no 3

Gibbs, P. and Costley, C. (2006) An ethics of community and care for practitioner researchers. In *International Journal of Research and Method in Education* vol. 29 no2 pp 239–249

Guile, D. and Fonda, N. (1999) Managing learning for added value. In *Issues in people management* London: Institute of Personnel Development

HM Treasury (2002) SET for Success: the supply of people with science, technology, engineering and mathematic skills. London: HM Treasury. Available from: http://www.hmtreasury.gov.uk/documents/enterprise_and_productivity/research_an d_enterprise/ent_res_roberts.cfm. Accessed 11th July 2006

IWBL (2007) www.mdx.ac.uk/www/iwbl/

Lave, J., and Wenger, E., (1991), *Situated Learning: Legitimate Peripheral Participation* Cambridge: Cambridge University Press.

Lester, S. (2004) Conceptualising the practitioner doctorate. In *Studies in Higher Education* 29 (6), 757–770

Maxwell, T. (2003) 'From First to Second Generation Professional Doctorate'. In *Studies in Higher Education* 28(3): 279–291

Nowotny, H., Scott, P. and Gibbons, M. (2001) *Re-thinking Science: knowledge and the public in an age of uncertainty* Cambridge: Polity Press

Portwood, D, & Thorne, L. (2000) Taking Work Based Learning to Doctoral Level. In Portwood. D. & Costley, C. *Work Based Learning and the University: New Perspectives and Practices*. Birmingham: Staff & Educational Development Association (SEDA Paper 109)

Quality Assurance Agency for Higher Education (2004) Code of practice for the assurance of academic quality and standards in higher education, Section 1: Postgraduate research programmes. Bristol: QAA. Available from http://www.qaa.ac.uk/academicinfrastructure/codeofpractice/section1/postgrad200 4.pdf. Accessed 15th July 2005.

Scott, D., Brown, A., Lunt, I., and Thorne, L. (2004) *Professional Doctorates: Integrating Professional and Academic Knowledge* Milton Keynes: Open University Press.

Stephenson J., Malloch, M., and Cairns, L. (2006) Managing their own programme: a case study of the first graduates of a new kind of doctorate in professional practice'. In *Studies in Continuing Education* 28 (1): 17–32

Thorne, L. E. (2001) Doctoral level learning: customisation for communities of practice. In B. Green, T.W.Maxwell and P.Shanahan (eds) *Doctoral Education and Professional Practice: The Next generation.* Armidale: Kardoorair Press

UK Research Councils (2001) Joint Statement of Skills Training Requirements for Research Students. Available from http://www.grad.ac.uk/jss Accessed 16th May 2006

UKCGE (2002) Professional Doctorates The UK Council for Graduate Education

http://www.ukcge.ac.uk/filesup/ProfDox.pdf Accessed 30th June 2006

UKCGE (2005) Professional Doctorate Awards in the UK The UK Council for Graduate Education

10

Combining Academic Study and Professional Practice: The Story of the Doctorate in Psychotherapy

Derek Portwood

***

On the brink of its ninth anniversary, the Doctorate in Psychotherapy (by professional studies) (DPsych) has passed the cardinal test of all social enterprises. It has survived, and given that it is the product of a small private institution, registered as a charity and without state subsidy or external sponsorship, that is no mean achievement. Evidently, it has recruited 100 candidates demonstrating the doctorate has an appeal. But what is that? And how has it kept its appeal? What cost has been involved? What benefits have accrued? What lessons have been learned?

Obviously there's a story to be told. This chapter attempts to tell the story. Following the example of the DPsych itself which examines its candidates on the basis of what it calls 'descriptors' (a shorthand version of criteria of learning achievement), these will be used to explore and examine the genesis, development and outcomes of the DPsych. The descriptors are organised into the broad categories of professional context, professional knowledge and professional practice. How has the DPsych measured up to and what has it made, is making and could make of them? This story is told from those perspectives.

Professional Context

'Metanoia Institute was founded in the 1980s (becoming a registered charity in 1994) within the professionalising processes of psychotherapy and counselling. Its particular contribution was to meet psychotherapy training needs. Accordingly, it built up a suite of programmes which have been recognised by the profession's accrediting bodies (BACP, UKCP, BPS). In the mid 1990s it enlarged its remit and produced three Masters programmes in collaboration with Middlesex University. Shortly afterwards, it added two undergraduate degrees. It completed the different levels of its awards with the validation of the DPsych in 1998.

'The immediate context of the DPsych, therefore, is a private, non profit making organisation located in a web of academic and professional relationships, primarily with a public university (Middlesex) and the abovementioned set of professional accrediting bodies. All these influence, of course, its standards, protocols and structures. Eligibility for admission to the DPsych, for instance, is professional registration and a Masters degree or equivalent professional achievement.

'As its host institution, Metanoia provides the DPsych with systems of governance, support and accountability and requires it to contribute to the Institute's mission to promote and advance excellence in psychotherapeutic and counselling thought and practice.

'Overarching all these structural connections, however, the DPsych is placed in the broad professional context of psychotherapy with its ethos, values and purposes of contributing to human mental welfare. Egalitarian, caring and collaborative principles are fundamental to psychotherapy and the culture and practices of the DPsych have been shaped and directed accordingly.

'Given then this multidimensional context, what have been the implications and consequences for the DPsych?

Professional bodies

'The link with the professional bodies has mainly been informal, notably through DPsych candidates holding offices and performing roles within them. This has enabled those bodies to become acquainted with the work of the DPsych but a fuller relationship has yet to be explored. The initiative for this may be Metanoia itself rather than the programme on its own. However, in the spirit of work based learning (WBL) which espouses partnership, the link with the professional bodies has the potential to be developed to mutual advantage such as collaborating in conferences and publications to disseminate knowledge generated through the programme.

University

'The relation with Middlesex University, on the other hand, is necessarily formal. The DPsych's modular structure, credit system and WBL ethos are modelled on the university's Doctorate in Professional Studies (D Prof). Hence, as the validating body, Middlesex must ensure standards and quality assurance. Consequently, it plays a central part in all the regulatory systems and assessment tasks of the programme. It provides monitoring, double-marking and chairmanship of assessment panels and boards. It sanctions the appointment of external examiners. It requires quality assurance and monitoring reports.

'Furthermore, as the DPsych is a joint collaborative programme between the two institutions, Middlesex has also developmental and resourcing roles. Candidates on the DPsych are registered students of Middlesex University and, thereby, are afforded and have access to the various learning facilities and resources of the university. It also provides a complaints procedure if the matter cannot be settled through Metanoia's own procedure.

'Key university staff facilitate co-operation. A link tutor, for instance, provides a communication channel between the programme and the host university school. Also, a senior university academic chairs the programme's Assessment Board and also its Board of Studies which includes representatives from all year based cohorts of the programme. In turn, the DPsych has its own team representatives on the relevant university Board of Studies and research committee.

'Put like this the relationship sounds fruitful and fulfilling and in many respects it has been but not without frustrations. Jenifer Elton-Wilson, the designer and first programme leader of the DPsych, in her doctoral study (2000) of the inception and first year implementation of the programme portrayed the relationship as possessing dragon-like features. A dragon, she pointed out, can be benevolent as in the East but also malevolent as in the West.

'Three areas of difficulty have been noticeable. One is that of communication and consultation, with the DPsych often learning post hoc of developments and decisions, affecting its own style and arrangements, which have been taken independently by the university. A second area has been that of administration where the DPsych for a long period experienced difficulty in finding out and satisfying the university's requirements for various recording and reporting activities. The final difficulty has arisen from the university's criteria for external examiners. These are entirely academic in nature and pay no regard to professional eminence as such. Seeing that the professional development of psychotherapy is at an early stage, the pool of appropriately qualified psychotherapists is small. Prohibitions arising from not allowing potential examiners even slight connections with the programme and then severely restricting the number of examinations they can undertake have imposed heavy demands on the leadership of the programme in the search for permissible examiners.

'Improvements, especially in the first two cases, have been made but if one was to embark on this venture again, high priority would be given to investigating, arranging and agreeing administrative matters and communication before the programme became operational.

Metanoia Institute

'As for being part of the Metanoia Institute, not often can one say that a vision for an initiative emanates from a committee but it did for the DPsych. Metanoia's Board of Trustees, advised by its Management Committee, not only envisaged the DPsych but championed and invested substantially in its inception and implementation. Metanoia did this in a focused way by basing decisions on commissioned market research on comparable programmes and potential clientele. It then appointed a senior psychotherapist to design and subsequently lead it. Most importantly, the Metanoia commitment was not short term. Only now, after nine years, is the programme becoming financially viable. The continuing faith and practical support of the Management Committee and Board of Trustees have been critical for the success of the DPsych.

'But the debt of the programme to its host institution goes deeper. The values and bonds of Metanoia have never been tested so sorely as when a serious fire in its premises in Ealing in 2004 meant that all its work was evacuated for 14 months. Hotels, church halls and temporary office accommodation became its sphere of operations. The dedication, care, resilience and efficiency that this demanded spoke volumes about the qualities of Metanoia and its members who, as in all adversity, could have either split or cemented their relationships. The DPsych, like the other programmes, met the challenge and, in the process, forged stronger links within the Metanoia community.

Psychotherapy field

'Encompassing the multidimensional structural context, is the field of psychotherapy itself. Still at an early stage of professionalisation, it lacks some of the unifying features of established professions such as clear jurisdiction, career structure and knowledge control. Indeed, comprising an array of perspectives, its members tend to emphasise practice from the standpoint of one perspective or another. Research has not been a prominent feature, even at the master's degree level.

'These are complicating factors for a professional doctorate, rising epistemological and knowledge competency questions. Although these can best be left until the section on professional knowledge, the orientation of the DPsych as a programme for practitioners undoubtedly accounts for much of the interest it has stimulated. Notably, few applicants have had advanced research expertise whereas all have had experience of private practice. Indeed, the pioneers of the programme believed that doctoral studies would focus on that area of work whereas, in line with occupational trends in psychotherapy and counselling, few now do so. The shift in the lifetime of the DPsych has been to an organisational focus within the NHS, government agencies, other workplaces and local communities. Whatever the work context, however, the appeal of the programme is to use the actual context and its concerns for the focus of the research. Thereby, it produces outcomes of value to the candidate and their professional situation.

'The DPsych Handbook (2006/2007: 27) expresses its position as follows:

'The philosophy at the heart of this doctorate is the belief that professional practice and research in psychotherapy are inseparable. The quality of relationship and engagement with clients, colleagues, students, supervisees and attention to evaluating practice and leadership in training and in the provision of psychotherapy services, provide an overview of what constitutes the basis of an excellent and proficient practitioner.'

'Excellence in practice naturally involves ethical as well as pragmatic considerations. In its early stage, the DPsych was mindful of ethical issues but only formalised them after six years at the prompting of the external examiner. With hindsight, the issue should have had this fuller treatment from the outset because it affects not only the quality of research but also the quality of relationships which are at the heart of psychotherapeutic practice.

'On the subject of relationships, collaboration and community figure prominently in the vocabulary of psychotherapy. The DPsych embraced these concepts enthusiastically, crystallising its vision of the doctorate as:

A Community of Scholarly Practitioners Contributing to a Community of Practice

'In reality, however, the profession's disposition towards individual therapy and the individualism of academic awards has tempered the realisation of that vision. Plainly, as will be shown later, graduates have made significant contributions to practice but these are the work of independent individuals and the DPsych cannot yet claim to be a community of scholarly practitioners. Perhaps recent attempts by staff members to achieve a fuller team identity are a first sign. Also vehicles for this purpose such as the use of internet, conferences, publications and alumni association are being considered and developed. The message, however, is plain. Rome, as they say, was not built in a day.

'A final feature of psychotherapy that needs to be considered is its spread worldwide. Apart from strong interest from Ireland and some isolated cases from the Caribbean and Scandinavia, the DPsych has been confined to the United Kingdom and almost exclusively to England. It is just beginning to plan its spread internationally and is looking to its partnership with the IWBL at Middlesex University and their network of overseas regional centres to take that ambition forward. More immediately, it is seeing the introduction of the DPsych by Public Works as a possible means of engaging and involving leading figures from other countries.

Summary

'In summary, therefore, the professional contexts of the DPsych have on the whole proved to be fertile ground. They have helped to clarify its vision, shape its provisions and, significantly in the case of Metanoia, have morally and financially supported its endeavours. In turn, the DPsych has become a major addition to Metanoia's inventory of programmes and has considerably enhanced its research profile. More broadly, it has opened up a new route for continuing professional development at the highest level for practising psychotherapists and counsellors. On the other hand, it has struggled with a clash of professional and academic cultures and different institutional systems of working. It has yet to take full advantage of all the development opportunities which its contexts offer and particularly is at an early stage of realising its vision as a community of scholarly practitioners. These topics will recur as we now consider professional knowledge and then, finally, professional practice.

Professional Knowledge

'Unquestionably the subject of research methodology has received more attention from the DPsych team than any other area of the programme. There are a number of reasons. Methodology is fundamental to achieving original contributions to knowledge which is the key criterion of doctoral assessment. Whether or not candidates have perceived methodology in this light, it is evident that the relation of methodology to assessment has made the subject an anxiety-ridden experience for many of them.

'The lack of a research tradition in psychotherapy and counselling courses has meant that a majority enter the DPsych with little formal research training and competence. A minority, however, are advanced in this respect, several having taught research methods at university level. This unevenness of experience and competence has posed a serious pedagogical issue for the module tutor. Various tactics have been used including special sessions for the uninitiated on the basics of research techniques. One result was the disruption of group cohesion leading to the abandonment of the experiment.

'The disparities in experience and competence also raised the issue of whether or not an accreditation exercise should enable exemption from the module. Again, this was abandoned and participation was made compulsory partly in the interests of group continuity and cohesion but mainly because it was found that even experienced researchers honed their knowledge and techniques within a peer group setting. While not a complete antidote to the anxiety issue, the sharing and caring features of this approach have helped, particularly when the prescribed sessions were supplemented with tutor-facilitated group activities on a voluntary basis.

'This pedagogical approach has promoted a positive tone to the research module especially when the orientation of the methodology has emphasised research and development and not research in an abstract sense. This has given the module a key status in the eyes of the candidates because they no longer see it only as a means to serve the execution of the final project but rather intrinsic and integral to all their doctoral work.

'Thus the initial review of professional learning took on a new understanding when therapeutic practice was conceived as a kind of research exercise. Similarly, the production of the pivotal learning agreement became recognised as a research exercise in its own right and not simply an occasion to describe and justify the final project's methodology. Involvement in the module, the title of which, after four years, changed significantly to Research Challenges, enabled a more perceptive and critical presentation of claims for accreditation at levels 4 and 5. Finally, when the style of the Professional Knowledge Seminars (referred to below) became more interactive and interrogative, the candidates were able to use, test and elaborate the learning they had gained from the research module.

'Obviously, the different tutors (three, so far) have put their own imprint on the module. All, however, have drawn on the research repertoire of the social sciences from a psychotherapeutic perspective. All too have needed to relate the passion which candidates have for their interests with the traditional dispassionate stance of research. One tutor coined the concept of creative indifference as a result. The current tutor has highlighted the notion of practitioner research and explores it from a Gestalt perspective.

'To give a flavour of the pyschotherapeutic influence underpinning the eight sessions of the Research Challenges the current tutor's opening session is aimed at creating a learning culture based on the following principles:

1. Come Prepared to Share Your Reality and Evidence With Others. Speak with the authority of your own experience.

2. Explore and Question Everything That Happens: Remain curious and sceptical; engage in ongoing exploration of the social events that arise and remain curious to the effects of these upon yourself and others.

3. Experiment With Being Different And Play With New Ideas: Risk opening yourself to others and reducing your usual guard; be prepared to explore new ways of expressing, being you and of being with others.

4. Respect Yourself and Others: Try not to leak confidential material about others or their research inquiries beyond the group nor share sensitive information you are privy to without prior consent; take responsibility for sharing or holding onto your own secrets.

5. Act On Your Beliefs: Choose for yourself when to opt out of activities which appear wrong for you; do not collude in situations that embarrass your personal value system.

6. Clarify The Intention Behind Your Interventions: Try to be clear if you are attempting to support a point of view, to challenge the same or seek clarification.

7. Be – Here – Now: Share your feelings and thoughts so that others might appreciate your position.

(Barber, 2007)

'The Research Challenges module, accordingly, is not cast in the usual mould of describing approaches and techniques, but rather takes up the theme of research and development using a psychotherapeutic intelligence and processes. In consequence, candidates tend to favour qualitative and human inquiry approaches and while tutors do not underplay the role of quantitative methods and their relation to qualitative ones, the candidates themselves tend to become dismissive of natural science perspectives and methods. Similarly, little coverage or credence is given to methodologies from the arts (e.g. literary criticism).

'All this makes the Tutor's task exceedingly demanding. It also gives an indication of the complexity of the professional knowledge underpinning, being developed produced by the DPsych.

'The ultimate expression of that knowledge is in the final Doctorate projects. Their status is marked by informal and formal layers of oral and written assessment. The project themselves take many forms but, as was clear from the discussion of the Research Challenges module, they must go beyond informative purposes to reformative and possibly transformative outcomes.

'Recognising that additional support is needed to achieve such outcomes, the programme appoints an academic consultant to work with the candidate's academic adviser (these roles will be discussed shortly). Being projects, however, the objectives will be practical as well as intellectual. And being at doctoral level, the knowledge must bestride propositional, procedural and practical forms. In consequence, DPsych projects usually produce an artefact (for example, book, DVD, training manual) accompanied by a critical commentary describing and discussing the knowledge processes and competencies involved in the genesis, development and uses of the artefact. The emphasis is on criticality which also characterises claims for accreditation at level 5 where evidence of completed projects is submitted as part of the candidate's doctoral work. Hence, the professional knowledge is not a narrow version of performativity but includes contemplative knowledge or rather intersects contemplative and performative forms.

Reflection
'This level of knowledge capability is largely achieved through reflective thought. Accordingly, reflection parallels research in importance for revealing, developing and producing professional knowledge in the

DPsych. The initial doctoral exercise of reviewing personal and professional knowledge sets the tone and direction for the whole doctoral experience. Reflection is critical for every element of the doctorate. DPsych candidates respond positively because this mirrors their professional belief and practice.

'The DPsych, however, is designed to sophisticate their capability and use of it. Specifically the programme promotes reflexive dialogue through a range of peer group activities and especially a series of professional knowledge seminars. These were one of the innovatory features of the DPsych compared with the generic DProf. Leading authorities in psychotherapy are invited to lead a day long seminar on their specialist subject. Having been supplied beforehand with selections of the presenter's work, the seminars themselves use this information not simply for further elaboration but rather for interrogation of the whys, hows and consequences of the presenter's knowledge. In short, they are exercises in reflexive dialogue. Candidates must attend at least six of these seminars as well as an introductory session on the nature of professional knowledge. The whole experience is assessed by an essay on how it has affected their work on the doctorate.

'The version of reflection which the DPsych promotes is, therefore, a combination of personal reflection and reflexive dialogue. It sees this as vital, for instance, for articulating and permutating the relation of tacit and explicit knowledge which the programme highlights as a source of knowledge creation.

'In sum, the DPsych promotes and produces praxis, a combination of theory and practice. All its activities from the initial Review through the Research Challenges module, Accreditation Claims and Learning Agreement to the Final Project are designed to encourage and exhibit that form of knowledge. The underpinning twin processes of research and reflection enable its achievement.

Collaboration

'But good intentions, even good practice may not achieve desired results. The DPsych is no exception largely because of its individualising ethos and structures. While promoting group work, reflexive dialogue and collaborative research throughout the programme, it culminates in assessing the individual. Only one project out of the twenty which graduates have presented has been a collaborative production by two candidates and assessed as such.

'From a professional knowledge viewpoint, it is worth noting what the authors wrote about their joint experience. After saying that the scale and scope of the project put it beyond a single person's competence and endeavour, they observe:

'Our project represents the ultimate expression of working with difference. Two persons from different ethnicities with differing life experiences came together to contribute their diverse perspectives to produce one piece of work. This was not a simple, linear process... We challenged ourselves by facing the feelings that emanated from our obvious difference and found a source of togetherness within our way of working...The fact that we found a way through these challenges is a testament to the authenticity of our communication and to our determination that our relationship would continue to be strong and deep enough to work together in the spirit of true collaboration.' (Caleb & Chowdhry 2005)

'Despite this declaration, questions at the oral presentation focused on: Who did what? Who wrote what? and so on, thereby exposing the individualistic tenor and form of academic assessment. No such questions were addressed to other candidates whose Acknowledgments pages revealed their dependence on and indebtedness to many colleagues. The regulations for the DPsych allow collaborative projects but the dominating norm of individuated summative assessment means that the social sources, co-operative mechanisms and collaborative forms of professional knowledge do not receive formal recognition. Psychotherapists tend not to challenge this, not least because of their own biases. A possible solution is a suggestion already made to the DProf by one of the DPsych team to create a distinct team category of assessment. The forthcoming re-validation of the DPsych may follow this up. In any event, the reference to collaborative practice leads to a consideration of the workings and outputs of the DPsych as examples of and contributions to professional practice.

Professional Practice

'The vision of the DPsych, as mentioned earlier, is to create and develop a community of scholarly practitioners who contribute to the community of practice. Practice in psychotherapy is mainly about meeting the mental needs of people through therapy. This may take many forms but, whatever the context, the essential feature of professional practice is the therapeutic relationship on an individual or group basis. The immediate implication for the DPsych is consequently the quality of its own internal and external relationships. Does it practise what it preaches?

Staff team

'Starting with the staff team, all its current ten members are employed part time. Opportunities to meet either casually or formally are consequently severely restricted. Creating team identity and values, therefore, become critical responsibilities for the programme leader who in any case represents the team's interests on the Management and Academic

Committees of Metanoia and the Board of Studies at Middlesex. In this situation a special relationship is needed which goes beyond the usual leadership attributes and styles to incorporating some kind of insider experience. This familiarity with the ethos and culture of the programme gives the team confidence and encourages collegiality.

'Fortunately, for the DPsych, the first leader designed the programme and both her successors have graduated from it. This means they have got quickly into the job and also aware of necessary and desirable changes.

'It is just as well that this is the case because induction and training for new staff is minimal. The DPsych has a mentoring system but has recently recognised its inadequacies and is examining additional provision.

Candidate collegiality

'Nonetheless, there is a collegial spirit in the team and the programme seeks to create a collegial style among the candidates themselves. In the first part of the programme, formal and informal sessions relevant to all the early modules are organised for each year cohort and electronic communication is encouraged between them.

'A different story unfolds in the second part of the DPsych. Scarcely a Board of Studies passes without lengthy discussion of the isolated experience of candidates in the later stages of their studies. Obviously candidates are then preoccupied with the concerns of their individual projects and the commonality of earlier doctoral exercises is lost. Also the fact that they are working on differing time scales disaggregates cohorts.

'Anticipating this problem, the inital design of the programme tried to counter it through the professional knowledge seminars. Up to five of these are held each year and are open to all candidates. Naturally the primary intention of the seminars is to develop candidates' criticality but another outcome has been finding common interest with colleagues from other cohorts leading to dialogue and collaboration. The programme administration, in any case, publicises to all candidates the research interests of each one in the hope that this too will foster dialogue – and, co¬operation. Other compulsory and voluntary group sessions relating to the execution and assessment of projects have gradually been introduced.

'Perhaps the most significant development has been a re-examination of the personal support system for candidates undertaking their projects. All candidates from the outset of their programme have an academic adviser who provides their main link to the programme and a range of guidance services. The original conception of this role was that the adviser would be heavily involved in the first part of the doctorate up to and including the Learning Agreement, then less so in the second part when an academic consultant would take on the major task of supporting the candidate in their project work. Probably the fact that consultants were rarely members of the core team led to the link between the candidate and programme becoming more tenuous.

'Anxieties on this score were voiced leading to a reappraisal of the adviser's scheduled contact hours which became three hours per semester for the duration of the doctorate. This meant that the balance of contact by the adviser and the consultant was adjusted in favour of the adviser. Experience has confirmed that this has ameliorated the sense of isolation. The problem, though lessened by all these tactics, still persists and remains an abiding item on the team's agenda.

External relations

'Regarding the programme's external relations, few links have been made with external agencies. Mention has already been made that connections with professional associations are through individuals and the same applies to other organisations. This is clearly an under utilised resource. For instance, taking the case of the signatories of Learning Agreements, candidates are required to obtain endorsement from relevant authoritative figures of the value of their proposed projects. The notional nature of the exercise questions its worthwhileness. The programme does not follow up the endorsement with any kind of further involvement of the signatories in the candidate's work. Plainly to take advantage of the good offices of the signatories, let alone establishing relationships with their organisations, would further the programme's intention to contribute to the community of practice. This says something about the exclusive culture of academic programmes and perhaps even more that concepts such as partnerships are largely rhetoric.

'But while the contribution of the programme as a corporate body is only now beginning to happen through a proposed series of publications and public events, the contributions of its candidates and graduates are another story. A spate of books, journal articles and training manuals have been published. Prisons, hospitals, universities, regional authorities and local communities have adopted proposals of new systems of working and training put forward by the candidates. Graduates, in particular, have been in demand as conference speakers and consultants. More fundamentally still, their work has provided new or enhanced models and insights into therapeutic relationships and practices. However, as yet another sign of how long radical developments take as well as what characterises a mature organisation, the programme only recently has begun to review, research and capitalise on this reservoir of learning.

'Of course, professional practice is not exhibited by artefacts alone but rather in the commitment and capabilities of practitioners. Reflective and critical thinking, research mindedness and competence – these are what graduates of the programme persistently identify as the major outcomes of their study. In so far as these are central characteristics of a community of scholarly practitioners, the DPsych, in its ninth year, may be seen as on the way to realising its vision.'

References

Barber P (2007) *Guidelines For An Inquiring and Learning Community*, Handout, Research Challenges Module, Doctorate in Psychotherapy, London: Metanoia Institute

Caleb R & Chowdhry P (2005) *An Inquiry Into The Role of University Counselling Services: A Collaborative Model of Institutional Support*, unpublished DPsych report, London: Metanoia Institute/Middlesex University

Elton-Wilson J (2000) *Creating A Community of Scholarly Practitioners In Order To Serve A Community of Professional Practice: The Challenge of the First Year*, unpublished DProf report, London: Middlesex University

DPsych (2006/2007) *Doctorate in Psychotherapy by Professional Studies: Programme Handbook*, London: Metanoia Institute/Middlesex University

11

The Development of a CPD Framework for GP Vets by Experienced Practitioners

Annette Fillery-Travis, David A Lane and Jonathan Garnett

***

The divide between academics and practitioners is evident throughout the professions. The difference in perspective between the two communities impacts at the very heart of professional practice. The most striking example is knowledge transfer and the difficulties of linking academic research efforts through to impact upon practice. However there is a more indirect, but no less significant, effect and that is on the design and assessment of postgraduate professional development. Within the academic context, postgraduate education still implies to many a specialisation in one aspect of the professional knowledge base. On the other hand, the seasoned practitioner is increasingly seeking to have their expertise as a generalist acknowledged, and further developed, within formalised certification procedures.

This raises the issue of how this expertise is constituted and how it can be developed and accredited. As professionals we identify that the trend towards grounding practice firmly in the available evidence is not a trend that can be ignored. However, it is a trend that must be adapted and refined if evidence based practice is going to be sensitive to different populations and contexts for delivery (Mace and Moorey, 2001). Similarly, for professional groups where the discipline is based in science "CPD" activity needs to reflect evidence of effectiveness and, as such, it must relate to context and delivery of service.

In considering the impact of scientific evidence on our practice, Sturdee (2001), comments that, when contemplating the nature of evidence, we must be concerned with some key questions including:

- Who decides what counts as evidence?
- What status should an outcome be given?
- What is the best way to use this information?
- Who will be its principal exploiter?
- What is the likely impact of this information?
- Who will benefit most (and least) from it?

The questions Sturdee poses serve as a reminder that we are not dealing with simple questions about best practice but rather that there are likely to be winners and losers, depending on how the constructs of science and evidence are defined and by whom. These issues were highlighted by one profession, general practice veterinary surgeons, when considering their CPD provision into the future. They were concerned to examine how those in general practice could continue to offer unique value to their clients. This question was of particular note as veterinary general practice had not traditionally been seen as an area in which advanced training certificates were available through the regulatory process.

To address this the Royal College of Veterinary Surgeons asked the practicing arm of the profession, The Society of Practicing Veterinary Surgeons (SPVS) to consider the development of a general practice award. This body approached the Professional Development Foundation. Based on the discussions a collaboration was agreed between SPVS, PDF and the National Centre for Work Based Partnerships at Middlesex University to generate a unique research led approach to developing a new award in general practice. (CertAVP(Vet GP)).

Continuing professional development as a means of improving practice

Where different forms of knowledge are equally valued as appropriate for different purposes, there is the potential for practitioners to engage with their science more collaboratively for client benefit. Within general practice this knowledge emerges from a combination of the science of medicine, and the experience of practice. Reflection on each, and between each, can inform and enhance the effectiveness of the service to clients. Unfortunately, there was little research on which to draw to inform this debate as general practice in the veterinary world had not received the same attention as general practice in human medicine. As Guest (2001) has pointed out, it was once possible to obtain an initial qualification linked with training and be reasonably confident about keeping well informed. Attending the occasional course or conference and reading appropriate journals was enough and most professional bodies did not require you to commit to formal, ongoing continuing professional development. However, the last decade has witnessed the introduction of compulsory re-accreditation emerging in some professions and compulsory CPD in others. The forms of CPD that are recognised have also been widened to acknowledge the value that practitioners gain from engagement with their community of practice (Garnett, 2004).

Ensuring the impact of our learning through identifying frameworks for CPD

Learning is (or at least should be) a lifelong process. Senge (1990) goes as far as suggesting that to practice a discipline is to be a lifelong learner.

However, Guest (2001) maintains that professional bodies will be seen to have made real progress with their lifelong learning policies when advertisements appear asking not just for qualifications but for people whose learning is up to date and related to the work they will be doing today and in the future. So how can we achieve this for the GPVet?

Within this context a number of possibilities emerge, including models of science/research/audit, reflective practice and work based learning (WBL). These are considered next.

1. Models of science, research and audit in clinical practice

The training of veterinary surgeons is grounded in the science of medicine which is then applied to both animal and human problems. However, this begs the question 'what type of scientist are we when we practice as GP Vets?'

For example if we view the consultation as a focus of practice using a systems framework we go beyond an individual clinical diagnosis and recognise that we are balancing our individual objectives within the context of the organisational practice in our setting with the objectives of the client and needs of the animal. It is not a simple system; many factors influence the information given and the take up of any treatment. Otherwise, why do clients leave a practice discarding the prescription offered on the way out? Specifically, it requires us to look not at the beliefs of individuals (ourselves as practitioners) but the effects of the system (our activity as part of it) on life chances of the animal and objectives of the client. Engagement with alternative modes of knowledge beyond the clinical are needed (including business management) and these need to form part of CPD.

2. Reflective practice

Alongside the central role of the scientist as a basis for the practitioner is increasing recognition of the importance for advanced practice of the concept of the self-reflective practitioner. As reflective practitioners, GP Vets must appreciate the critical importance of self-awareness and the need to reflect on their own practice from this perspective. This self-awareness is extended to 'the importance of diversity, the social and cultural context of their work, working within an ethical framework, and the need for continuing professional and personal development' (BPS, 2004, 17). Increasingly Vet GPs are and will be required to show in their CPD record that they have been able to identify personal development needs, plan appropriate development activities to meet identified needs and reflect upon learning and its application to practice.

3. Work based learning

An additional framework for thinking about CPD is the rapidly developing discipline of WBL. Work based learning is not about the location of learning (in the sense of the old style sandwich courses) but rather about forms of learning specific to practice and how they may be developed and applied. Our work can be a source of learning to improve and critically challenge practice. Ongoing experience from organisations such as the National Centre for Work Based Learning Partnerships (Middlesex University) and the Professional Development Foundation has led to the development of ways in which practitioners can share learning and research about learning from analysis of their practice. Particular tools that have added value to the CPD debate include:

- A Learning Review, including a personal knowledge and skills audit in order to establish what knowledge and skills the practitioner has acquired to be applied to future learning.

- Programme Planning, to create learning that aligns service focus, client and personal need, stakeholder commitment and access to related structural capital.

- Work based research that addresses the forms of analysis applicable to the issues that the practitioner faces in order to capture, use and enhance the structural capital of the organisation.

4. Models of intellectual capital

Schön makes the point that our professional artistry needs to be understood in terms of reflection – in action, and as such it can play a central role in the description of our professional competence. The concept of reflection in action has resonance with work in the field of action learning (Revan, 1998), learning conversations (Thomas and Harri-Augstein, 1985), de Bono's Parallel Thinking (1995) and intellectual capital models (Burton-Jones, 1999; Stewart, 1997). Thus, learning within context becomes central to our CPD. There is also the potential for the university based world of science and the work based world of applied practice to collaborate here thus breaking down the science practice divide. Garnett (2004) has identified key contributions that university/work based partnerships can make to building intellectual capital within work based projects.

- Focus on organisational objectives to ensure the knowledge it develops has a performative edge and is thus of value to the organisation.

- Develop strategies for working with tacit knowledge, by focusing reflexive practice to enhance individual knowledge recognition, creation, dissemination and use.

- Fully exploit and reinforce the crucial role of structural capital in fostering knowledge recognition, dissemination, creation and use.

- Explore the nature and implications of the apparent lineage between WBL, knowledge creation, organisational decision making and bounded rationality.

The partnership between the work place (practice) and the university (science) provides a powerful resource to overcome the research practice divide and adds substantial benefits to both. What is clear, however, is that if our learning is to impact it needs to be part of a process of knowledge creation and exchange. It has to be embedded in a knowledge culture comprising systems, values and behaviours that transcend individual values, and even the values of single organisations (Rajan et al., 1999).

So how might these ideas be used to develop the GPVet?

The Professional Development Foundation is dedicated to working with practitioners and professional bodies to explore new ways to create effective CPD, as well as innovative solutions to development issues. It has, in partnership with NCWBLP at Middlesex, a set of work based Masters Degree programmes developed for and with professional bodies. Thus, it was in light of this experience that SPVS approached PDF to determine a way forward to consolidate the CPD of vets within a framework. The resulting SPVS/PDF/NCWBLP partnership provided an opportunity for experienced vets to come together to shape a research project that could inform the needs of GP Vets for continuing development and advanced standing.

The veterinary profession

- The veterinary profession is predominantly made up of small business units in which practitioners can be employees or alternatively partners of the business.

- CPD provision was predominantly clinical with an average spend of over £2000 per year.

- Vets, as graduated, are expected to practice with little apprenticeships or internship. Historically, informal mentoring systems had provided support for new qualified Vets. However, resource constraints within an increasingly business orientated practice context had reduced the duration and accessibility of such support.

- There is a move away from a dominant mode of service provision through local small businesses towards corporate ownership of practices. Many believe this to be driven by a 'feminisation' of the profession and the aspiration of many in the profession for an improved worklife balance where the need to work out of surgery hours – 'on call' – is greatly reduced.

- There is evidence of a relatively high level of suicides within the profession and a significant 'drop out' rate of graduates from the profession within first few years of practice.

CPD provision for the Vet General Practitioner

SPVS was concerned with the lack of coherence in the CPD provision for GP vets. There was no recognition of general practice as a distinct professional arena and to obtain any formally recognised further qualifications post graduation, required the Vet GP to specialise within a particular clinical area e.g. dermatology. This specialisation was accredited through a certificate system provided by the RCVS. However, at the time this project was being considered it was running with an 80% drop out rate. SPVS were a well established professional body but they did not have the infrastructure nor the allocated funds to commission a full research project into redesigning the CPD provision of their peers.

The research premise

In light of these considerations PDF suggested that the research was best carried out by Vets themselves and the design of a certificate in Veterinary general practice could be considered as an appropriate issue for practitioner research. As insider researchers GP Vets would:

- Have a good knowledge of the historical and current issues.
- There would also be an implicit level of trust from their fellow professionals and
- Vets would have automatic access to networks, both formal and informal, which would be able to contribute to the debate.

Within a work based Masters degree they would undertake the task of establishing the desirability, feasibility and demand for a post graduate qualification in veterinary general practice.

Work based learning Support

The PDF aims to enable those in practice in a variety of professions to generate advanced learning from practice. Typically these are master degree programmes negotiated between PDF and a professional body, but can include individually developed learning plans. The NCWBLP provides expertise in the development of WBL and a range of awards at undergraduate and post graduate levels whereas the PDF, in partnership, provides significant experience of developing professional competence based learning in the work place and in translating practitioner needs into viable programmes of learning. The PDF's preferred mode of support is through facilitated learning sets of practitioners who support each other in their learning.

Methodology

The methodology is effectively action learning whereby the students meet at approximately monthly intervals for five hours to support each others' learning and undertake a piece of research. In this construct of an Action Learning Set we identify three fields of knowledge: the knowledge and perspective the participants bring to the Set, external forms of knowledge (literature and expert input) brought into the Set by request of the Set and the knowledge created by the Set through synthesis and dialogue.

In this instance two groups of students were formed based on geographical area (one of six and one of three practitioners). Their background was as follows; eight were practice owners, one was employed and one worked as a solo vet (a practice owned and run by a single vet). eight practiced as small animal Vets whereas one had a predominantly equine practice. Although all were in general practice, one was politically active within SPVS council and one had been a past member of SPVS Council. The rest had no previous background either in work for their professional societies or in committee membership.

Research Activity

The scope and depth of the research activity required by the overall aim was identified within the Sets themselves and formed part of their joint work. It can be described in the following stages:

1. Identification of a Shared Concern

The initial discussion of the Sets identified an overarching, ambitious target for their work:

The development of a postgraduate qualification in veterinary general practice.

2. Consultation with the Profession on the Shared Aim

One of the first outputs of the Sets was the identification that their aim should be achieved through collaboration with the entire profession – a postgraduate qualification designed by GP Vets. The Set clearly identified the academic practitioner divide as being evident in the curriculum design of previous qualification programmes. The academic perspective was thought to be over represented, with little acknowledgement of the value of practice experience in shaping optimum service to clients. The Sets response to this challenge was to undertake a consultation on the shared aim (identified above) with the entire profession. This was achieved through the distribution of a questionnaire by the journal Veterinary Record. This journal is available to the majority of Vets in the country and hence nearly every Vet would have sight of it. The questionnaire sought to identify the perceived needs of the profession for CPD in the future, both in content and mode of delivery.

3. Individual tasks

Each vet then identified research questions and issues to explore which appealed to their particular interests. These were:

1. The historical perspective. The development of the profession over the last 30 years, and the need for support of general practice.
2. Current and future challenges for the profession.
3. The importance of communication skills in consultations.
4. What is clinical audit? What are the attitudes within the profession towards its introduction? Raising standards in general practice.
5. Encouraging research in general practice.
6. The challenges facing solo vets and rural vets.
7. Post graduate learning and the development of clinical expertise.
8. Assessment of learning through learning diaries and portfolios.

Each was explored through an individual work based research project over 12 months.

4. Common task

The Sets adopted a competence based approach to professional development with a context based analysis. The central task to this was the development of a framework of professional competencies identified as appropriate for the Vet GP. An individual's development as a professional could then be mapped against such a list of competencies.

5. Design of a CPD Framework for the profession identifying the constituent elements

At the end of their research the Sets came together, by common consent, to consolidate their work within a report to the profession identifying the requirements and appropriate content for a postgraduate certificate in advanced veterinary practice for the GP Vet.

Throughout this course of work the Vets were supported in a variety of ways:
- The facilitator of their Learning Set was drawn from PDF faculty and also acted as their academic advisor providing initial feedback and information on the academic requirements of the course.
- A virtual learning environment was provided where the students could maintain contact with their peers, post their reflections and access resources such as literature and module manuals.
- All modules of the Masters programme were accompanied by full distance learning manuals which fully identified the requirements of each module.

In line with action research principles, members of the group continually put their research and work before their peers. This was initially done by posting on community forums, such as the SPVS discussion list, and then later through presentations at SPVS conferences and other professional events. One member was elected onto the work group looking at the introduction of a modular certificate at RCVS and later stood for election to Council. This full engagement with their community of practice (in the broadest sense) and the dissemination of the results throughout the process of research resulted in a wide recognition of the group's aim and robust debate throughout the research process. One of the Master Vets was a long-standing member of the SPVS Council. He had been instrumental in setting up the initial enquiry to PDF/MDX and was a passionate believer in the shared aim. It was through this Master Vet that continual contact was maintained with SPVS and one of the authors, D.Lane, also visited the Council meetings on an annual basis. The group were keen to also keep RCVS informed of their progress particularly in view of the ongoing review of their Certification process. The engagement of the group with their community developed significantly within the work.

Outcomes

The impact of the groups work was significant at a number of levels. In September 2003 the Group presented their work to the RCVS Council recommending a modular Certificate for Vet GPs covering professional and clinical skills assessed at Postgraduate Certificate level to allow direct mapping onto the university credit system (SPVS Masters Group 2004). These recommendations were accepted by the Council as being of use to their working group.

Discussion

The reflections of the Vets who undertook this programme, and those of their facilitator and supporting faculty, identify clearly the high impact and relevance of the practitioner research undertaken within the Action Learning Sets. The critical engagement of peers, during a structured enquiry into the shared concern, had promoted a depth of dialogue and exploration which enabled one participant to say:

> 'This dialogue has enabled us to say passionately and with complete integrity that this [development] has been done in the profession, by the profession, and for the profession'

This speaks to the high value the Vet practitioners place not only on the academic standards of their CPD but also upon its explicit currency within their profession i.e. general practice vets. By using practitioner research as the form of enquiry the Vets achieved their goal of maintaining rigor and integrity whilst placing the focus and purpose within the realm of practice.

An essential element to the integration of CPD within practice was the definition of the competencies of a professional vet. The work of the Sets quickly identified and acknowledged that they were more than day one (straight out of vet school) competencies but defining them fully proved difficult. The Sets spent a significant amount of time on this but did not fully agree on the outcomes. Further work will be necessary to explore the contributing and generic issues such as the development of 'professionalism' within this context; how can the process be supported and how can it be assessed. The scope of the required work and its potential impact upon the work of the individual GP Vet was identified by one Set member as:

> 'Being able to treat the ordinary, day to day, common conditions to 'best practice' standards and to learn from what goes well and also from what goes badly for you, and being able to carry this out in such a way as to build a rapport with clients, practice team members and practice owners, is what makes an experienced general veterinary surgeon.'

If currency is to be sustained and allowed to evolve with practice, then the assessment process must mirror the multidimensional aspect of the competence it seeks to assess. Conventional methods of assessment in veterinary science such as multiple choice questionnaire and technical essay were quickly identified as too limited to assess the learning of professionals within the midst of the ambiguity and uncertainty of practice life. As identified within a final reflective essay of one Set member:

> 'Gone are the days of having to memorise text books and produce the perfect case study – and forward to the real world of being a busy general veterinary practitioner where few cases present as they should.'

WBL assessment, as experienced by the Set members through their degree programme, clearly offered a route for assessment which could address issues of evidence based practice and the systemic perspective required of work within practice.

It was, however, the role of reflective practice in the development of the professional which was most explored and fully experienced through the work of the Action Learning Sets. The development of self awareness and the need to reflect upon their practice from this perspective is not part of the conventional CPD of a Vet GP. Its development is, in essence, the central theme to the Masters programme but it was within the Sets that this reflection was made public. This sharing of reflection was first within the 'safe' confines of the Set and then, upon agreement, within the wider profession. Raelin (2000) identifies public reflection to be at the heart of WBL; part of the process of knowledge creation and exchange which develops communities of enquiry and intellectual capital within organisations and professions. The Vets from both Sets were enthusiastic in their promotion of public reflection upon their shared concern. They contributed to online discussion groups, workshops and conferences, continually seeking to engage their peers with their reflections and research. The mode of these exchanges was often far from the goal of dialogue, and at times challenging. But, in essence, the process did develop a community of enquiry; drawn from practice and academia (albeit highly informal and made up of very disparate views) but fully engaged in debating the future of CPD for GP Vets.

This debate has continued subsequently and, in 2006 the final format of the Certificate in Advanced Veterinary Practice was unveiled by the RCVS. It does not differ in any major respect from the structure recommended by the SPVS Master Vets Report. Within the specialisms offered is the CertAVP(Vet GP).

On a personal level all the Vets successfully completed their degrees and five went on to do professional doctorates. The RCVS recognised the Masters degree and the award ceremony was held at the RCVS London offices in 2004.

Acknowledgements
The authors would like to thank the entire SPVS Masters group for their enthusiastic contributions to the programme and this work. Their engagement and perseverance in the pursuit of their vision has learning for us all.

References
BPS, 2004, 17

Burton-Jones A (1999) *Knowledge capitalism: business, work and learning in the new economy* Oxford: Oxford University Press

De Bono E (1985) *Six Thinking Hats* London: Penguin

Garnett J (2001) Work based learning and the intellectual capital of universities and employers. In *The Learning Organization*: 8 (2): 78–82

Garnett J and Nikolou-Walker E (2004) Work-based learning. a new imperative: developing reflective practice in professional life. In *Reflective Practice*, 5 (3) 297–312(16)

Guest D (2001) Human resource management: when research confronts theory. In *International Journal of Human Resource Management*, 12(7): 1092–1106.

Lane D and Corrie S (2005) *The Modern Scientist Practitioner* London: Routledge

Mace C, Moorey S, Roberts B (2001) *Evidence in the Psychological Therapies: A Critical Guide for Practitioners* New York: Brunner-Routledge

Raelin J A (2000) *Work-Based Learning: The New Frontier of Management Development* New Jersey: Prentice Hall

Revans R (1982) *The Origins and Growth of Action Learning.* Bikley: Chartwell-Bratt

Senge P (1990) *The Fifth Discipline: The Art and Practice of The Learning Organization*: New York: Doubleday-Currency

SPVS Masters Group (2004): Meeting the post-graduate educational requirements of the General Practitioner Veterinary Surgeon in the United Kingdom: RCVS

Sterdee P (2001) Evidence, influence or evaluation? Fact and value in clinical science, in *Evidence in the Psychological Therapies: A Critical Guide for Practitioners* (ed) Mace C, Moorey S, Roberts B New York: Brunner-Routledge

Stewart T, (1997) *Intellectual capital: the new wealth of organizations*, New York: Doubleday-Currency

Thomas, L and Harri-Augstein S. (2001) Conversational science and advanced learning technologies (ALT): Tools for conversational pedagogy *Kybernetes* 2001, 30(7/8), 921–954

12

Transnational Corporations: The Irish Centre Experience

Nick Hodgers and Andrew Hodgers

***

Introduction

The founders of the Irish Centre for Work Based Learning Partnerships (ICWBLP) fervently believe that management science can best be furthered by practising managers making sense of their activities by developing new insights and making these explicit in a manner and timeframe that is relevant to fellow practitioners. Considerable experience is based on practising managers and involvement with Action Learning and Action Research. WBL as defined by Middlesex University was considered to be the most appropriate way to fulfil this objective – the continuing development of relevant and timely management knowledge.

We believe that individuals, as a consequence of their activities, develop 'real time' individual solutions to individual issues which can and often are generalised into new methodologies and theories of practice. We see WBL programmes as a way of formalising and extending this activity. The decision to insist that only Centre staff that come from the field of management, and have additionally completed a postgraduate WBL programme, can deliver such programmes appears correct. We work primarily with 'leading edge' fast moving multinational corporations whose competitiveness is largely dependent on continuous improvement.

We see WBL as a process through which practitioners and their sponsor organisation can generate, manage, and make explicit the knowledge which is imperative for their sustainable success.

As one senior manager put it;

'Things happen so fast in this business that we have to keep inventing it as we go along'

WBL programmes provide a structure and process for capturing and generalising this inventiveness for the originator's benefit.

In addition to creating and making explicit new knowledge for practice, we believe that workplace methodologies for generating and testing new knowledge can provide viable alternative research methodologies than those predominantly used in the academy; we see WBL programmes at the Masters and Doctoral level as ideal for formalising methodologies of participant research.

Those who fall in love with practice without science are like a sailor who steers a ship without a helm or compass and who is never certain whither he is going (Leonardo Da Vinci)

We see our participants not only as practitioner researchers but also as practitioner scholars.

The background to the Irish Centre for Work Based Learning Partnerships

The Irish Centre for WBL partnerships was founded in 2003 with the coming together of the National Centre for Work Based Learning Ireland and the Middlesex University National Centre for Work Based Learning Partnerships.

The founders of the National Centre for Work Based Learning Ireland and subsequently the Irish Centre for Work Based Learning, Professor Noel Mulcahy, and Nick and Andrew Hodgers have for over four decades now been driving change and advances in management education and practice both within the academy and the professional world of practice in the areas of 'work related learning'. In the 1970s Professor Mulcahy recognised the need for management practice to be formalised. Following discussions with Reg Revans he established the worlds' first Action Learning Masters programme (also known as the Management Practice Programme MPP) set up in conjunction with University of Dublin (Trinity College) and the Irish Management Institute. This programme differed from the traditional theorised Action Learning model proposed by Revans in the 1960s in that managers on the Management Practice Programme did not have to leave their companies to go to other companies or work in Action Learning sets as mandated in the Revans model, thus placing the Management Practice Programme participants in a position to learn from their own work role, a feature also of the Middlesex University WBL programme.

An inaugural candidate and graduate of the first Masters in Management Practice Programme was Centre co-founder Nick Hodgers.

Nick Hodgers in his capacity as a Partner in Kollmorgen Corporation USA was involved with further developing the learning at work model. Kollmorgen corporation worked with Peter Senge at MIT and references are found in *The Fifth Discipline* (1990); *The New Management: Moving from Invention to Innovation* (Senge, 1985) and *Metanoic Organisations* (Kiefer and Senge 1984).

Peters and Austin in a review of Kollmorgen highlighted the work based learning initiatives that Hodgers was implementing in their book *A Passion for Excellence* (1985).

From our collective experiences in both the academic and professional world we felt that management practice is enhanced when conducted within a framework and through a process which gives credibility and visibility to the very real and valuable knowledge being generated. By making explicit much of the implicit knowledge of management practice, management as a profession can be further recognised and formalised.

The collective vision of the Centre at inception was;

(i) To further develop the philosophical and epistemological base of activity based learning (Action learning and Work based learning); this was to be achieved by collaborating with the university, candidates and their sponsoring organisations and by the Centre sponsoring Doctoral level research. (Currently three Doctoral programmes under way).

(ii) To deliver WBL programmes to the large multinational sector in Ireland.

(iii) To provide best in class performance in the delivery of WBL programmes to the target client base. This was to be achieved by the development of an optimal model of organisational structure and appropriate organisational responses that could effectively connect the differing operating procedures and expectations of the university and the client.

Status

Over the period of time that the Irish Centre has been in existence (three years) it has enrolled 27 Masters and 15 Doctoral candidates, both individual candidates and company sponsored groups, from various multinational corporations. Three Doctoral candidates are also sponsored by the Centre itself whose projects relate to the development of a WBL Centre internationally associated with Middlesex University. The projects which are nearing completion focus on the development of optimising the interface between the client base and the provider in terms of structures, systems, procedures and research epistemologies.

The other Doctoral and Masters projects are specific to enhancing the performance of the sponsoring companies across the full spectrum of their key activities.

Client focus

An early realisation of the founders was that the Irish Centre systems and procedures needed to be compatible with those of their client base (multinational corporations) particularly in the case of regulatory requirements, vendor approval and finance cycles. The International Organisation for Standardisation ISO 9000:2000 Management Systems Standard was identified as the framework to achieve this.

'ISO 9000 satisfies a number of significant and even critical strategic and corporate requirements in a changing industrial and marketing environment. Chief amongst these are marketing considerations, legal aspects, management and productivity and changing customer-supplier relationships' (Rothery 1993).

The International Organisation for Standardisation states that the 'ISO 9000 has become an international reference for quality management requirements in business to business dealings.' 'The ISO 9000 family is primarily concerned with "quality management". This means what the organisation does to fulfil:

- the customer's quality requirements, and
- applicable regulatory requirements, while aiming to
- enhance customer satisfaction, and
- achieve continual improvement of its performance in pursuit of these objectives. ' (ISO 2007)

Despite the above there appears to be a very limited take up of the standards by Higher Educational Institutions in Europe. No universities in the UK and Ireland were found to have ISO 9000 compliance as entities. The Centre's action at the outset was to put in place a framework for:

(i)   developing a customised Quality System Model for the delivery of work based study programmes

(ii) a quality system and operating standard that match the requirement and quality standards of the client organisations

(iii) achieving certification to the ISO 9000:2000 standard

The key requirements for this programme are:
(i)   a model which will be in conformance to ISO 9001:2000

(ii) a model which will have the ability to react to the diversity of needs presented to the ICWBLP by each client organisation

(iii) a model with the ability to interface effectively with Middlesex University

(iv) a model which will facilitate the continuing development of the Irish Centre for WBL.

The Centre recognises that the development of a quality system model and operating procedures is necessary for creating a continuously improving learning organisation. Secondly, the development of a quality management system conforming to international standard ISO 9001:2000 will offer the Centre a unique and competitive advantage over other higher education providers who cannot provide quality system standards matching that of the client organisations.

From our experiences client companies also have expectations of

providers in the areas of:
- Excellence in the provision of service(s) – Responsiveness
    - o We define and measure responsiveness by two dimensions, Timelines (velocity of response) and Completeness (the ability of the response to move the client / provider dyad to the next stage of operation.

- Innovative approaches to the delivery of service e.g.
    - o Flexible admissions policies: a rolling admissions (continuous enrolment) policy operates at the Centre where client cohorts have an anytime start during the calendar year, this also applies to individual students
    - o Continuous Assessment procedures: procedures for no semesterisation and rolling assessment and Centre approval boards
    - o Financial receipt and payment procedures as per client requirements
    - o Vendor Approval procedures: ongoing commitment to achieve certain regulatory standards as deemed necessary by the corporation in order to remain an approved supplier
    - o IT systems compatible with client company's e.g.
        - ■ Voice Over Internet Protocol (VOIP) communications
        - ■ Instant Messaging (IM)
        - ■ E-mail (both open source and licensed platforms) with integrated scheduling where the Centre can schedule meetings, timetables and events in the candidates and client company's calendar systems.
- An understanding and acceptance of their business requirements and activities (their business model)
    - o confidentiality agreement and intellectual property belonging to client
    - o Recognition and acceptance of their 'cutting edge' business practices and use of such practices as research / enquiry methods. This further refines their practices through reflection and application.

Work Based Learning and Industry

The literature has highlighted the need for adaptability, viability and responsiveness in companies to enable them to cope with ever changing environmental conditions. Environmental conditions also drive companies to strive for greater efficiencies and effectiveness in their operations. Both corporations and some academic institutions operate at the forefront/

cutting edge in their respective domains. However it is often the case that knowledge generated in-company is not considered groundbreaking, novel etc until a critical mass has developed and this knowledge then flows back down the line where it is picked up by other companies and utilised. Usually it takes a large multinational corporation to reveal the secret of its success or to develop/endorse a particular approach before it is widely adopted. Examples are the development of Six Sigma by Motorola in the 1980s as a business improvement process, when Motorola revealed that the 'secret' of its turnaround was elimination of waste and wasteful processes through this in-house developed methodology.

Jack Welch former CEO of General Electric Corporation stated that "Six Sigma has spread like wildfire across the company and it is transforming everything we do". The methodology has been adapted by hundreds if not thousands of corporations worldwide and has also been taken up by some of the largest services companies.

Toyota's lean production manufacturing system is another example where lean manufacturing, Kaizen and Ho-shin planning have been adopted by hundreds of corporations and companies worldwide. However the academy is often slow, possibly reluctant, to pick up on, or endorse these practitioner developed methodologies or give formal validation to them, leaving corporations to blaze their own trail and establish their own corporate universities, professional institutes, professional societies and so on for the dissemination and further development of this knowledge.

Frequently this knowledge is disseminated outside the corporation as a new business trend. In our case WBL programmes at Masters and Doctoral level provide a structure, and process for such knowledge development and an academic validation of it.

Unlike normal university students, practitioners in corporations operate in a high velocity change environment where significant projects come and go relatively quickly, in many cases, less than one year. In these cases it is important to facilitate the practitioner to fit his programme around approximate project start times. Practitioners and companies often cannot and sometimes do not want to wait for the academic cycle to come around. It was found that continuous enrolment and 'ad hoc' assessment are important requirements of the client base. Requirements that are at odds with a university's normal operating procedures, which are typically developed for large numbers of individual students pursuing taught programmes. The Centre provides flexibility in this regard.

Insider Management Research

In delivering the WBL programmes into predominantly the management arena we found that, as Thietart (2000) suggested, the nature of management research is very broad and has an inexhaustible mine of questions. These questions can vary according to their subject aims and the research approach adopted and the richness of the management field is not limited to research questions. The diversity of the theoretical foundations and methodologies that researchers can draw from adds an additional degree of complexity:

- Multiple paradigms coexist, diverse techniques are employed, numerous theories are developed and utilised.

- Research feeds on multiple experiences and from these can emerge a better understanding of the phenomena that management researchers wish to study.

- A diversity of approaches, without rejecting any one of them 'a priori' is a source of richness and discovery in a field still far from being as formalised as that of other sciences, (Thietart op.cit).

Tranfield and Starkey (1997) state that management research "is concerned to build a body of knowledge which documents, codifies and articulates a problem and the solution set concerned with understanding and improving the practice of management." Jarvis (1999) also states that a new phenomenon has emerged in recent years, where practitioners in many occupations are undertaking a great deal of their own research.

He suggests several reasons for this:

- Research practice itself is undergoing rapid change

- More knowledge is being legitimated pragmatically rather than either logically or empirically.

- The high status of theory is being questioned

Our experience to date supports this view.

We also perceive that our candidates find the approach of Arbnor & Bjerke's (1997) three basic methodological approaches i.e. the analytical, the systems and the actors, more compatible with their professional experiences and their 'theories in use' then the more traditional social research texts. In fact some have pointed out the similarities between Action Research methodology and problem solving and issue resolving methods in common use throughout the business world, for example the Six Sigma frameworks for Business Process Improvement.

We have found that it is important that the provider and programme advisers share the same mental models as the participants, a view endorsed by the participants themselves.

Perspective

The Irish Centre for WBL partnerships was set up as a Not for Profit Company and its Memorandum of Association lists as its main objective:

'To advance education of the public by the promotion, support and undertaking of education in particular "work and activity based learning". To do so in the private and public sector for institutions, corporations, groups, individuals and in so doing facilitate lifelong learning in individuals and continuous organisational learning in institutions and corporations', (Memorandum of Association 2003).

To date the Centre has focused on postgraduate activities and currently has 15 Doctoral candidates and 27 Masters candidates. These are predominantly engaged in multinational organisations in senior management roles. The Centre is sponsor to three Doctoral projects which are nearing completion. These projects, whilst they are focussed on the development of an optimum interface between the client base and the provider in terms of structures, systems, procedures and research epistemologies, have additional important dimensions:

(i) the development of the Centre's own faculty, rooted in WBL and practice

(ii) providing insights for the enhancement of WBL epistemologies (subject for future publication).

With the development of the Centre's own faculty further progress will be made towards the objective of the Centre as above. Opportunity will also be extended to other constituencies and individuals who to date have been disadvantaged and not adequately catered for by the traditional education system. As also indicated in the objectives, the Centre is willing to share and collaborate with other educational institutions in this regard.

The experience to date in working with leading multinationals is providing insights into how formalised WBL programmes can provide a coherent process for organisational learning by structuring the transformation of tacit knowledge to explicit knowledge. Practitioners in their work setting generate pertinent knowledge through 'sustained collective inquiry into everyday experiences,' (Wyatt 1997).

It is the epistemology of such inquiry that is of fundamental interest to us, as it should be appropriate to the context of the inquiry. "Knowledge is understood in relation to the context in which it was generated' Raelin (2000).

As indicated previously postgraduate candidates of the Centre argue and we agree that research methods at their level in industry are constituently comparable with methods emanating from the Social Sciences but are labelled differently. Work based learning programme providers need to be cognisant of this. This understanding is enabled by shared mental models with the participants, their context, conception of reality and pre-understanding. The participants have particular ontological perspectives which are derived from their experiences both academic and work related, which are further shaped by their operating contexts and their methods in use. It is considered vital therefore that the participant's advisors/supervisors understand and are intellectually comfortable with the participant's perspectives, contexts and methods in use. Likewise it is not unrealistic to expect that the academy's assessment is also in tune with these particular circumstances. The advisor/supervisor has a significant role to play in aligning the academy's assessment criteria with the participant and the sponsoring organisation's ontological perspective. This is particularly relevant where the participant's organisational context demands an approach consistent with Ceruti's (1994) view of the internal and external observer.

We believe that the epistemology in use should most appropriately be based on what is termed 'natural epistemology' (Ceruti op.cit) and stems from the works of Maturana and Varela, Jantsch, Laszlo, Bateson, Capra, Maruyama and others. Our instincts and understanding have been reinforced in this regard over the last three years working with 15 Doctoral and 27 Masters candidates predominantly within industry. We find that the work of Arbnor & Bjerke (1997) is a practical and usable step in that direction.

The Centre's memorandum of association cites as an objective "continuous organisational learning in institutions and corporations". This involves recognition of the dissonance between activity cycles in leading business entities and most educational institutions. Increasing the velocity of 'learning cycles' is a major differentiating factor between competing businesses. Such businesses tend to be 'Time' driven. University processes on the other hand are 'Stage' driven. The challenge for the interfacing WBL Centre is to facilitate rolling enrolment, and rolling assessment whilst avoiding unreasonable and unnecessary queuing at the university process stage gates. Such a flexible interface between dynamic business and the academy is in our view the major challenge facing educational providers, if they are to participate at the 'cutting edge' of business knowledge generation which is increasingly being done in-company. Collaborative, in-step, WBL postgraduate programmes offer the common ground where Business-Academy synergy can be enhanced and new knowledge generated, validated, collated and disseminated to the benefit of national economies.

References

Arbnor, I. & Bjerke, B. (1997) *Methodology for Creating Business Knowledge*, 2nd edition, London: Sage.

Bateson, G. (1972) *Steps to an Ecology of Mind*, New York: Ballantine.

Bateson, G. (1979) *Mind and Nature. A Necessary Unity*, New York: Dutton.

Capra, F. (1975) *The Tao of Physics* Suffolk: Chaucer Press.

Capra, F. (1982) *The Turning Point* London: Wildwood House.

Ceruti, M. (1994) *Constraints And Possibilities, The Evolution of knowledge and the Knowledge of Evolution* Lausanne: Gordon & Breach.

International Standards Organisation (2007). *ISO 9000; 2000* [online]. Available from: http://www.iso.org/iso/en/iso9000-14000/understand/inbrief.html

Jantsch, E. (1975) *Design for evolution. Self-organization and planning in the life of human systems* New York: George Braziller.

Jarvis, P. (1999) *The Practitioner Researcher; Developing Theory from Practice* San Francisco: Jossey Bass.

Kiefer, C., & Senge, P. (1984) 'Metanoic Organizations'. In *Transforming Work* John D. Adams, ed., Alexandria, VA: Miles River Press.

Laszlo, E. (1972a) *The systems view of the world. The natural philosophy of the new developments in the sciences*. New York: George Brazillier.

Laszlo, E. (1972b) *Introduction to systems philosophy. Toward a new paradigm of contemporary thought* San Francisco: Harper.

Laszlo, E. (1987) *Evolution: The grand synthesis* Boston: New Science Library.

Maruyama, M. (1974) Paradigmatology and its applications to cross-disciplinary, cross-professional and cross-cultural-communication. In *Dialectica*, 28, 135–196.

Maturana, H., Varela, F. (1985). *The Tree of Knowledge* Boston: New Science Library.

Peters, T. and Austin, N. (1985) *A Passion for Excellence* Glasgow: W. Collins Sons & Co.

Raelin, J.A. (2000) *Work Based Learning, The New Frontier of Management Development* Upper Saddle River, NJ: Prentice Hall.

Rothery, B. (1993) *ISO 9000* 2nd edition Gower Press UK

Senge, P., (1990) *The Fifth Discipline, The Art & Practice of The Learning Organization* New York: Doubleday.

Senge, P. (1985) 'The New Management: Moving from Invention to Innovation', System Dynamics Group, Sloan School of Management, Massachusetts Institute of Technology, Cambridge, MA

Thietart, R.A. (2001) *Doing Management Research* London: Sage.

Tranfield, D. and Starkey, K. (1997) 'The nature, social organisation and promotion of management research: toward policy'. Keynote session at the British Academy of Management conference. London Business School / QEII Conference Centre.

Wyatt, S. (1997) John Dewey meets the bottom line. *OD Practitioner*, 29 (4): 5–12.

13

Negotiating Learning with SME Managers

Barbara Light

***

Introduction

This chapter focuses on the dynamics of learning and knowledge generation in work based management programmes, accredited by Middlesex University, that I designed and delivered over several years to more than 400 first/second tier managers in the north east London SME sector. I focus on the key programme features, consider how the co-creation of knowledge transformed the initial pedagogic model, and analyse the opportunities, problems and benefits for the learners. From this experience, I also raise some crucial issues for the future role of universities in the new knowledge economy as knowledge demonstrably begins to shift away from academia into a multiplicity of sites.

The Context

The SME sector is commonly perceived as reluctant to engage with learning, often having little time or resources to spare, and regarding what universities might offer as beyond or irrelevant to its needs. This perception is corroborated by King's (2007:28) findings in a recent report into employer engagement with higher education that employers need small chunks of learning delivered at appropriate times, that are 'demand led... with learning outcomes ...linked to business performance outcomes'. Given this premise, it was therefore important to develop an outreach programme directly meeting SME managers' needs that was work based, short, intensive and highly focused. The perception of university level learning as usually irrelevant to SMEs' specific needs was further confirmed by a survey of the programme participants, many stating that these programmes represented their first opportunity to engage with higher education. The main reasons given for participation were: confirmation from the university that their practices measured well against current thinking; the desire to acquire new competences and ways of dealing with work issues; and the added bonus of an award (Certificate or Diploma) to enhance status.

Funds to run the programmes over four years were obtained in partnership with MU Professional[1] from the European Social Fund (ESF)

---

1 The university's outreach unit

under the European Union Objective 2 regeneration project targeting the Lea Valley area of London. The programmes were open to all new or existing managers; no previous qualifications were required, but some managerial experience was a prerequisite and was tested through a brief questionnaire on the programme application form or by telephone interview.

Key programme features

Both the Certificate and the Diploma consisted of four modules that were accredited by Middlesex University at 40 credits Level 1 or 2, followed by a 20 point work based project. One-day module workshops were held over a four-week period with a final action-learning workshop for applied learning and project outline design, delivered off campus directly in the Tottenham regeneration area in the MU Professional training rooms. This was advantageous as it created a business-like atmosphere more suited to the programme and participant typology than a university campus could offer, but concomitantly disadvantageous as it prevented easy access to university learning resources such as the library for project research. Additionally, a catch22 situation existed as ESF fund parameters only paid for successful outcomes with verifiable official certificates, so a decision was reluctantly taken to register and fund post-programme only those participants who completed the written assignments and projects, thereby blocking access to university learning resources, which required a password provided on pre-payment of fees. Whilst this situation could potentially have presented an embarrassing impasse, participants generally tended to use the internet or public libraries for their research.

The programmes were intensive, competence based and highly focused on real situations, enabling participants to seek confirmation of their own practices and to find solutions for their problems. Workshop materials were designed and written to include theoretical content, relevant scenarios, and activities that stimulated participants to reflect on, analyse, share and evaluate their own practice, knowledge and competences. Topics included:

- communication skills
- managing performance
- recruitment and retention
- managing meetings and negotiations
- team building, motivation, and leadership

Module learning outcomes provided participants with opportunities to analyse and improve current individual and organisational management practices, acquire new management competencies, influence and change personal and staff behaviour, and implement new work strategies.

Participants were required to research and incorporate additional material to enhance their knowledge, to demonstrate they met the Middlesex level descriptors in assessed work, and to:

- attend the workshops
- participate in workshop action learning sets through group/whole class activities
- complete four short module assignments of between 1200–1500 words each that evaluated their own learning and demonstrated how this would be implemented in their own work situations
- research and write a final 4000 word project focused on implementing and evaluating organisational change and reflecting on learning
- complete a learning log[2] that identified learning gained throughout the duration of the programme

Tutorial support and feedback was provided throughout the contact time with the addition of email/telephone support for the duration of the project research/write-up. Typical projects included: identifying new approaches and solutions to work situations or problems, implementing systemic or strategic change, or planning new businesses.

Participant profile
Participants ranged widely in sector, in age, in management experience, in job position, in organisational influence and in academic level. Many were from minority ethnic backgrounds with English as a second language that caused significant difficulties when it came to writing their assignments for assessment. There were also cultural differences in approaches to management, albeit the one commonality was that they were all working in the UK, and therefore needed at the least to implement current legislation, if not conventions. This at times led to difficulties as participants' issues, theories and practices were shared and often contested in the workshops; however, concomitantly this process engendered problem solving and ultimately possibly improved practices.

Pedagogic approach
When I began to develop the programmes, I had assumed that the majority of participants would not hold qualifications and would therefore welcome the opportunity to learn from the university 'knowledge holder' in a top-down model of knowledge transfer. However, this assumption was immediately challenged in the workshops when I realised that whilst the participants were indeed officially 'unqualified', they possessed significant

2 Not formally assessed

knowledge, experiences and competences that had been developed in the work place through years of practice and that in many cases demonstrated higher-level learning than the module materials provided.

The pedagogic approach thus shifted into one of 'knowledge brokerage', where I facilitated a learning environment using the course propositional material as a baseline that allowed 'real world' experiences to surface and be used as more meaningful contextual examples, rather than the artificial 'scenarios' I had written. In the role of knowledge broker, I acted as an agent for change, linking the different 'dispersed social systems' (Cope, 2000:155) of individual participants', their organisations and the university into a coherent knowledge creation partnership creating and testing a new body of living theory based in practice (Whitehead & McNiff, 2006). The bi-directional academic/practitioner knowledge flow (shown in Figure 13.1 below) functioned in this way: firstly propositional (academic and practice based) knowledge was tested against individual practices, then new concepts were collaboratively developed in the workshops into collective knowledge that produced tradable academic assets[3] and individual/organisational assets of new knowledge and practices.

Figure 13.1 – Co-creating knowledge with the SMEs

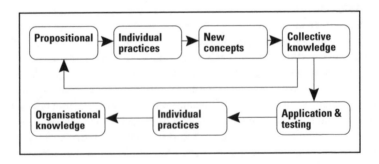

Although each unique learning situation lasted only a matter of weeks, during this time participants skills, knowledge and capabilities (human capital) were transformed into collective intellectual capital that was then articulated and legitimated in the two knowledge domains: in the academic domain through workshop discussions, through assessed written assignments and awards[4]; and in the work domain through codification into the structural capital of systems, procedures or products such as plans for

---

3 The original Certificate was rewritten and the knowledge contributed to the Diploma developed two years later

4 And ultimately through university accreditation of the new Certificate/Diploma

new businesses, reorganisation of working methods, administrative, management or recruitment systems, or new marketing strategies (Edvinsson & Malone, 1998). In a small survey of previous participants who had returned for the Diploma, when asked to evaluate how learning from the Certificate programme had changed or affected their organisation, one participant stated that he had 'created a structured organisation able to deliver results in a timely and more efficient way' and had been able to develop a more 'mature organisation able to compete effectively with the challenges ahead'.

This dual and reciprocal legitimisation, where 'knowing as description' interacted with 'knowing as prescription' (Barnett, 2000:18), supports the notion that the foundations of knowledge are changing from academic theory to working action. Borne out by my experience with these programmes there is also an argument here for mutual legitimisation by recognising that formal and informal learning are interrelated and present in all learning situations, and that neither can claim superiority (Colley et al 2003), and that work based knowledge/competences and academic knowledge can be meshed together into new or competent knowledge.

Issues

One of the key issues of this programme was the mismatch between the management practitioners' knowledge and experiences and their inability to express themselves within the standard academic and linguistic requirements. Many found the idea of sustained pieces of writing off-putting or too time consuming and were therefore unable to complete the written assignments, and if they did, some failed to meet the assessment criteria because of poor written English or paucity of academic capability. It was not possible for financial reasons to provide study skills or language support, and given the level of their experience in practice, would participants have appreciated such support, or would they have felt humiliated?

This was a conflicting situation – whilst on the one hand enabling access by not requiring pre-entry qualifications, concomitantly the university denied awards to those who were unable to reach the required academic standard of formal assessment. Different assessment methods might have enabled the participants – as autonomous agents of personal learning – to demonstrate that learning had occurred, for example, by the use of self-assessment against pre/post course defined competencies and demonstration of subsequent enhanced practice and knowledge in a report, or through peer group or mentor assessments (Jarvis, 1998; Boud, 1995).

The Middlesex approach to WBL as a field of study recognises that work is a site of multidimensional knowledge production (Costley, 2000), and the quantity and quality of practitioners knowledge was self evident in the programme workshops, but when dealing with professional practitioners the university also has a responsibility to commence a paradigm shift to fully recognise and reward high level learning on its own terms, rather than on the university's fixed level (generic or subject based) criteria and quality assurance systems, although the use of APEL partially enables this recognition.

From this experience with the SME practitioners, I began to understand that there was potentially a case for both fuller recognition of work based knowledge and a more symbiotic relationship between universities and the work place.

Proposing new university and work place relationships

In the new knowledge economy, academic knowledge is becoming increasingly sublimated to market needs and demands shifting from mode 1 science to mode 2 knowledge production (Gibbons et al, 1994) where knowledge is valued for its capacity to enhance performance through skills, competences and lifelong learning discourses. Examples of this can be seen in the expansion of vocational courses using National Occupational Standards, in foundation degrees, in graduate apprenticeships or in learning frameworks. This trend supports dominant free market, neo-liberal ideology that considers knowledge in terms of its utility and tradability, but is limiting in both discourse and application with an inherent risk of marginalising the 'truth-seeking' aspect of knowledge (Lyotard, 1984) and potentially significantly altering the future role of universities.

Scott (1997) notes how the massification and marketisation of intellect affects higher education – mechanisms of control are manifest in the emergence of discourses such as learner centredness, learning outcomes and ECTS/CATS schemes; in the subjection of universities to continual financial audit/reward schemes and the control of research through the relation of outcomes/outputs to the provision of finance. Increasingly, cognition is being substituted by instrumental and vocational practices – notions of competence – that focus on what learners can 'do' with concomitant loss of critical ability. Furthermore, the need for compliance with European and national policies increasingly obliges universities to account for themselves in terms of utility, and, in this new ontology, universities and work need to find innovative ways of engaging in collaborative knowledge generation (Boud & Solomon, 2001).

If universities look beyond their boundaries and begin to validate their own knowledge in the real world through enhanced partnership with the work place (Barnett, 2000), rather than remaining as validators of work situated knowledge, then it will be possible to forge a more symbiotic and balanced relationship. Organisations and individuals often perceive universities as irrelevant to their learning needs because of a top-down model of teaching (or of knowledge transfer) that more closely resembles a school classroom, or because they are unresponsive to real work-focused practices and research needs. If knowledge is transferred, inquiry and reflection can be impeded as transfer is not dialectical – it has inherent power structures of knowing and ignorance, it is linear and static and implies a unidirectional flow of information. Knowledge transformation, on the other hand, is a dynamic, multidirectional flow requiring more than one willing partner in action and can simultaneously encompass a variety of contexts – as demonstrated in this case study with the SMEs. Unfortunately, common discourse still often holds that partnerships should transfer knowledge to the work place rather than transform it within the work place.

With closer links to organisations, universities could use their professional research capability to help codify and enhance organisational explicit and heuristic knowledge and develop curricula and learning methodologies that are responsive and developmental. As sites of power shift, organisations, universities, and others, such as research bodies, all need to recognise the value that each site holds and engage with each other through complex understandings in an egalitarian 'open world ontology' (Tsoukas, 2005:5). Partial engagement or maintaining exclusive power over knowledge negates the intrinsic knowledgeability of all stakeholders, risking entrenchment or even irrelevance in an era of global change.

Innovative institutional attitudes and ability to implement change will increasingly decide the positions of universities as preferred partners in knowledge creation in the twenty first century. Nowotny et al (2004:93) suggest that universities need to de-institutionalise as inside/outside boundaries no longer make sense in mode 2 knowledge production realities, and also need to adapt to new knowledge configurations and alliances in 'synergistic activities'. As boundaries between work based and academic based knowledge elide, universities must reposition themselves in order to remain key players in the field of knowledge and WBL programmes help universities to become collaborators rather than competitors with organisations (Boud and Solomon 2001).

Building on the example of the SME programmes, course materials could be regularly renewed in a 'real-time, real-world' mode, however, in order to achieve this, academic systems need to be simplified and mental models need to change to enable recognition/validation of work based knowledge. At Middlesex , despite over ten years of developing and using innovative WBL methodologies, the general academic programme structure and supporting systems remain predicated on full-time students, posing limits on mature and experienced learners based at work. Additionally, these learners must take (and pass) certain mandatory modules in order to gain an award – however, the knowledge and competence they already possess is highly contextualised, relevant, and often specialised beyond academic knowledge and should, therefore, be appropriately recognised in a full APEL award.

Conclusion

In the new knowledge economy, there is a continuing tendency to elevate learning acquired in a formal institutional setting above the knowledge found in the work place; conversely, competence is increasingly considered as more desirable and valuable than knowledge – reflecting the vocationalisation of higher education into skills delivery. Barnett (2000:29) calls for knowledge based in the work place to be 'structurally reflexive' and scrutinised and reviewed by professionals and academics in order for knowledge to be recognised as such, but I argue in this chapter that knowledge based in and emanating from the work place is already valid and valuable in its own right, and does not necessarily require scrutiny, although it does benefit from codification. A paradigm shift is required that not only recognises and validates work based knowledge, but also acknowledges that the work place can be an equal (or sometimes superior) generator of knowledge, thus opening new ways for universities and organisations to collaborate.

References

Barnett, R. (2000) Working Knowledge in eds. Garrick, J. & Rhodes, C. – *Research and Knowledge at Work* – London: Routledge

Boud, D. (1995) *Enhancing Learning through Self-Assessment* – London: Kogan Page

Boud, D. & Solomon, N. eds. (2001) *Work Based Learning. A New Higher Education?* – Buckingham: SRHE & Open University Press

Colley, H.; Hodkinson, P. & Malcolm, J. (2003) *Informality and Formality in Learning – A report for the Learning and Research Centre* – Leeds: Lifelong Learning Institute, University of Leeds

Cope, M. (2000) *Know your Value. Value what you Know* – Harlow: Pearson Educational

Costley, C. (2000) *The Boundaries and Frontiers of Work Based Knowledge* – in eds. Portwood, D, & Costley, C. – *Work based Learning and the University: New Perspectives and Practices* – Birmingham: SEDA Paper 109

Edvinsson, L. & Malone, M. (1998) *Intellectual Capital* – London: Piatkus

Gibbons, M.; Limoges, C.; Nowotny, H.; Schwartsman, S.; Scott, P. & Trow, M. (1994) *The New Production of Knowledge: The Dynamics of Science and Research in Contemporary Societies* – London: Sage

Jarvis, P.; Holford, J. & Griffin, C. (1988) *The Theory and Practice of Learning* – London: Kogan Page

King, M. (2007) *Workforce Development: How Much Engagement do Employers*

Have with Higher Education? – Council for Industry and Higher Education – www.cihe-uk.com

Lyotard, M. (1984) *The Postmodern Condition. A Report on Knowledge* – Manchester: Manchester University Press

Nowotny, H.; Scott, P. & Gibbons, M. (2004) – *Re-thinking Science – Knowledge and the Public in an Age of Uncertainty* – Oxford: Blackwell

Scott, P. (1997) *The Crisis of Knowledge and the Massification of Higher Education* – in eds. Barnett, R. & Griffin, A. *The End of Knowledge in Higher Education* – London: Cassell

Tsoukas, H. (2005) *Complex Knowledge* – Oxford: Oxford University Press

Whitehead, J. & McNiff, J. (2006) *Action Research Living Theory* – London: Sage

Themes in Work Based Learning Development

14

Partnerships in Higher Education

Katherine Rounce

***

Introduction

Academic accreditation of non-certificated learning that is gained outside of the formal institutions of higher or further education is still a relatively unknown aspect of higher education. The accreditation of organisational learning – programmes of learning devised and managed by organisations – is even less well recognised. Yet at Middlesex University this forms an important aspect of our work, not just in Work Based Learning (WBL) but increasingly within the professionally orientated aspects of university provision for example the police, health care and business. Engaging in academic accreditation brings both challenges and rewards to both parties and it is these that form the basis of this chapter, in particular the focus is on partnership working and organisational development; adult learning and quality enhancement are also addressed.

Academic Accreditation

Accreditation is a formal activity of the university; as such it is supported by processes and procedures that ensure rigorous quality enhancement and forms part of the annual report to the Academic Board. The initial focus, following an approach to the university, is consideration of the capacity of the organisation to develop learning outcomes and an assessment strategy as it is these that will form the basis of the proposal. A link tutor is appointed and the eventual developed proposal is presented to an Accreditation Board consisting of academic staff and an external examiner. The Board may decide that a proposal be accepted in full, or with recommendations, or conditions, for change, may be requested and unless these are met prior to the activity starting, accreditation is not awarded. The partnership is then governed by a binding Memorandum of Co-operation issued by the university and which sets down the expectations and requirements of each party giving approval for up to six years. The Memorandum includes a financial agreement. Once the programme has started, an annual monitoring report is developed by the organisation and the link tutor and presented to the Accreditation Board.

It is important to note that the use and ownership of the knowledge and learning that is developed remains the intellectual property of the organisation and the university cannot use it for its own purposes. It is the quality assurance processes and attainment of academic levels that are the province of the university.

Partnership Working

The framework that guides developments in accreditation seeks to provide clarity to users, but whilst there are opportunities for creativity and learning, as with any new venture, there is also the potential for misunderstanding and tensions. The most critical area for avoiding these is that of the partnership that develops between the organisation and the university. This is particularly so in WBL, as the very title indicates the knowledge that is to be gained and developed cannot be the sole province of the university. It is contextualised and focused to an individual or organisational need. Additionally there needs to be a strong element of praxis, of knowledge that is to be enhanced and, more critically, used within a particular environment. This is a strong feature of organisational learning where professional development may be designed to meet individual needs within a particular organisational context and with a specific and visible outcome. Thus the organisation may have very strong views about the expression of learning and these may not always be compatible with university expectations.

Collaborative partnerships are generally acknowledged to be hard work. They can be difficult to manage and need continuous nurturing for them to develop the trust that is necessary for them to flourish. Research by Trafford and Proctor identified five key characteristics for effective partnerships: good communication, openness, effective planning, ethos and direction, (Trafford and Proctor, 2006). Vangen, in earlier work highlighted both the importance and difficulties in building and managing trust, yet without this collaborative projects, which are essentially what accreditation of organisational learning are, may be seriously threatened (Vangen, 2003). At Middlesex University we take these issues seriously as they are at the heart of developing the shared values and trust that are necessary for the quality assurance and enhancement processes to be effective. The key to all this is the appointment and practices of the link tutor.

The link tutor role

Once the university is approached by an organisation that wishes to gain accreditation and following consideration of the proposal, a link tutor is appointed who is responsible, on behalf of the university, for the quality assurance processes. Formally this role is focussed on monitoring, ensuring that the appropriate academic levels are met and on joint production of the Annual Monitoring Report that is presented to the Accreditation Board. However it is the informal aspects of the role and the development of shared understandings that are key to a successful collaboration and programme of learning. The link tutor acts as a 'critical friend' advising on academic levels and language, aiding the development of the learning outcomes and assessment and smoothing the path between the organisation and the university (Rounce et al 2007). Nonaka and Takeuchi, in their work on knowledge generation, advise that organisations should not be afraid of a little 'creative chaos' and that bringing people together with different knowledge and experience is one of the critical factors for knowledge creation (Nonaka and Takeuchi, 1995). From the perspective of organisations, our experience suggests that gaining consensus is critical to further work when it is of importance that parity and agreement is achieved; whilst a little chaos may be creative, too much can be destructive.

Case Study: The Local Authority

The Local Authority (LA) had a problem: it was keen to promote and provide a programme of professional development to its staff designed to enhance their motivation, knowledge and skills at work and considered that a partnership with a university would help with this. This case study demonstrates the use of learning outcomes and assessment to enhance management practices and to support projects that would contribute to the authority 'Best Value' targets. Additionally it demonstrates the influence of accreditation in the development of new knowledge and new business for the university.

Background

The LA had worked with the business arm of the university to design a programme with the key themes of enabling and developing new skills and knowledge that would enable middle managers to work more effectively in a modernised local authority. The programme was driven by competencies identified by the LA based on the principles of a learning organisation and demonstrated against the LA's Management Competency Framework. The programme was a success; in June 2001 it had been one of the four finalists in the 'CSM Customer Services Excellence Team Awards' – so why seek academic recognition? By the second cohort some problems were appearing, most noticeably participants tended to miss study days and completion of project work was patchy. Accreditation had originally been considered and rejected, but following a review in 2002 after two cohorts had completed the programme it was decided that academic credit might provide the 'carrot' by which full participation might be achieved.

The Programme Process

The programme was divided into three parts:

Creativity, learning and judgement
Leadership and political sensitivity
Strategic thinking and planning and partnership working.

The key task when the university was approached was the design of learning outcomes and an assessment that would meet the level 4 (Masters level) criteria and achieve the competencies specified by the LA. This level was chosen as representative of the thinking and application that such managers should demonstrate. The target was an assessment that integrated new learning, demonstrated competencies and contributed to the 'best value' targets. This was achieved by a small group including the university link tutor, the course leader and the training manager and produced an assessment that combined formative and summative work and was designed to integrate all aspects of learning into workplace effectiveness and to include elements of self and workplace assessment with traditionally assessed project.

The assessment tasks were broken down into a learning agreement; a personal project and a group project as follows:

The development of a Learning Agreement with the line manager, in which the specific competencies, which the participant would focus on, were identified and which would then provide the focus for the individual's application of learning.

The Personal Project which would be agreed between the manager and the individual and would satisfy a departmental need (and there were many of these), allow attainment of the competencies and meet the requirements of a university project.

The Collaborative Project which tackled a 'Best Value' project identified by the departments and to which groups were allocated by the Authority. Each group was 'sponsored' by a senior member of the LA and tackled a significant organisational problem. At the end of the course, these projects were presented to senior managers and officers. Group projects are notoriously difficult to assess and so the assessment of this focused on partnership working and critically on:

- The experience of doing a group project
- Personal input to the group and the project
- The public interface with the organisation.

The assessment process was accompanied by the Learning Agreement and the 'Sign off sheet'. This was designed in three parts, each completed by the participant and the manager:

167

Part 1 'overview of the project and development of competencies' – a self appraisal of both the content of the project and their experiences such as change, unexpected barriers, development of competencies and effect on the department.

Part 2 'effectiveness of the programme for the participant and section' required the manager to appraise the impact, both personal and departmental of the project and specifically the development of the competencies.

Part 3 'final review' in which the individual made a final appraisal of their learning, their personal development and impact on the organisation.

Project assessment. The assumption by the LA was that as the university was awarding the credits, this was where projects would be assessed. This however did not fit either usual practice or the ethos of partnership and integration, and so a 'reading party' consisting of a course leader, business studies lecturer, LA training manager and the link tutor was formed to assess the work in terms of the self-appraisal, organisational impact, achievement of level 4 criteria and subject effectiveness.

The effects

The assessment was well received by the participants who welcomed the synergy between enhanced effectiveness at work and academic achievement. Although it was not compulsory, virtually every participant completed the assessment. Standards of work were good on the whole, but there was a small group of people who felt that they had been coerced into being on the course and were therefore compelled to complete the assessment and who tended to submit incomplete work.

Whilst the personal project concentrated on personal development and organisational improvement, with some very impressive results, it was the group project that had the greatest organisational impact. The senior managers were very impressed by the calibre of the work and as a result two things happened which had wider organisational impact. First, the LA awarded a prize for the best project and also held an award ceremony.

Additionally two other events had impact on the university: as a result of requests by participants, the university was asked to provide a project module that would then enable participants to gain a Postgraduate certificate in WBL Studies and a Masters programme for senior managers was also commissioned.

Outcomes

The LA felt that accreditation provided a quality assurance process to the programme

The hoped for outcomes of attendance were not met

Participants who felt that they had been forced onto the course felt coerced into completing the assessment, despite assurance to the contrary, and the extra work appeared to fuel their resentment

Despite the voluntary nature of the assessment virtually all participants submitted the assignments and the overall quality of work was high

The 'sign off sheet' proved to be the most valuable aspect as it had the dual role of contributing to the assessment but more importantly it engaged the manager in the learning and development of the participant

The participants had the opportunity to gain a Postgraduate Certificate in WBL (Management and Leadership).

Discussion

Elements of personal learning, 'credentialism' and social learning were all present and were, to some extent, demonstrated in the reflective self appraisals where participants frequently commented on their reasons for completing the assignment, the challenges that they faced and learning acquired. There were participants whose major focus was on gaining credit and using this to support applications for promotion, those who considered that 'not taking part' would be seen as lack of commitment and those who gained real enthusiasm for learning. But although it was a minor part of the overall assessment (10 credits out of 40), it was the group project that had the greatest impact and this was due solely to the importance and public value placed on it by the LA. The celebration of success and acknowledgement of achievement by the groups had a real impact and was the driving force for the extension into a university award.

Conclusions

In our experience, accreditation and WBL attracts the mature student who may not have the traditional background in schooling and examinations but who has a commitment to work and to the learning that they acquire through it. Particularly, accredited learning appears to go someway towards removing the structural barriers that inhibit attempts to embed lifelong learning, such as cost, time, managerial support, place, gender and family (Coffield, 2000) – what Rees has referred to as a 'framework of opportunities, influences and social expectations that are determined independently' (Rees et al, 1998). Whilst we would guard against making the exaggerated claims so often associated with lifelong learning, the investment required from organisations to run their own programmes frequently leads to independent evaluation of the work, and it is from this and from internal evaluations that we draw our information, we do not make any claims to having research evidence, although we are aware of the need for this.

The multi disciplinary nature of the programme encouraged the articulation of tacit knowledge and particularly the sharing of this between different groups and teams. Accessing, articulating and valuing such knowledge can be extremely difficult where people work in 'silos', viewing other departments or organisations, or even teams as rivals rather than partners. Evidence from the local authority evaluation indicates that contact between participants has continued, particularly between those who worked together on projects. Whilst Eraut warns that 'tidy maps of knowledge and learning are deceptive' he suggest four 'good practical reasons' why we would want to make tacit knowledge explicit:

To improve the quality of a person's or learner's performance

To help to communicate knowledge to another person

To keep one's actions under critical control by linking aspects of performance with more or less desirable outcomes

To construct artifacts that can assist decision making or reasoning

(Eraut, 2000)

These are congruent with the intentions of the programme, which aims to develop new knowledge amongst practitioners, to enhance practice within the organisation and to ensure rigour of achievement through the quality assurance processes of the university. Whether these intentions will reach a critical mass or are maintained is the responsibility of the organisation themselves; however the greatest risk to such achievements is possibly the constant restructuring that is symptomatic of the current public sector climate. There is real potential within the programme to contribute to organisational learning and achievement as well as that of the individual participant. It would be most unfortunate if the constant changes in structures, roles and personnel common to such organisations led to the loss of such knowledge, as Nohria described, resulting from the re-engineering exercises of the 1990s (Nohria et al 2003).

Apart from the organisational changes that can disrupt attempts at learning, social contexts of learning can stifle any innovation and learning, exaggerating power relationships, inequalities and competitiveness. In the busy lives of people, embarking on a programme of study can be yet another source of stress – yet not participating may be viewed as failure or lack of motivation – both potentially powerful influences on career progression. This is on the whole an ignored but important part of WBL and was perceived to be the experience of a small number of participants in the LA programme. Additionally the public sector is not very good at creating incentives. Shipley takes the view that 'if the link between organisational performance, capability and individual learning is accepted, the challenge for management is to create an environment in which employees engage willingly in performance-focused learning' (Shipley 2001: 144). Shipley and others suggest that a range of inducements e.g. remuneration, career progression or recognition are the most effective mechanisms for this (Shipley 2001). This is a real challenge for the public sector where career and succession planning or reward for performance is not the norm, a factor that was later identified by evaluation of the programme.

At a different level, the notions of partnership that are central to our work is congruent with the new model of knowledge described by Gibbons as mode 2 knowledge (Gibbons et al, 1994). Gibbons talks of mode 1 knowledge (discipline specific, university-centred process) and mode 2 knowledge (trans-disciplinary based knowledge production process in which knowledge is produced at the site of application and with the co-operation of users and stakeholders). Gibbons asserts that mode 2 knowledge which is problem based is a superior form, more suited to modern thinking and practice. According to Lyotard (1984) and Barnett (2000) this represents not just a threat to the university, but the end of it in its current form – as it will be therefore no longer the sole guardian or legitimator of knowledge. But the real value to the university is the opportunity for exposure to current professional thinking and practice that can stimulate many other aspects of academic work. Additionally it brings new business to the university through commissioned programmes and via individual applications. It is a partnership with the potential for gains on each side but much depends on the quality of the partnerships that underpins understanding and processes at every level.

References

Barnett R., 2000. Working knowledge. In: J. Garrick, C. Rhodes, eds. *Research and knowledge at work.* pp16–31 London: Routledge

Coffield F., 1999. Introduction: Past failures, present differences and possible futures for research, policy and practice. In: F. Coffield, ed. *Speaking truth to power.*

Eraut M., 2000. Non-formal learning and tacit knowledge in professional work. *British Journal of Educational Psychology*, 70, 113–136

Gibbons M., Limoges C., Nowotny H., Schwartzman S., Scott P., Trow M., 1994. *The New Production of Knowledge: The Dynamics of Science and Research in Contemporary Societies*, London: Sage Publications

Lyotard J.-F., 1984. *The Post-modern Condition: A Report on Knowledge.* Manchester: Manchester University Press

Nonaka I., Takeuchi H, 1995. *The Knowledge-Creating Company.* Oxford: Oxford University Press

Nohria N., Joyce W., Robertson B., 2003. What Really Works. *Harvard Business*

Review On Point. July, http://www.hbr.org

Rees G., Fevre R. and Furlong 1999. 'Participation in post-compulsory education and training: a regional study' Swindon EXRC End of Award Report

Rounce K., Scarfe A. & Garnett JR 2007. A work based learning approach to developing leadership for senior health and social care professionals: a case study from Middlesex University in *Education and Training* Volume 49 Number 3 2007 218–226

Shipley N, 2001. Smart Work: What Industry Needs from Partnerships. In: D. Boud, N. Solomon eds. *Work-based learning: a new higher education?* Buckingham: Open University Press

Trafford S. and Proctor T. 2006. Successful joint partnerships: public – private partnerships. In *International Journal of Public Sector Management* Vol 19, No 2, pp 117–129

Vangen S. 2003 Nurturing collaborative relations: building trust in inter-organisational collaboration , *The Journal of Applied Behavioural Science* Vol. 39 No 1, pp5–31

15

The Quiet Revolution: Developments in Europe

Barbara Light

***

Introduction

The European Union agenda for developing a globally competitive knowledge economy is forcing radical educational change through implementation of the Bologna Process[1] that aims at transparency of national higher educational frameworks within the European Higher Education Area (EHEA). As a consequence, new educational concepts such as work based learning (WBL) and an increasing focus on skills and competences for employment are slowly starting to become part of European higher education discourse and practice, although these are often highly contested and resisted by regional politics and by academic institutions and their practitioners. In 2001, realising that WBL was little known in Europe, I contacted three universities in Italy, Germany, and Belgium to introduce the Middlesex WBL models, which were received with both interest and some scepticism as to the academic validity of such programmes. However, there was sufficient interest to enable the founding of a partnership that would focus on developing WBL and in 2003 the DEWBLAM[2] project obtained funding from the European Union Socrates Grundtvig fund for a three year period.

DEWBLAM was a highly complex and diverse partnership operating in different educational fields and in diverse cultural, linguistic, economic and socio-political domains. It was constituted by eight higher education institutions and four private research or employers' organisations in Belgium, the Czech Republic, Finland, France, Germany, Italy, Spain, Switzerland, and the UK, all with differing levels of pre-understanding and practices of WBL. For example, Middlesex University[3] (UK) and the Université des Sciences et Technologies de Lille[4] (France) had considerable experience whilst the Belgian Katholieke Hogeschool, Limburg after early

---

1 See www.dfes/gov.uk/bologna for further information

2 Developing Work Based Learning Approaches and Methods

3 Middlesex has operated a full range of work based programmes for over twelve years

4 Lille has developed technicians into engineers using the VAE system – Validation des Acquis de l'Éxperience. National decrees have also created the opportunity to gain full awards through VAE.

contacts with Middlesex, had acquired some experience by developing a degree in special educational needs that enabled access to the second semester via APEL[5]. However, the other partners – the Czech Republic Univerzita Karlova Praha, the Finnish Abo Akademi, the German Fachhochschule Aachen, the Italian Università di Firenze and the Spanish Universidad de Granada commenced the project with no pre-existing experience of WBL.

The principal project aim was to develop common theoretical and practical definitions and features of WBL that were European in origin and orientation, forming a common European platform that was to be the basis for understanding WBL concepts, and that could also be utilised to inform the development of pilot programmes specific to the single higher education context. The first year of the project focused on research into the existence of possible national WBL practices, and into the legal and institutional barriers and opportunities that might prevent or encourage the application of WBL. In the second year, the common European WBL platform was collectively developed in workshops and via the community website. In the third year the partners focused on piloting work based programmes or approaches, and on the dissemination of findings to external audiences through local events, publication of papers, and a final European conference.

The transformation of epistemologies

The context that best helps to position DEWBLAM and its struggles to define and implement WBL is that of the new postmodern reality, and a key issue underlying the project discourses has been that of modernity versus the postmodern, consonant with the struggle between the traditionally conceived knowledge domains of the Enlightenment and those now being constructed and legitimated through performativity. Lyotard (1984) has argued that the modernity characterised by dominant Western discourses of science, progress, and rationality and the educational systems to support these, is losing relevance in this era of plural truths, uncertainty and rapid changes. Indeed, knowledge itself is becoming increasingly commodified (Edwards, 1998) and performative[6], where knowledge is valued as to its saleability and utility (rather than its "truth") and is legitimated through its capacity to enhance and induce performance in the work place (Edwards & Usher, 2000).

In the European arena, these new constructs are visible as higher education begins to comply with EU protocols and to engage with the new

---

5 Accreditation of Prior Experiential Learning

6 I use the term "practice based" synonymously with "performative" knowledge throughout this chapter

realities of knowledge. This is occurring at national implementation levels and also at local levels as national and European funding strands become more focused on lifelong learning competencies and employability – fully corroborated by the aims of DEWBLAM that had to match the European funding parameters. Four years ago, the DEWBLAM partners had barely heard of WBL – today, all are implementing pilot programmes and have contributed their own understandings to the common WBL platform.

Through developing the common work based platform and individualised pilot programmes knowledge epistemologies were quietly and subtly transformed, but this transformation was not fully and consciously foregrounded within the partner institutions. Indeed, institutional engagement with this paradigm shift was often unwilling, and strong academic opposition to WBL was experienced by the German and Czech partners, despite the presence of high level champions in the executive. Other partners experienced different degrees of opposition, for example, despite initial difficulties but ultimately driven by pragmatic local economic and social needs, Granada successfully developed and implemented in conjunction with industrial partners a pilot award in "Subtitling for the Deaf and Audio-description for the Blind" that offered both "traditional" and innovative WBL pathways. However, despite the fact that both Italy and Finland have legislated to allow the use of APEL procedures[7], this is "relatively ineffectual" (Adams, 2006:39) and the universities of Florence and Abo struggled to identify appropriate WBL or APEL approaches.

More favourable conditions prevailed for other partners such as the University of Lille, which has been operating WBL degrees for over ten years. Indeed, France has been in the forefront of modernising its higher education system through legislation (from 1985–2002), allowing full awards through the demonstration of life and work experiences and competences, as well as enabling differentiated entry to taught degrees through accreditation[8]. The UK HET[9] system allows independence for universities, so WBL and APEL practices are varied and acceptable, although not currently enshrined in legislation. However, to some extent, despite twelve years of awarding degrees in WBL, the new Institute at Middlesex has suffered from similar non-acceptance of its epistemology from colleagues across the university. Even here, much still needs to be done in order for work to be fully recognised as a locus where knowledge is independently generated, as well as being a recipient of academic knowledge transfer.

---

7 Devolved to regional governments in the case of Italy

8 APEL system known as VAE – Validation des Aquis de l'Éxperience

9 Higher Education and Training – term used across Europe and emblematic of the new vocationalisation

The internal project environment

Given this background of diverse multiple realities and epistemologies compounded by the differing cultures, practices, and pre-understandings of partner representatives, it was vital to establish a common discourse and a common domain in order to move the project forward and to create the transformative knowledge required to implement WBL approaches. Discourse is never singular, as a variety co-exists in any situation, nor even equal in power relations (Edwards and Usher, 2000), but it is through amalgamation or convergence that domains can be contested and constructed. Initially, the discourse of the work based approaches coined by Middlesex was pre-eminent, supported to some extent by that of the University of Lille. A clear example of this was in the common WBL platform I first drafted that was naturally closely aligned to the Middlesex model, but later editions changed with increasing focus on competences as Middlesex WBL discourse became less dominant, and new common understandings of WBL were negotiated.

In the European partnership, multiple narratives textualised and contextualised the differing practices specific to each institution and nation, therefore it was challenging to construct a meta-narrative that could be individually relevant to and owned by all its constituent members and yet act as a common domain. Influencing factors included:

*   national legislation
*   academic/work knowledge, pre-understanding and practices
*   institutional, cultural, and individual discourses
*   languages
*   traditions
*   social practices

Using the media of meetings, seminars, and web communications, the partnership negotiated understandings of WBL epistemologies and practices (the meta-narrative), and established the common ground and common domains that were expressed in the project aims. The culmination, or product, was the jointly developed, dynamic European common WBL platform; however, in order to make sense of this in single contexts, it needed to be justified and rationalised through individual and localised constructs of meaning (Weick, 1995) that informed the local WBL pilots.

To illustrate how learning and knowledge creation occurred across challenging "positional differences" (Lee & Boud, 2003:195), in a shared domain, I have adapted the concept of the four Ba[10] – originating, interacting, cyber and exercising – that Nonaka & Konno (1998) had amalgamated with the phases of the SECI[11] knowledge conversion model:

*   Originating (socialisation phase) where emotions and mental models

are shared
- Interacting (externalisation phase) where joint meanings and concepts are created and knowledge transformation commences
- Cyber (combination phase) a virtual and collaborative environment where existing and new knowledge is combined
- Exercising (internalisation phase) where an individual iteratively learns and creates knowledge through active participation

Whilst Nonaka and Konno's concept is presented as a static deterministic model with ordered linear progression, for DEWBLAM, the process of knowledge creation was more dynamic, iterative, and chaotic as represented in Figure 15.1 below. Here, new knowledge was transformed continuously through application in different ways and in specific contexts, and then transferred back to the cyber core (community web site) enabling the development of different meanings, mental models, understanding, and further learning.

Figure 15.1 – The "Ba" in DEWBLAM

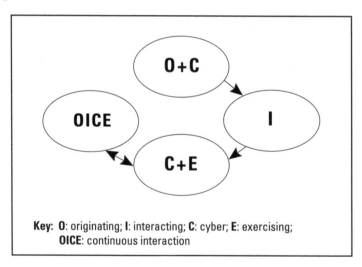

Key: **O**: originating; **I**: interacting; **C**: cyber; **E**: exercising;
OICE: continuous interaction

During the first project phase, the partners shared their mental models of WBL and their external operating conditions in meetings and on the web (O+C), these were transformed (I) and combined with new knowledge and active participation (C+E). With the growth of maturity, there was

10 Coined by Japanese philosopher Kitaro Nishida
11 Socialisation, Externalisation, Combination, Internalisation – developed by Nonaka & Takeuchi (1995)

continuous, and at times, seemingly chaotic interaction (OICE), as knowledge was generated in separate sites, filtered back to the centre where it was scrutinised, and added to, before being applied in the single contexts. Above all, the "ba" was a shared interactive physical/virtual space, evolving as partners contributed their own contexts.

Tensions

One of the key issues that caused considerable friction over the three year project was that of perceived knowledge withholding – aimed at one institution in particular for not transferring its programme assets wholesale, despite its significant leadership of the project. This was problematic for a number of reasons: firstly as the intellectual capital of the university in question had been developed over many years, it could not be handed over without some commercial transaction; secondly the DEWBLAM project aimed to develop distinct indigenous work based programmes or approaches and had to avoid cloning a particular WBL model; and finally, it was more productive to engage all partners and stimulate the creation of knowledge, which found expression in the common European work based learning platform and guidelines and in the different applications.

Other tensions that affected the complex DEWBLAM partnership were:

1. **Relationships and personalities** – partners needed to supersede barriers of personality, nationality, and attachment to the local in order to create meaningful knowledge through interactions, social learning, and the exchange of experiences, knowledge, and information (Tissen et al, 1998). However these interactions were often tense, and small alliances were formed by project end, detracting from the holistic "ba".

2. **Language and cultures** – eight native languages were spoken by the 13 partner organisations (Czech, Dutch, English, French, German, Italian, Spanish, Swedish[12]) with English as the first and German as the second officially registered language for communication, but these differences of national and organisational culture and identity expressed through languages, systems, behaviours, and attitudes had to be backgrounded in order to reach common understanding and a collective identity through the use of the meta-narrative.

3. **Experiences and understanding** – initially differed widely but by project end some partners had gained direct experience by implementing programmes that either contained elements of learning based in the work place or used professional competency frameworks. However, all partners were able to grow in understanding through

---

12 The Finnish partner institution was from the Swedish linguistic minority

contributing to conceptualising the common platform and the guidelines for developing WBL programmes.

4. **Willingness, requirements, and resistances** – all partner representatives were personally willing to participate in the project but in several cases (Italy, Finland, and Germany), the respective institutions posed resistances. For example, academics at the Fachhochschule Aachen continued to resist the implementation of a WBL programme, questioning the validity and legitimacy of research and learning occurring outside of the academy – this was despite some executive support, involvement with European modularisation, and winning a national prize for innovation (February, 2005) through its participation in the DEWBLAM project. There might possibly have been less resistance had an influential academic represented the university, rather than a member of the administrative staff.

5. **Contexts, regulations, and legislation** significantly impacted on acceptance or resistance to WBL. In the German example, despite European agreements and national law that allows for WBL, the state of Rheinland-Westphalia refused to permit Aachen University to implement WBL programmes. In other national contexts, WBL was legally allowed but was deemed by the institutions to be too innovative (such as in Italy or the Czech Republic).

The process of growing work based knowledge in the European partnership

Nonaka & Takeuchi (1995) identify three key characteristics of knowledge creation: the use of figurative or symbolic language, the sharing of personal knowledge, and the use of ambiguity and redundancy. The language used during the DEWBLAM project was that of academia and current business usage, but although there was a definitive shift from "pure imagination...(to)... logical thinking" (ibid:16) as initial ideas moved to practical implementation, it would have been difficult to find common symbolism, given the diversity of the partnership. The second characteristic of sharing personal knowledge was an essential part of the process of knowledge creation, supporting the authors' contention that an individual's personal knowledge is transformed into organisational knowledge and can be the starting point for new knowledge. Ambiguity and redundancy, understood as conditions that enable new ways of thinking to emerge from chaos or the creation of "common cognitive ground" (ibid:18) also resonate with the DEWBLAM process which seemed to be endlessly chaotic as numerous and often repetitive discussions took place, before the common WBL platform provided a focal point and enabled the development of some pilot programmes.

Figure 15.2 below traces the stages of knowledge creation and development from inception to impact, identifying both the key features and the complex processes involved.

Figure 15.2 – Stages in DEWBLAM work based learning developments

FEATURES	PROCESSES
1. Creation of a common vision	Harmonisation of perceptions through meetings, socialising, virtual communication
2. Institution of a democratic approach	Establishment of consensual decision making, incorporation of diversity and levels of pre-understanding
3. Transfer of knowledge	Papers, workshops, seminars, presentations
4. Sharing of knowledge	Research and communication
5. Codification of knowledge in platform	Conceptualisation of WBL theories, writing
6. Collective and individual learning	Internalisation of knowledge leading to new experiences and applications
7. Development of WBL experiences	Identification of suitable resources, approaches, and disciplines
8. Pilot programmes and support systems	Testing and initial evaluation, reflection on practice
9. Embed WBL theories and practices	Institutionalisation through systems and new mental models, validation of experiences and practices
10. Establish a community of practice	Sharing and reviewing new knowledge internally and with wider audiences through papers, seminars, and conferences
11. Contribute to changing learning/knowledge economies	Analysing significance and local impact of WBL on institutions, learners and environments. Reports to internal/external stakeholders.

1 & 2. Creation of a common vision and democratic approach – in order to develop a common vision that could drive and sustain the whole partnership, differing perceptions, goals, and practices needed to be aligned; although the objectives had to be set by a core group of partners (from the UK, Italy, Belgium, and Germany) before the project obtained funding from the European Union. To obtain the collaboration of all partners in achieving this, formal meetings and informal socialising opportunities were used that motivated and valued people for sharing their knowledge. A democratic, consensual, and inclusive approach to decision making was agreed during the first meeting inviting all partners to participate in the steering group meetings, thus enabling and empowering all to have an equal voice and equal value, despite the fact that initially there was an inner core, a leader, and a coordinator.

The language of communication was English – spoken and understood with differing levels of expertise – but more important than language difficulties were the definition of the common vision, common understandings and of the meta-narrative. Pre-understandings differed widely as has been previously noted and caused substantial tensions when these were foregrounded; however, ultimately, these differences added to the overall knowledge capital. Tissen et al (1998:171) hypothesise that Europeans "...eagerly seek out concepts, theories and methodology to improve performance", and this was indeed the case with much discussion over epistemologies.

3 & 4. Knowledge transfer and sharing – whilst the significant expertise of Middlesex and Lille Universities was called upon to leverage theoretical and working knowledge (Dixon, 2000), both avoided wholesale transfers of explicit systems. This was because the recipients were unlikely to have identical contexts to enable exploitation, the project aims were to develop indigenous programmes, and there were important issues of ownership as it was not in the commercial interests of the universities to freely transfer their knowledge assets. Therefore, the features of the WBL systems already in operation were shared in meetings, seminars, and workshops, but the finely detailed processes were not.

5. Codification of the common WBL platform was pivotal in centralising and generating conceptual knowledge, acting firstly as a theoretical framework and source that partners could interpret and apply in their specific contexts, before reflecting on and filtering their experiences back to enhance the platform.

6. Learning was individual, collective, and institutional, beginning to change practices and have an effect on social environments. Reflecting the differences in contexts, one partner highlighted the "mental impact" on key institutional figures that enabled both the planning of a WBL programme despite resistances and a new way of thinking about organising learning; whilst another partner considered that WBL approaches should be standardised across the EU before having an impact on local education policies. One of the prime drivers of change was the requirement of the European Union to align higher education awards and to meet the perceived needs of the new knowledge economy through professional profiling, the increasing vocationalisation of education and through competency frameworks[13]. This requires a paradigm shift from learning per se to learning fit for purpose, concomitantly becoming a less socially "dangerous" activity as it increasingly focuses on changing practices rather than questioning established societal systems (Jarvis et al: 1998).

7, 8, & 9. Develop pilot programmes and experiences – as the partners began to adapt and apply relevant elements of the platform, the pilots needed to be tested, evaluated, and institutionalised through supporting systems.

10. Communities of practice are still being established both internally and externally to individual institutions as new knowledge is shared with wider audiences through workshops, papers, seminars, conferences and so on. Open seminars were held in Aachen and Prague in an attempt to overcome local resistance, and this should gradually diminish as WBL becomes part of discourses and understandings – particularly when economic needs drive the search for new sources of learners and income, and as focus increases on knowledge partnerships between business and higher education in order to meet the requirements of the EU knowledge society. Framing WBL within a European community of practice will benefit all partners, enabling multidirectional knowledge flows and international referencing that strengthens indigenous practices. This is already visible in examples such as Granada which incorporated aspects of the Middlesex practice to include a research module in their new programme, or Middlesex which drew on the Lille experience to offer a full APEL doctorate and also organised the July 2007 UALL[14] WBL Network conference to include European perspectives.

11. Learning and knowledge economies change at a slower pace than institutions, but there is growing recognition at European and at partnership level that there is a need to engage directly with businesses and to incorporate their learning requirements into the higher education agenda. Work based approaches are ideal as economies change from supply led to demand led with concomitant effect on cost and educational programmes, and partners have implemented programmes that were jointly developed with industry. The "social partnership" aspect of both the local and the European learning economies is constituted through formal legal agreements and institutional frameworks and is enhanced by social dialogue, mutual understandings, and trust (Nyhan et al, 2003) – in this

---

13 See for example the Tuning project aimed at aligning HE frameworks –
    www.unideusto.org

14 Universities Association for Lifelong Learning (UK)

perspective, the DEWBLAM partnership can contribute to education and can impact on a wider European economy as well as on each local or regional cluster.

The common European WBL platform

The common European WBL platform is an ambitious attempt to define core common concepts and key features of WBL pertaining to European educational and social contexts. It is both theoretical and practical, emerging from the partners' understandings and from new practices as elements of the platform were applied in pilot programmes. It aimed not only to conceptualise WBL and to give guidance to partners on the implementation of work based programmes but was also intended at project end as a guide for other interested institutions and to provide a baseline of work based theory and practice that could contribute to European educational protocols.

Inevitably, the first versions represented the Middlesex WBL practice but partners' emerging understandings and practices gradually altered the focus, ultimately reflecting more the conceptualisation and practice of vocational competence rather than a broader open ended definition. This emphasis on competence development was due to several factors. Firstly, a dual vocational/academic educational system from secondary school to university level has traditionally coexisted across Europe, which may have contributed to pre-understanding of WBL as work training for apprentices or as work placements for students applying their school/college acquired knowledge. Secondly, with the new focus of the EU on the competitive knowledge society, practice based knowledge is becoming more valued within European discourses, but this is understood as competence or job related skills. Thirdly, the whole concept of WBL was new to the majority of the partners, and, therefore, a discourse of WBL as a knowledge creation system was perhaps too complex to comprehend. Finally, it may simply have been due to market forces as job related competences/skills programmes are potentially easier to sell to businesses than those with an academic focus.

The platform firstly proposes definitions of WBL in higher education; detailing distinctive features such as accreditation processes, blended learning methodologies, enhanced professional competence and the meeting of strategic objectives. It then focuses on the role of partnerships in defining professional profiles, in developing programmes and in learning agreements; on the pre-conditions and requirements necessary to implement the development of WBL programmes and programme structures; and finally on programme structures and clearly defined learning tools and environments. However, whilst this is a wide ranging document, there is only sufficient space in this chapter to analyse three definitions of WBL.

The first platform draft proposed a single definition:

• learning at, through and for work

By version six, this had been replaced by multiple notions that WBL was:

• a matrix combining formal, informal and non-formal learning
• a knowledge transformer
• a higher education enabler responsive to social demands and to emerging areas of transdisciplinary knowledge

The final definitions in version eight proposed that:

• WBL is an educational and training approach in which competence development is given a central position, and in which prior and experiential learning, formal learning, informal learning and non-formal learning complement each other in the progress towards formal recognised and accredited qualifications by the HET institution.

• WBL is an experience centred teaching and learning approach in which the learner will develop competencies in multiple contexts, especially in the work place and because of the work place. The learner undertakes a theoretical (applied) scientific project, which is essential and relevant for study and work environments.

• WBL takes place in a context of structured partnerships and environments and brings about a definite added/surplus value and social capital for all parties involved, namely the workplace, the HET institution and the learner. All three parties share equal responsibilities in the learning process, which engages learners of all kinds in structured learning programmes designed, agreed upon and supported by the three parties, and managed by the HET institution. The process lies in the hands of the learner, which entails the fact that s/he is responsible for their own learning experience and the ensuing transition. A reflexive approach and attitude is a fundamental concept in the personal competence development process.

The definitions of WBL, commencing from a simple statement in the first version, were undoubtedly enriched, contextualised, and enhanced by the final version. But is it necessarily a reflection of what experienced UK practitioners might consider WBL to be in higher education, and have the essential elements of work as a context and an enabler been lost? What is the role of knowledge in the final definitions or is WBL seen here as an arena where learning is 'taught' and is merely instrumental in acquiring a predefined set of competences and gaining a qualification?

In the UK, the term 'work based learning' is employed in a variety of ways to cover a range of learning levels, meanings, and contexts – from vocational training based partially or fully in the work place that may use National Occupational Standards (NOS) to enhance professional development or provide CPD[15] courses, NVQs[16] or foundation degrees; through student internships or work placements that may use the work place as a medium for teaching or supporting part of a set curriculum; to programmes that offer partial or full high level learning opportunities to participants based around their work contexts. Whichever interpretation is used, WBL is certainly part of the new agenda for economic relevance in higher education.

Brennan (2005:4) proposes the notion that the curriculum of WBL in higher education entails learning that is identified and demonstrated through activities occurring in the workplace, that is not taught on campus, nor restricted to narrow performance related learning (such as in the NVQ system), nor to preparation for employment. Garnett (2004)[17] emphasises the focus of high level critical thinking on work in order to facilitate the recognition, acquisition, and application of individual and collective knowledge, skills, and abilities and to achieve outcomes of significance to the learner, their work, and the university. These two notions contribute to broader understandings and practices of WBL in higher education, referred to, for example, by Brennan and Little (1996) or Boud and Solomon (2001), whilst Connor (2005) posits a contrasting view that focuses on gaining knowledge and competencies in the workplace and, in this sense, is closer to the DEWBLAM definitions.

The philosophical grounding of the Middlesex approach in viewing WBL as a field of study (Portwood and Costley, eds. 2000), rather than as a new mode of 'transmitting university based learning to the work place' (Garnett, 2005:80), potentially validates any learning occurring in any place of work, lifting it to comparability with academic research and learning and thereby creating a 'professional researcher/learner' who might be based either in an organisation or in a university. It is this openness that contributes to the success of the Middlesex model of WBL, and it is precisely the narrowness of the DEWBLAM propositions that caused me such unease.

Critical analysis of the platform definitions against current thinking and practices of WBL as posited above, points to reductionism and instrumentalism where any concept of the role of knowledge as key to learning has been lost, and where learning based at work is seen merely as

---

15 Continuing Professional Development

16 National Vocational Qualifications

17 In inaugural lecture

an approach or mode of teaching and learning in order to acquire/develop pre-defined competencies – rather than recognising that work engenders learning. Such definitions refer to earlier educational positions where learning was only recognised when matching a prescribed set of course outcomes and denigrates the possibility that high level learning is already present in the work place and may need explicating and validating, rather than adding to by 'training or courses'. This focus on vocational competence acquisition is pre-eminent in new European higher education discourses, exemplified by the types of programmes that the DEWBLAM partners began to pilot, and perhaps experienced UK practitioners need to engage more with forums across Europe to ensure that learning and knowledge based at work achieve higher status and wider understanding and recognition.

The potential impact of DEWBLAM

The knowledge created through DEWBLAM needs to be firmly located within economies, but also needs to remain dynamic and capable of adaptation contributing to the performance of individuals, organisations, regions and countries (Lundvall & Borras, 1999). However, the increasing dominance of notions of competence (as exemplified in the EU Tuning project, and in the platform definitions above) represents a danger in too closely defining what a student is expected to do at the end of a course of study without allowing for the pre-existence or the development of transdisciplinary tacit or explicit knowledge. This echoes the shift of knowledge epistemologies from rationality towards performativity, employability and utility, with concomitant risks of losing sight of knowledge as communal wealth.

What significance might DEWBLAM have within localised economies? In the first instance, the higher education institutions might become more community focused, offering programmes that include work based and APEL systems and are adapted to local needs; working in partnership with a wide range of industry and social stakeholders to develop and deliver these. Secondly, the impact that DEWBLAM might have on local environments could be situated within the context of the European social model that aims to 'find a balance between economic and social objectives' (Nyhan et al, 2003:30). By providing new opportunities for lifelong learning and validating existing learning, the partner institutions can make a significant contribution to both the social and economic aspects of the social model. Furthermore, they could gain conceptually by impacting on established mental models, by enabling greater creativity in developing new programmes and gaining a leading competitive edge over other educational institutions, whilst individual partners have also enhanced their own professional knowledge and practice.

With the accession of Eastern European countries whose economic and social models differ substantially from Western Europe, DEWBLAM potentially presents a role model for new EU members to draw on, concomitantly offering opportunities for educational innovation as embedded traditional, rational and linear HE models confront postmodernist epistemologies. Additionally, DEWBLAM can contribute to the learning and knowledge economy through the development of intellectual capital – the combined knowledge capital produced by the partnership, and the structural capital that codifies and transforms this into useable (and tradable) systems or pilot programmes (Edvinsson & Malone, 1998). However, the knowledge that remains tacit can only have a limited effect – it is up to the partnership to ensure that all knowledge generated as a result of the project is transformed into a set of actions that will innovate the new realities of higher education. So long as legislation and established protocols remain dominant in both discourses and in operational systems, potential conflict between old and new paradigms will continue, and the dichotomies and struggles between sites of knowledge creation and learning remain.

In conclusion – what impact could DEWBLAM have on Middlesex University? Significantly, it has already drawn directly on the Lille model for its new doctorate – the DProf by Public Works that offers an award via the recognition of prior work. Secondly, it could develop more programmes jointly with industry or professional institutions, using professional profiles or National Occupational Standards, and making better use of employer resources for tutoring and assessing. Finally, it could use the DEWBLAM platform and experience as a lens to reflect and inquire into its own practices.

References

Adams, S. (2006) *The Recognition of Prior Learning in the Context of European Higher Education* – in eds. Corradi, C.; Evans, N. & Valk, A. *Recognising Experiential Learning: Practices in European Universities* – Estonia: Tartu University Press

Boud, D. & Solomon, N. eds. (2001) *Work Based Learning. A New Higher Education?* – Buckingham: SRHE & Open University Press

Brennan, L. (2005) *Integrating Work Based learning into Higher Education. A Guide to Good Practice* – Bolton: University Vocational Awards Council

Brennan, J. & Little, B (1996) *A Review of Work Based Learning in Higher Education* – Leeds: DfEE

Connor, H. (2005) *Work Based Learning – A Consultation* – Council for Industry and Higher Education www.cihe-uk.com

Edvinsson, L. & Malone, M. (1998) *Intellectual Capital* – London: Piatkus

Edwards, M. (1998) *Commodification and Control in Higher Education* – in eds. Jary, D.& Parker, M. – *The New Higher Education* – Stoke-on-Trent: Staffordshire University Press

Edwards, R. & Usher, R. (2000) *Research on Work, Research at Work* – in eds. Garrick, J. & Rhodes, C. – Research and Knowledge at Work – London: Routledge

Garnett, J. (2005) – *University Work Based Learning and the Knowledge-driven Project* in eds. Rounce, K. & Workman, B. *Work based Learning in Health Care* – Chichester: Kingsham Press

Jarvis, P., Holford, J. & Griffin, C. (1998) *The Theory and Practice of Learning* – London: Kogan Page

Lee, A. & Boud, D. (2003) *Writing Groups, Change and Academic Identity: Research Development as Local Practice* – in Studies in Higher Education – Volume 28 No.2 – Carfax Publishing

Lundvall, B. & Borras, S. (1999) *The Globalising Learning Economy: Implications for Innovation Policy* – Luxemburg: Office for Official Publications of the European Communities

Lyotard, M. (1984) *The Postmodern Condition. A Report on Knowledge* – Manchester: Manchester University Press

Nonaka, I. & Konno, N. (1998) *The Concept of "Ba": Building Foundation for Knowledge Creation* – California Management Review Vol. 40, No.3 (extract in www.cyberartsweb.org)

Nonaka, I. & Takeuchi, H. (1995) *The Knowledge Creating Company* – Oxford: Oxford University Press

Nyan, B. et al (2003) *Facing up to the Learning Organisation Challenge* – Luxembourg: CEDEFOP Reference Series 41–1

Portwood, D. & Costley, C. – *Work based Learning and the University: New Perspectives and Practices* – Birmingham: SEDA Paper 109

Tissen, R., Andriesson, D. & Lekanne, Deprez, F. (1998) *Value-Based Knowledge Management* – London: Longman

Weick, K. (1995) *Sensemaking in Organisations* – California: Sage

16
The Core Components: Teaching, Learning and Assessing

Barbara Workman

***

Teachers who inspire students to learn are generally considered to be effective at teaching. However, to learn effectively usually depends more on the student's motivation and capacity to learn than the teacher's ability to teach. In the current climate when knowledge is easily generated, used and discarded rapidly, depending on the elearning fad of the moment, it seems reasonable to suggest there have to be some enduring characteristics of teaching that help learning to happen. When learning from work, it must be acknowledged that all workers have an opportunity to learn from their work, but not all learning is good, neither is it always effective nor does it always enable progressive learning. However, the WBL programmes endeavour to use some key teaching, learning and assessment theories and interventions in order to maximise experiential learning from whatever source, whether that be full or part time, paid or voluntary work, life experiences or domestic responsibilities. This chapter will identify specific teaching, learning and assessment strategies which make a positive contribution to an individual's learning, and on which the Middlesex WBL programmes are predicated. It will consider some of the theoretical frameworks which underpin our learning approaches. It will discuss how the development and use of level criteria have provided benchmarks by which programmes are managed and assessed and how this contributes to a sound academic framework in which the student is able to negotiate an individual programme, become an autonomous learner, developing skills of lifelong learning and inquiry in order to meet personal and professional development needs.

Reflection, adult learning and experiential learning
Theories related to learning through reflection upon experience such as Kolb (1984) and Schön (1987) have informed the WBL curriculum and are integrated within each stage of the WBL programme to facilitate learning from reflection. Theories of adult learning have also informed our approach to WBL, in particular those which recognise the social construction of learning such as the humanistic view that adult learning is shaped by individuals' self identified learning needs with the teacher as facilitator, rather than the repository of all knowledge (Rogers, 1983). The andragogical approach (Knowles 2005) that recognises and values learning

from experience, stimulated and motivated by the need to know, also makes a significant contribution as well as the political imperatives that drive lifelong learning, the agenda for widening access and participation and employer engagement in education.

There are four curriculum components in the WBL programme, each with different types of learning activities and assessment requirements:

1. Review of learning (APEL) and accreditation; compilation of portfolio of experiential learning supported by evidence and a reflective essay
2. Programme planning; a negotiated three way learning agreement between the student, employer or sponsor and the university
3. Research and development; portfolio of learning and a project proposal with critical commentary
4. Work based projects; a real time work based project

These build upon one another as indicated in Figure 16.1 below.

Figure 16.1: Core components of WBL programme (Garnett 2001)

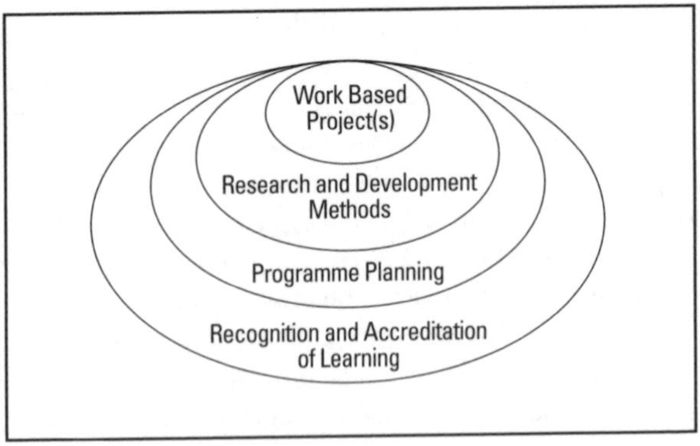

The programme starts with the review of learning and accreditation claim, which captures the student's attention as the assessment relies on a compilation of their personal learning, together with evidence to support their APEL (Accreditation of Prior experiential Learning) claim. It draws on the work practices and experience gained through and at work for the individual and forms the basis for the rest of the students' programme by being accredited with academic credits. This then forms the foundation of an individually negotiated programme, building upon an individual's experiential learning and providing the focus for future learning. Such learning may come from accredited organisational training programmes or continuous professional development, or from other experiences and activities outside a traditional academic teaching environment. These are explored through the use of reflective activities and are assessed as

'General' credit or 'Specific' credit. General credit is awarded for learning demonstrated by the claimant, and does not have to demonstrate an exact match with taught programmes. Specific credit matches specific learning outcomes from programmes which the claimant has chosen to demonstrate s/he has the equivalent learning from a source other than through taught programmes in the university. General credit is favoured by the majority of the students as it reflects their real world experiences.

Progression through the programme is then enabled by a three way negotiated learning agreement between the student, their employer/sponsor and the university, and identifies the learning that will be undertaken in the form of work based projects, and/or taught modules where applicable. Appropriate methods of learning and assessment for that individual's programme will depend on negotiations with the student's adviser to ensure a good fit between the proposed learning and assessment strategies. The move onto new learning is preceded by a research and development module, which encourages the student to learn methods of critical appraisal and inquiry to equip themselves with new knowledge and learning skills for their proposed new learning in the form of projects.

As the curriculum is of the workplace and work is the curriculum (Boud 2001) there are a great range of differences in terms of project outcomes that WBL must accommodate. For example, the demands of the project work of an office manager will be very different from someone who teaches dance or reviews risk assessment in a shipping company. The projects therefore, will be presented differently and reflect the vast range of areas of expertise, but may not all rely on a standard written submission. They may include the creation of an artefact, together with a critical commentary of its creation, or it may be an evaluation of a video of practice or a portfolio record of the development of a corporate policy. Consequently, the methods of learning and assessment must respond to and cater for different modes of presentation, but also provide standard criteria that can provide a consistent and rigorous assessment framework for both undergraduate and postgraduate levels and across subject areas.

Biggs (1999) states that good learning and teaching activities are those which enable the student to reflect upon, question and analyse new ideas and information. He identifies four characteristics which promote this within a curriculum: a well structured knowledge base, appropriate motivational context, learner engagement in the task and interaction with others. The WBL programme meets these criteria in that the knowledge base that the student brings is knowledge of their own subject area and work context, supplemented by new learning which is facilitated through the programme, but highly focused and relevant to their work. The context provides the motivation and application to work, particularly as the content is negotiable. By beginning with exploring their own learning learners become intrigued with what they know, but also how much they do not know, and are stimulated to find out more.

Recognising that learning at work is not confined to classrooms, but is liberated into the workplace through interactions with colleagues and clients, or through work and management systems, centres the learner in the learning experience rather than learning being teacher centred.

The learning cycle as described by Kolb (1984) underpins the learning stages inherent within the WBL programme. This is particularly evident in the final project when the student undertakes a project that is founded on work practices and contributes to work as a whole. The new knowledge not only contributes to the organisation, but the learning from the process, including insights into organisational behaviour and networks, equips the worker/student with new understanding of their organisation and profession. The knowledge that is required in such an assignment usually contains only a limited amount of disciplinary knowledge, perhaps newly applied to changing and enhancing practice, but is supported and defended by the intellectual case made through taking account of the academic requirements as well as organisational needs (Costley 2007).

Figure 16.2 Kolb's (1984) Learning cycle as overlaid upon the WBL curriculum framework.

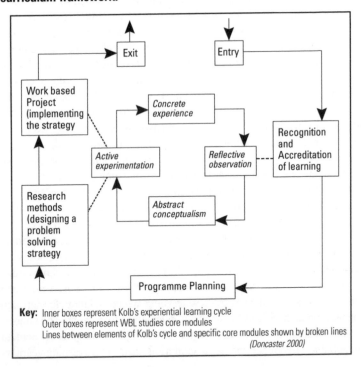

Key: Inner boxes represent Kolb's experiential learning cycle
Outer boxes represent WBL studies core modules
Lines between elements of Kolb's cycle and specific core modules shown by broken lines
(Doncaster 2000)

Assessment in Higher Education (HE) is considered to have a number of functions which include directing learning, promoting learning activities and focusing aspects of learning behaviour (Bryan & Clegg 2006) as well as providing feedback on quality assurance aspects of the programme. These functions are the same whether it is WBL assessment within higher education or traditional assessment activities. Students have become increasingly strategic in the way they allocate their time and effort to learning and see assessment tasks as taking priority in their programme (Gibbs 2006). Students take their cues from academics as to the assessment within a course and may not explore wider aspects of new theories because, pragmatically, they have limited learning time in which to maximise their academic success and this is achieved by focusing only on the assessed task (Gibbs 2006), thereby limiting the range of subject knowledge which they study. The challenge therefore for an academic programme, is to integrate key learning into the assessment task in order to ensure that the learning is undertaken; thus it follows that the assessment shapes the curriculum (Shacklock & Morgan 2002). In WBL, work is the curriculum (Boud 2001), and so assessment that is closely aligned to work activities will motivate the students and enable them to extend their knowledge and skills in line with work and assessment demands.

In WBL there are additional assessment pressures as individuals must function competently in the workplace as well as submitting academic assignments, as all the WBL students are primarily workers studying part time rather than full time students working part time. The challenge therefore for WBL in HE is to provide assessment tasks that align assessment requirements with individuals' learning needs, whether those are intellectual challenges or achievement of practical competences. This includes aspects of assessment that monitor individual performance and progress against course performance indicators and quality assurance standards, but which also broaden academic skills and knowledge, and engage individuals' in studying areas of preferred academic interest. The use of reflection facilitates and integrates the student experience with new knowledge and practice to gain insights as a practitioner (Schön 1987), to apply to future practice, and to develop and enhance knowledge in both academic and professional arenas (Major 2005).

Gibbs (2006) identifies the aims of assessment as having six main functions: capturing student time and attention; generating appropriate student learning activity; providing timely feedback which students attend to; helping students to internalise their chosen discipline's standards and notions of quality, marking and generating grades to distinguish between students or which enable pass or fail decisions to be made; and quality assurance which provides evidence for others to judge the appropriateness of the course. WBL programmes endeavour to fulfil these aims throughout the programme using a variety of teaching, learning and assessment strategies which will be further explored below.

Due to the nature of the WBL programme recruitment, there is potential for a wide range of subject focus. A second supervisor will be recruited to assist in the academic support and assessments, particularly of the APEL and project stages to ensure subject expertise. This provides academic support which reflects a subject discipline and its notions of presentation in academic and subject specialist work (Bryan & Clegg 2006). Where possible this will be sourced from within the university. Over the years the WBL group have been able to involve a wide range of subject experts from both inside and outside the university to provide specialist input and have consequently developed partnerships leading to increased involvement in WBL programmes as a whole. The WBL academic adviser remains involved with the student to ensure that the processes of the programme and progression are coherent. Brown (1999) suggests that employers, tutors and line managers are often best placed to assess learning undertaken outside the HEI, and indeed many work placement students have been assessed by employers on courses where WBL is used as a mode of study. However, as yet WBL has no consistent formal mechanism for involving a work manager or sponsor in the assessment process. There are some partnership programmes where members of the same learning community have been involved in assessment but this has not been widely integrated into our programmes and is recognised as a limitation of the WBL assessment process. For logistical reasons such as access to employers at peak assessment times, induction and assessor training, and resources restraint within and outside the university, this has not yet occurred as standard practice, maintaining the traditional view of assessment in HE whereby only the academics make the assessment judgments and students do not normally expect their employer to be involved.

Gibbs (1999) notes that feedback to students, when timely for it to be used within summative assessments, contributes positively to good assessment practice, and improves the learning experience of the student. Early feedback provides time for the student to use it to improve their work and also indicates whether they are meeting the expected standards and criteria and to what degree the work is meeting course expectations. Gibbs (2006) also suggests that peer assessment is helpful in providing students with formative feedback, either at interim points or when students are undertaking tasks without marks. This is a strategy that is used in some components of the WBL programme where the virtual learning environment (VLE) may be used to comment on shared work examples, or when students present their proposals for work based projects to their peer group for feedback and critique. These activities encourage the students to critique their own work and to learn to interpret it in the light of the WBL level descriptors and key performance questions, thus developing skills of comparative evaluation (Brown 1999).

Students are encouraged to gain feedback from their academic advisers in time for them to make adjustments before final submission. Draft work is expected to be sent to the academic adviser in time to allow a suitable turn around time, either by telephone, face to face or an email tutorial. Giving feedback to students with enough time to integrate it into final work, without being graded but with constructive comments, will enable students to learn from and use it to improve the quality of their work, and this has certainly been borne out by our experience. The WBL advisers actively encourage draft work as a way to monitor student progress and understanding of the assessment task. This may be the only contact that the WBL adviser has with the students as few WBL students attend the university campus during their programmes and are therefore reliant on alternative teaching strategies, such as reading draft work, to get feedback and interact with their adviser. The onus, therefore is on the students to become self directed learners, taking the initiative in contacting their adviser, seeking out information to inform their inquiry and pursuing locally based policies and information. Because each student's programme is very individual they find it hard to transfer commonalities of feedback from VLE to their own particular situation and therefore its use to support teaching and learning has been slow.

Case study

Peter works as a community nurse. He identified a health need in his locality that needed easily accessible information. As the final project in a Bsc (Hons) WBL (Community Nursing) he worked collaboratively with colleagues to introduce and evaluate a health information leaflet, which was rapidly adopted by other local health care practitioners as being responsive to local health promotion needs. As a distance learning student and one that did not find studying easy, he sought advice during the project process by means of sending draft work by email for his adviser to comment on and make suggestions, supported by telephone tutorials, and paced to meet his personal time requirements. He never met his adviser until the final oral presentation of the project, when he came in person to present his project. He graduated with a first class honours degree, having responded well to advice and academic direction, and developing academic and critical enquiry skills far beyond those anticipated when first entering his profession.

Criterion Referenced Assessment Level Descriptors

To aid marking and grading of work, WBL level descriptors have been devised to provide assessment criteria for all curriculum components. Each module has learning outcomes designed to apply the level descriptors to specific assessment tasks, but all assessments involve the use of the level descriptors. With criterion referenced assessment, it is possible to say what the student must be able to do, teach them to do it, and then assess their ability to do it (Biggs 1999). As all the WBL assessments are strongly qualitative in nature, the expectations of what a piece of work at a particular academic level looks like, can be captured and expressed within these qualitative statements. Eleven key criteria have been generated and specific interpretations for each academic level have been derived from them, so that all assessors and students can refer to the level descriptors at a given academic level. The level descriptors are also mapped against programme specifications for the range of undergraduate and postgraduate programmes.

The level descriptors reflect the following key areas of assessment and are linked to programme outcomes by the numbering. As part of the work of the Centre for Excellence in teaching and learning, the stems have been developed further by expressing the meaning of each descriptor in more accessible language to assist students to make the transition between work and academic jargon, and prevent terminology from becoming a barrier to learning. Figure 16.3 below states the stem and its interpretation.

Figure 16.3: Level Descriptor Stems and their meanings

A1	**Identification and appropriate use of resources of knowledge and evidence:** select and choose information and evidence from a range of options, justifying your choices and use in your discussion. Different sources of learning can be used to illustrate and inform learning, if you explain how these contributed to your decisions.
A2	**Selection and justification of approaches to task:** provide a rationale for a chosen approach to a given situation, and discuss the range of available and suitable alternatives, demonstrating the application of an evidence base/criteria which utilises a range of underpinning knowledge and understanding
A3	**Ethical understanding:** apply and interpret a variety of moral codes and ethical practice that direct people's decisions and behaviour, particularly when applied to professional roles, expectations & organisations.
B1	**Analysis and synthesis of information and ideas:** disentangle a variety of elements of an idea and reconstruct and combine them in different ways to demonstrate alternatives or implications of an idea.
B2	**Self appraisal/ reflection on practice:** critically consider own actions and motives and understand more about how and why you or others might think or respond in particular ways, and how these insights might impact work with others.
B3	**Action planning leading to effective and appropriate action:** demonstrate measurable outcomes using appropriate strategies and interventions supported by relevant knowledge and understanding

B4	**Evaluation of information and ideas:** rigorously weigh alternatives and evidence in order to make reasoned and informed judgements
C1	**Application of learning:** use new learning to inform, develop and/or improve your own or other's practice activities
C2	**Effective use of resources:** demonstrate use of sources and/or location of information, knowledge, skills, equipment/ materials and personnel that are available and use them to inform and develop practice for yourself and/or others
C3	**Effective communication:** communicate in a variety of ways including construction of an appropriate level of academic argument, use correct grammar and syntax to communicate your ideas in writing, including use and application of other modes of communication which may be verbal, physical, performance orientated or artistic etc as appropriate.
C4	**Working and learning autonomously and with others:** demonstrate taking initiative, involving and including others within your sphere of influence and practice.

Further building upon each of these level descriptors is important within each module and a holistic approach to assessing the full range of abilities is taken, especially in relation to negotiated project modules. The benefits of this approach means that learning builds upon previous knowledge and develops in complexity (Biggs 1999). Assessment by criteria reflects the current level of complexity and how it matches the module objectives rather than how it compares across students, thus being very appropriate for WBL students who are often developing trans-disciplinary skills and to a lesser degree, subject discipline knowledge. A holistic approach to assessment recognises the intrinsic meaning of the overall assessment therefore making it difficult to be proficient in one aspect and inadequate in another and still pass (Biggs 1999). Consequently, WBL students must demonstrate not only achievement in their analytical abilities or problem solving skills, but also application to the context of their work.

Assessment Characteristics

The use of criterion referenced assessment provides a fairer and more accountable assessment regime than norm referencing as the student is measured against standards of achievement rather than against each other (Dunn et al 2002), thus fulfilling the Quality Assurance Agency (QAA) requirements for equity and accountability in assessment. These assessment criteria are stated and made available to the students at the beginning of their programme so that application is transparent at the outset. The process of devising and using criterion referenced assessment has been criticised as requiring considerable negotiation to identify agreed criteria, although some suggest that the descriptive standards echo competence statements and are perceived as being reductionist and task orientated, resulting in subjective assessment decisions (Dunn et al 2002). These criticisms may be apposite to positivist subject disciplines whose grading systems traditionally follow a specific distribution curve or normative assessment. Within WBL, which reflects a constructivist curriculum philosophy (Biggs 1996), once assessors have become accustomed to the range of criteria available, a responsive and structured approach to assessment feedback develops which extends to the student's evaluation of their own academic work.

To demonstrate the applicability of one such criterion at a variety of levels, the figure below shows an example of how a criterion stem is developed to relate to each academic level, indicating the context and level of academic complexity expected of the student. (Figure 16.4)

Figure 16.4 C4. Working and learning autonomously and with others

Level 1: (certificate)	Working and learning autonomously and with others will be in a familiar context and may contribute to effective team working
Level 2: (intermediate)	Working and learning autonomously and with others will often be in a familiar context and may influence effective team working
Level 3: (graduate)	Working and learning autonomously and with others may span a range of contexts and is likely to challenge or develop the practices of others
Level 4: (Masters)	Working and learning autonomously and with others and/or within a team will span a range of contexts, often in a leadership role, and is likely to impact upon personal and professional understanding

Case study example:

Geraint is a manager in public sector services. He undertook a WBL project at Masters level to investigate the initiation of a change of service provision to clients. By using a series of action research cycles he consulted all interested parties and stakeholders and subsequently designed service changes that took government imperatives, service restraints, clients preferences and colleagues experiences into consideration, resulting in a new service that met stakeholder needs, as well as developing his personal understanding of organisation and service development. This project was therefore assessed in the practice area by the virtue of being put into actual practice and demonstrated stakeholder consultation resulting in an improved public service. This project activity clearly reflects the above level descriptor at level 4 as it demonstrates the involvement of others in the project as well as the leadership and sphere of influence required of the project leader.

If this descriptor is applied to another WBL project at graduate level, learning outcomes can be written to reflect the level criteria as follows:

Application to a level 3 WBL project as a learning outcome:

• Level 3: (graduate)

Working and learning autonomously and with others may span a range of contexts and is likely to challenge or develop the practices of others

Becomes:
• Identify, analyse and evaluate your role and, as appropriate, the role of others in the project. If applicable include taking the lead role in the project and demonstrate how you have taken your ideas forward.

• Take responsibility for overseeing other collaborative aspects of the project work, clarifying the areas in which you have worked particularly with others.

As WBL students use work projects which are real at work to fulfil their award requirements, these learning outcomes are achievable because of the applicable real time nature of the work activities and required outputs. The student is able to develop project management skills as part of the learning process. Reflection upon the progress and outcomes of the project and the development of their own skills of critical enquiry and evaluation is expedited by the formal record within the academic project report of the processes involved. There is an oral presentation of the work to academic advisers, but by virtue of the fact that it was undertaken at work, it comes into the real work domain. Being able to see the impact of a project in the 'real' world does much to integrate learning of new knowledge into the practice context, as well as providing motivation for personal learning (Dunn et al 2002) which is congruent with adult learning theory (Knowles et al 2005, Rogers 1983). Should the student encounter difficulties during the lifespan of the project, alternative strategies and interventions may also be tried, tested and incorporated into the learning. Biggs (1999) argues that learning from direct experience and being allowed to make errors and find alternative solutions to practical and intellectual problems recognises the social contexts and learning communities in which authentic assessment occurs, and that a model of alignment of the curriculum which links learning outcomes to assessment tasks and criteria makes learning meaningful for both individuals and groups. This is evident within the WBL assessment process as each assignment the student successfully completes builds upon previous learning and directs future learning within the work environment. This aspect also confirms the reliability and validity of the assessment activities, as the level descriptors provide a consistency of assessment criteria across a variety of subject areas and transdisciplinary work activities, thus demonstrating reliability and application of new knowledge within a real situation, hence demonstrating validity.

Case Study

A cohort of six students completed a Masters programme whilst working as Cancer service improvement leaders nationally within the NHS, several of them working to modernise services to speed patients through the waiting lists for surgery or diagnostic treatments. Their backgrounds varied from health care professionals, such as nurses, to administrators who had demonstrated a flair for project management. The programme started by recognising the in-house training provided by the NHS in service improvement techniques and processes, for which each student made an individual accreditation claim by portfolio. It concluded by each student working on projects in their own NHS Trusts. These projects included: reducing waiting times for urological and gastro-intestinal investigations; introduction of patient information for cancer services across an NHS Trust hospital; user involvement in designing cancer services; redesigning radiology and ultrasound services; and evaluation of video conferencing consultations. The WBL core curriculum provided an academic pathway that recognised the unique and influential roles that these students had in their own workplaces, and provided a framework within which they could gain an academic qualification. Three of the cohort gained a Masters with merit.

In terms of applying criterion referenced assessment the project work that they undertook required a clear application of A3; 'Ethical understanding' at M Level as stated in the learning outcomes for the project module:

> 'Show understanding of the project's underpinning values. Take account of the ethical implications involved in the project's development processes, methodology and likely outcomes. Show an ethical understanding of the specialised work contexts in which the project is undertaken, including full and critical understanding and sensitive application of appropriate prescribed ethical codes'.

All participants had to demonstrate that they had gained permission to pursue their projects within the ethical frameworks of the NHS; no mean feat in this day and age of rigorous clinical governance and legislative requirements to protect confidential data and vulnerable individuals. This also demonstrates that the learning gained from these projects had to be fit for purpose in order to meet government targets in reducing waiting lists.

Assessment Dimensions

Using qualitative assessment methods such as portfolios and projects promotes deep learning. The characteristics of deep learning include motivating the student to take responsibility for the learning task and recognition of its meaningfulness and appropriateness in relation to their practice, and which also requires a depth of relevant knowledge that encourages the student to ask questions and seek answers (Biggs 1999). For the teacher, this requires a facilitative teaching approach that seeks to develop what the student needs to know, and developing his/her problem solving and inquiry skills so that these skills are developed and transferred to future situations, without the teacher having to be the fount of all knowledge.

The assessment strategies also tend to stimulate divergent thinking. This is a learning approach which leans towards alternative thinking approaches, where there may not be a right or wrong answer, but where originality, usefulness, self-expression and creativity feature, whereas convergent thinking requires particular and specific answers, often with a scientific bias (Biggs 1999). Whilst studies suggest that convergent thinkers tend towards science and divergent thinkers towards arts, a mixture of the two approaches allows the development of a theoretical foundation from which to ask questions and creatively explore the unknown within a given context. Initially this can be challenging for the facilitator but WBL students tend to have a strong pragmatic element within their studies, and need both permission and opportunity to develop alternative thinking modes as part of their academic development, and therefore the facilitator has to adapt to the uncertainties of knowledge that this thinking might generate. The use of portfolios and projects as assignment activities allows the factual aspects of knowledge to be stated and evidenced and creative problem solving approaches to be applied and demonstrated.

Quality Assurance

Specific features of quality assurance are addressed specifically in chapter 17 by Garnett, but WBL is subject to the same quality procedures of double marking, external examining and moderating as in any other programme. Although assessment is usually contextualised within a specific work situation (Costley 2007) and is clearly moderated against transparent standards and criteria, for some reason traditional HEIs are unnerved by the thought of quality procedures within WBL. Building in a rigorous assessment framework as part of the programme development and ensuring that the university takes control of the processes and structures of the programme, but leaving the content to be evidenced by a number of different modes is similar in fact to standard HE procedures. The use of criterion referenced assessment ensures consistency of academic judgement for all subjects, thus emphasising the trans-disciplinary nature of WBL. The core features of any academic programme are the ability to critically appraise information, analyse and synthesise information and develop skills of problem solving and decision making within a given context. In WBL level descriptors and criteria make the assessment criteria explicit to all participants in the teaching, learning and assessment process, and can be used to make learning outcomes explicit, thereby enabling the curriculum to demonstrate its relevance and application to real time work.

Conclusion

WBL is designed to equip individuals with skills such as critical reflection and analytical enquiry in order to appraise their work and interrogate their own practice and that of others. Their knowledge may not all be from the academic institution, but is engendered from the work itself, suggesting that knowledge required to inform work may not originate from academia but from the work itself. This challenges the common understanding about the nature of knowledge within Higher Education (Portwood 2000) resulting in the concept of WBL in HE as being controversial and contested. However, the skills that are required to develop, extend and assess knowledge as fostered in HE in all graduate and post graduate programmes are evidenced in graduate transferable skills and these are also applied to our WBL programmes.

References

Biggs J. (1999) *Teaching for Quality Learning at University* Buckingham Society for Research into Higher Education & OUP

Biggs J. (1996) Enhancing Teaching through Constructive Alignment *Higher Education* 32, 347–364

Boud D. (2001) in Boud D & Solomon N (2001) *Work Based Learning: A New Higher Education?* Buckingham Society for Research into Higher Education & OUP

Brown S. (1999) in Brown S & Glasner A. (1999) *Assessment matters in higher education. Choosing and using diverse approaches* Buckingham The Society for Research into Higher Education and OUP.

Bryan C. & Clegg K. (Eds) (2006) *Innovative Assessment in Higher Education* London: Routledge

Costley C. (2007) Work-based learning: assessment and evaluation in higher education. *Assessment and Evaluation in Higher Education* 32 (1) pp1–9

Doncaster K. (2000) Recognising and Accrediting Learning and the Development of Reflective Thinking in Portwood D, & Costley C (2000) *Work based Learning and the University: New Perspectives and Practices* SEDA paper 109 Birmingham

Dunn L. Parry S. & Morgan C (2002) Seeking Quality in Criterion Referenced Assessment Paper presented at Learning Communities and Assessment Cultures conference, Northumbria 2002.
http://www.leeds.ac.uk/educol/documents/00002257.html Accessed 31/05/06

Garnett J. (2001) Models of Work Based Learning. Presentation, WBL Masterclass, July 2001

Gibbs G. (2006) Why assessment is changing in Bryan C. & Clegg K. (Eds) (2006) *Innovative Assessment in Higher Education* London: Routledge

Gibbs G. (1999) Using assessment strategically to change the way students learn – in Brown S. & Glasner A. (1999) *Assessment matters in higher education. Choosing and using diverse approaches* Buckingham: The Society for Research into Higher Education and OUP.

Knowles M.S., Holton III E.F, & Aswansu R. (2005) 6th Ed. *The Adult Learner* London: Butterworth Heinemann

Kolb D. A. (1984) *Experiential learning: Experience as the Source of Learning and Development* London: Prentice Hall

Major D. (2005) Learning through work based learning in Hartley P., Woods A. & Pill M. *Enhancing Teaching in Higher Education* (2005) London: Routledge

Portwood D. (2000) An Intellectual case for Work Based Learning as a subject, in Portwood D. & Costley C. (2000) *Work based Learning and the University: New Perspectives and Practices* SEDA paper 109 Birmingham

Rogers C. (1983) *Freedom to learn for the 80's* Columbus OH: Merrill

Schön D. (1987) *Educating the Reflective Practitioner: Towards a New Design for Teaching and Learning in the Professions* San Francisco: Jossey Bass

Shacklock R. & Morgan A. (2002) Developing Criterion Referenced Assessment http://www.hlst.heacademy.ac.uk/resources/link5/link5_4.html Accessed 2 February 2007

17

Enhancing Quality Assurance

Jonathan Garnett

***

Introduction

This chapter draws upon the Middlesex experience of preparing Work Based Learning studies (WBS) programmes for a range of internal and external quality reviews to identify key themes and issues relating to quality assurance and enhancement of work based learning (WBL) as part of the higher education curriculum. The main section of this book highlights that WBL programmes are derived from the needs of the workplace and of the learner rather than prescribed by the disciplinary curriculum of the university. Key features are a structured review and evaluation of current learning and the design and implementation of developmental projects that meet the needs of both the learner and their work. WBL programmes are often assessed with respect to a transdisciplinary framework of standards and levels (see Workman, chapter 16). The customisation of WBL to the needs of the individual learner and the concern for wider stakeholder interests (often employers) is part of the changing political economy of higher education as it responds to globalisation and the needs of corporate learning (Jarvis, 2001). Such "commodification" of higher education can be seen as placing quality assurance firmly within the discourse of modernism with an emphasis upon measurement of performance, productivity and customer satisfaction (Morley, 2003).

A distinctive feature of the Middlesex approach to WBL is that it not only focuses on the needs of work but explicitly focuses on WBL as a field of study (Costley, 2000). The "field of study" approach has led to WBL at Middlesex being subject to a range of formal evaluations as part of the university's internal quality assurance procedures and as part of external audits by the Quality Assurance Agency (QAA). In addition WBL was the focus of a successful Middlesex University bid to the Higher Education Funding Council for recognition and funding as a Centre for Excellence in Teaching and Learning. A summary of the typical characteristics of each of these evaluation exercises is presented as a "vignette". Each vignette is drawn from personal work based experience and as such is "subjective in nature and intimately linked to the individual or group generating it" (Baumard, 1999:17).

Vignette 1: Middlesex University Review of Academic Provision

In 2003 Work Based Learning Studies was subject to a Review of Academic Provision (RAP) as part of the routine cycle of university review. The focus of the RAP was the student experience rather than the curriculum. The programme team submitted a self evaluation document with a range of supporting evidence including external examiners reports, Board of Study minutes, annual review documents to a panel containing four internal and two external members. The full programme team including administrative staff met with the panel over a two day period. The panel also met with WBL students and had a range of telephone discussions with students aligned to Middlesex international centres in Cyprus, Greece and Hong Kong. The Panel expressed broad confidence in the quality of the student learning experience and the effectiveness of the procedures in place to optimise the learning experience and assure standards. Highlighted good practice was centred upon 'the highly responsive and flexible approach to learning that reflects students individual needs' (Middlesex University 2003). Recommendations to the Programme Team focused upon how to further expand the WBL provision. There were a series of linked actions required relating to tailoring the quality feedback mechanisms by questionnaire and Boards of Study to better meet the needs of work based students. In the area of student guidance and support there were recommendations for action relating to the needs of work based learners as off-campus students. For example the need to review induction to ensure consistency of information for a widely dispersed student body.

Vignette 2: Review by the Quality Assurance Agency as a Discipline Audit Trail

Work Based Learning Studies (WBS) was examined as a discipline audit trail as part of the Institutional Audit of Middlesex University carried out by the Quality Assurance Agency in 2003. In this case WBS was one of five 'discipline audits' carried out to examine at subject discipline level the University systems and procedures for assuring quality and maintaining the academic standards of awards. The programme team developed an extensive and detailed self evaluation document with supporting appendices. The main concern of the programme team in the preparation of the documentation was how to make an area of complex and innovative provision understandable to an external audit team. The programme team addressed this by use of examples and detailed mapping of points made in the evaluation document to supporting evidence. The audit was carried out over half a day and comprised a meeting with current and graduate students and a meeting with eight of the programme team. In addition the audit team examined a wide range of assessed work.

Within the context of a very positive institutional report 'the innovative and robust procedures in place for ensuring the quality of WBL' (QAA 2003) were highlighted as good practice. A specific concern in preparing the documentation had been that there was no subject benchmark statement for WBL . This was commented upon in the audit report but it was noted that there was evidence of WBL being informed by appropriate QAA codes and guidelines. It was also noted that 'since students work within individually negotiated schemes, there are no progression and completion data relating to cohorts of students' but that 'overall statistics for students engaged in all aspects of WBS are available and demonstrate how individuals can progress in flexible schemes at speeds which suit their particular circumstances' (QAA 2003:142). Aspects of good practice commented upon by the audit report included 'the detailed and supportive feedback which was meticulously articulated with programme and learning outcomes' (QAA 2003:145). This related to the mapping of module level outcomes and assessment criteria to programme level outcomes and the overarching use of academic level descriptors. The audit found a very high degree of conformity to university quality and assessment procedures and practices. The report concluded 'There was evidence that students saw their learning in WBS as enhancing their performance and that employers valued highly the benefits to the workplace arising from their students' experience' (QAA 2003:149).

Vignette 3: Middlesex University Enhanced Review

In 2005 WBS was considered by the university for review and revalidation. This was one of the first of a new style of reviews meant to combine the student experience focus of the Review of Academic Provision with the curriculum focus of review and revalidation. Unlike the previous two cases this represented an opportunity for the programme team to put forward and secure approval for change to the curriculum offer. Thus the preparation process and document submitted to the panel gave the opportunity for creative changes to be proposed in respect of the further development of WBL level descriptors and the validation of new modules developed as a result of operational feedback. A self evaluation document, draft student handbook, annual monitoring and external examiner reports were provided to the Panel (which included two external members with expertise in WBL) in advance. The evaluation document included a substantial appendix highlighting the nature of WBL as a field of study. The event was staged over one day and included meetings with senior management, the full programme team including administrative and learning support staff and face to face and telephone discussions with current and recent students. Revalidation was achieved with a small number of conditions but the event highlighted that despite the recommendations made in the 2003 Review of

Academic Provision there continued to be difficulties where off-campus students interacted with some central university services. It appeared that such difficulties often stemmed from the comparative flexibility of WBS programmes which placed different demands upon systems and structures developed primarily to meet the needs of full-time students.

Vignette 4: Consideration by the Higher Education Funding Council for England (HEFCE) for recognition and funding as a Centre for Excellence in Teaching and Learning in the area of Work Based Learning

In 2004 Middlesex University submitted an application to the Higher Education Funding Council for the award of a Centre for Excellence in Teaching and Learning. The evidence submitted as part of a two stage assessment process drew heavily upon the evaluative reports produced by the Panels described in vignettes one and two as evidence of "excellence" in teaching and learning, but also provided more flexibility for the programme team to define and evidence the nature of their excellent practice. The application to HEFCE stressed that the Middlesex WBL provision widened access to higher education at all levels and combined individual learning and organisational development. The flexibility and learner centred nature of the provision was highlighted as was the potential of the programmes to be relevant to the needs of individual work based learners, teams and organisations.

The Middlesex application was able to evidence excellent standards achieved by students not only in relation to standard university statistical data but also in respect of the high significance of WBL projects to the stakeholder organisation. For example WBS projects cited in the document submitted to HEFCE included the implementation of a knowledge audit process within a medium sized manufacturing company; a study of school truancy which was negotiated with the London Metropolitan Police. It was stressed that the impact of projects could be considerable and examples were given including the improvement of the reporting process of construction defects to learn from mistakes and thus increase customer satisfaction and company profits; an exploration of the emerging role of the Nurse Consultant in Elderly Care. While previous evaluation reported in vignettes one to three had tended to focus upon the success of WBL in providing customised programmes to meet the needs of individual students this document gave additional emphasis to working with and meeting the needs of their organisations (eg employer, voluntary, union, professional body). Attention was drawn to the development of different models of WBL to meet the needs of specific employers or professional groups such as Marks and Spencer, Ministry of Defence Police, continuing professional development for Vets, Leadership and Cancer Care initiatives in the

National Health Service and Small and Medium Sized Enterprises in North London.

Middlesex successfully argued that the proposed Centre for Excellence in Work Based Learning (CEWBL) would be uniquely positioned to impact upon work based learners who were full-time workers and therefore part-time students. The CEWBL would extend and further develop excellent practice by embedding elements of WBL excellent practice (eg reflective practice, accreditation of prior experiential learning, assessing work based projects) within other University programmes. CEWBL would explicitly support knowledge creating partnerships between the university and external partners. In order to do this the Centre would enhance the expertise of university staff in recognising, facilitating and assessing the use of transdisciplinary knowledge generated by accreditation of experiential learning and real life work based projects. In this way the CEWBL would be at the leading edge of developing and rewarding teaching and learning which would be of crucial significance if higher education was to fully contribute to the demands of knowledge-driven economies.

Themes and issues

The Middlesex experience is that WBL can score very well in standard performance measures such as recruitment, retention, academic achievement and student satisfaction and can further claim to be productive in terms of the significance of the programme (especially through real life projects) to a wide range of stakeholders. Common themes across the different types of quality evaluation were the advantages and challenges of providing highly customised work based provision and the use of generic learning outcomes and assessment criteria.

In all the quality evaluations WBL was commended as a highly responsive and flexible approach to learning, teaching and assessment that meets the needs of individual students who are at work. The high level of customisation, not only to meet the needs of individual students but also their organisations, is prized within the discourse of modernism which pervades quality assurance in higher education (Morley, 2004). In this respect WBL and quality assurance in higher education can be seen as part of the same modernising discourse.

However much of quality assurance as a 'technology' of higher education is predicated upon the desirability of standardisation which ' has deeply conservative underpinnings' (Morley, 2004:5) and in which the imperative is to perform and conform. The distinctive Middlesex approach to WBL as a field of study can be seen as a high risk approach for a university to take as it does not directly relate to subject benchmark statements which the QAA state 'provide authoritative reference points, which students and other interested parties will expect both to be taken into account when programmes are designed and reviewed, and to be reflected, as appropriate, in programme specifications' (Jackson 2002:154). The benchmark statements are intended to create a more explicit environment for learning by encouraging teaching teams and subject communities to set out what they believe are the main learning outcomes from programmes in a subject (Jackson 2002:140).

While WBS has been informed by other general codes or guidelines (eg placement, distance learning) the strength of the approach is the identification and articulation of WBL generic criteria which are mapped across academic levels and are explicitly linked to learning outcomes at the level of individual modules even when the content is negotiated by the individual learner. It is this transdisciplinary approach which allows WBL to be customised at the level of the individual learner (Osbourne et al, 1998) and at the level of individual organisations (Garnett et al, 2001). It is precisely the ability to assess the experiential learning of individuals for general credit rather than subject specific credit which enables recognition to be given to the full range of learning achievement of the individual (Garnett, 1998) rather than just that learning which matches the predetermined learning outcomes of a specific module which is in turn predetermined by the need to relate to standard subject benchmark statements. WBL requires an appreciation of 'forms of understanding that are sensitive to context, time, change, events, beliefs and desires and power' (Tsoukas, 2005:4). Thus while subject benchmarks are inevitably concerned with generalisation much of WBL is concerned with the complexity and depth of understanding of specific contexts (Garrick and Rhodes, 2000).

It could be argued that the absence of subject benchmarks focused the quality audits described in vignettes one to three away from consideration of WBL as a field of study to a more easily accessible focus upon the effectiveness of WBL as a mode of study. This shift places work based learners more neatly into conventional categories as part-time and distance learning students and has been helpful in highlighting the importance of focusing university support services on the needs of students who rarely, if ever, visit a university campus. However the mode of study focus obscures the distinctive position of WBL students which is that they are learning in an environment (the workplace) which is not under the control of the university and which has its own purposes (Garrick and Rhodes, Op. Cit). The success of WBL is in large part dependent upon how far the university programme is responsive to the needs of work and can draw effectively from the work context. The positionality of a WBL student within a specific work context makes WBL very different from a subject discipline based course delivered at a distance or a full-time university student 'out' on a work placement. The recent extension of the QAA Code of Practice to include WBL within the section which was formerly devoted to placement (QAA, 2007) is welcome in so far as it recognises the increasing significance of WBL but there is a major danger that the association of WBL with placement will blur the crucial distinction between them. The QAA precepts can be seen as grounded in the regulation of a supply side model of WBL. Given that the higher education institution has responsibility for the academic standards of all qualifications it awards there is an inevitable focus upon the higher education institution. For example precept one (QAA, 2007) states

"Where work-based or placement learning is part of a programme of study, awarding institutions ensure that its learning outcomes are: clearly identified, contribute to the overall and coherent aims of their programme, are assessed appropriately". Clearly in the context of WBL the employer could be expected to have a view on what constitutes appropriate assessment and an indicator of quality ought to be how such views are taken into account. Precept four states "Awarding institutions inform students of their specific responsibilities and entitlements relating to their work-based and placement learning." This seems to assume that the awarding institution is the sole driving force in WBL as provider of opportunities and designator of responsibilities. In fact WBL demands a partnership approach with the workplace which may well extend the learning opportunities available to the worker who is also a student. The work based learner will thus have a range of responsibilities to the higher education institution and to their employer. In most circumstances it is likely that the responsibilities will primarily be to the employer! The distinctive nature of WBL should be at the core of the evaluation not only of any higher education curriculum for WBL but also the evaluation of university systems and structures for supporting WBL programmes.

Development of the understanding of quality in respect of Work Based Learning

The Middlesex experience suggests that our current concepts of quality assurance and enhancement need to be broadened to meet the needs of workers and employers. An evaluation of a 'work based' learning programme relating to individual and organisational development would have to address issues relating to the relationship between the programme and the use and enhancement of the intellectual capital (Stewart, 1997) of the workplace. For example this might include regarding accreditation of prior experiential learning as an opportunity to enhance human capital by heightening the awareness of the knowledge and skills gained by the experiences of the individual worker and in so doing possibly making tacit knowledge explicit (Garnett et al, 2004). Evaluating the impact of a university WBL programme in intellectual capital terms might focus upon the effectiveness of the programme in drawing upon and enhancing the intellectual capital of the workplace and the university (Garnett, 2001). Such an approach would recognise the existing structural capital of the workplace, such as performance management systems, organisational competency frameworks, major training initiatives, and seek to use it to support individual WBL programmes. The long term effectiveness of WBL projects might be evaluated in terms of lasting impact upon the organisation or professional area. In other words has the project resulted in an enhancement of the structural capital of the organisation such as a change in process or procedures? This is a much richer agenda for quality than the supply side imperatives in the QAA code which focus upon control of the student experience by the higher education institution.

Conclusion

Higher education WBL clearly has the potential to perform well when measured within the prevailing quality assurance systems which put a premium on clarity of processes and outcomes and upon customer satisfaction. The wider scope of WBL stakeholders gives it the opportunity to exceed standard expectations in terms of perceived relevance to individual and organisational performance. Yet at the same time the work based rather than university subject discipline nature of the knowledge recognised, created and disseminated by WBL programmes is potentially at variance with the drive to standardisation of quality typified by subject benchmarking. For WBL as a field of study to be constructively and critically evaluated it is suggested that the implications of the epistemology of WBL would form an appropriate starting point and that this would lead to an intellectual capital analysis of the fitness for purpose of higher education WBL provision. Such an analysis would focus not only upon the human capital being developed but also upon the extent to which university programmes and other university support services were effective as 'structural capital' (Stewart 1997, Garnett et al 2001) to support knowledge recognition, creation, dissemination and use. Logically the fitness for purpose of quality assurance processes and procedures as structural capital would also be evaluated using an intellectual capital framework. In this way quality assurance and enhancement procedures for WBL programmes have the potential to contribute to a fuller understanding of 'quality' provision in higher education.

References

Baumard P (1999) *Tacit Knowledge in Organisations*, London: Sage.

Costley, C (2000) *The Boundaries and Frontiers of Work Based Knowledge* In, Portwood D and Costley C (Eds), Work Based Learning and the University: New

Perspectives and Practices, Birmingham, SEDA Paper 109.

Garnett J (1998) *Using APEL to develop customised work based learning programmes at postgraduate level*, Beyond Graduateness, South East England Consortium for Credit Accumulation and Transfer, Page Bros.

Garnett J, Comerford A and Webb N (2001) Working with Partners to Promote Intellectual Capital. In *Work-Based Learning: A New Higher Education?*, Boud D and Solomon N (Eds), OUP.

Garnett J (2001) Work Based Learning Programmes and the development of Intellectual Capital. In *The Learning Organisation*, 8 (2), 78–81.

Garnett J, Portwood D and Costley C (2004) *Bridging Rhetoric and Reality: Accreditation of prior experiential learning (APEL) in the UK*, A report for the University Vocational Awards Council, Bolton: UVAC.

Garrick J and Rhodes C (Eds) (2000) *Research and Knowledge at Work*, London: Routledge.

Gummesson E (1991) *Qualitative Methods in Management Research*, London: Sage.

Middlesex University (2003), *Review of the Academic Provision of Work Based Learning Studies*.

Jackson N (2002) *Growing knowledge about QAA subject benchmarking*, Quality Assurance in Education, 10 (3), 139–154.

Jarvis P (2001) *Universities and Corporate Universities*, London: Kogan Page.

Morley L (2003) *Quality and Power in Higher Education*, Maidenhead: SRHE and OUP

Morley L (2004) *Theorising Quality in Higher Education*, Institute of Education, Bedford Way Papers.

Osborne C, Davies J and Garnett J (1998) Guiding the Student to the Centre of the Stakeholder Curriculum. In *Capability and Quality in Higher Education*, Stephenson J and Yorke M (Eds), London: Kogan Page.

QAA (2003) *Middlesex University Institutional Audit Report*.

QAA (2007) *Code of practice for the assurance of academic quality and standards in higher education, Section 9 Work-Based and Placement Learning*.

Stewart T (1997) *Intellectual Capital*, London: Nicholas Brearley.

Tsoukas H (2005), *Complex Knowledge*, Oxford: OUP.

18

The Role of Research

Carol Costley and Paul Gibbs

***

Introduction

The research of Work Based Learning (WBL) academics is often related to the research of work based learners in higher education in that the learners are researching their own practice and the academics are researching the learning and related areas that inform that practice. The research of the learners and the research of the academics is unlikely to be on the same topic e.g. learners may be researching a way to improve an area of systems within their own work situation whereas academics may be researching aspects of how people learn at work, such as how workers reflect on their practice. This chapter does not focus on the work based research projects of the learner but on the research undertaken by academics within the broad area of WBL. This research encompasses a diverse range of research interests because in a fairly new and growing field and mode of study there is a broad range of areas that are in need of further investigation and consideration. These range from those whose interest is in the philosophical, pedagogical, psycho/sociological, economic and epistemological aspect of the field. These wide interests attract literature mainly from the UK and Australia but with an increasing interest from mainland Europe (especially the Scandinavian countries), Canada and elsewhere.

WBL research is often undertaken by practicing educators and experienced researchers from higher education who are linked to a prestigious and established research centre. There is also a growing literature from those who are course advisers and curriculum designers of WBL modules and programmes. These 'new researchers' undertake their research as a direct result of issues that arise from their teaching. There is a great deal of overlap between these two categories of researchers and the policy driven larger scale research of the first group is helpful and informative to the 'course adviser' category whilst the latter case study and curriculum development knowledge is informing to the first category of academic researchers (Costley 2007).

This chapter considers the research of the WBL research centre at Middlesex in particular and the related research of the learners in the centre. We then go on to consider how this kind of research can be underpinned and theorised, and how it can be recognised and funded. We conclude by looking to the future of research and WBL where we believe there will be major research initiatives in the field.

The WBL Research Centre (WBLRC) at Middlesex

The major focus for the WBLRC is the development and operation of a WBL higher education curriculum (at all levels from Certificate to Doctorate) that includes professional practice through partnerships outside higher education across diverse sectors. The WBL Centre for Excellence has taken a research led approach to curriculum and pedagogic development and the WBLRC is the agency for its research activities. The WBL approach adopted at Middlesex is based upon WBL as a field of study and not just a mode of learning and the research focus of the WBLRC is aligned so as to support and explore this approach to curriculum innovation. Special editions of journals have set out the case for WBL in higher education (JWPL 2007, AEHE 2007, TLO 2001, WBL e-journal 2007, RPCE, 2007).

To explore the research agenda for WBL it is therefore necessary to understand something about how the epistemological basis of 'the field of study approach' to curriculum came about. The programmes have not emerged from an existing academic department that had operated within a particular paradigm with an existing pedagogy. The programmes include the innovative Doctorate in Professional Studies (DProf) with its Doctoral project rather than thesis or dissertation. The field of Professional Doctorates then became an area of research and development at the Centre. The successful Doctorate in Professional Studies (c/f chapter 9) has been the topic of several publications by members of the research centre group, most recently, Stephenson et al (2006) and Costley and Stephenson (2008).

The DProf programme was designed to be equal in level and rigor to other Doctoral programmes (Thorne 2001) and develop the practice of people at work. It was not borrowed and did not emerge from existing subject based curricula within the university. It was from the outset designed for people working full time and who wanted to undertake higher education study, based on their current work and work experiences. Curricula were developed that relate to knowledge which is practice based and draws on practitioner led enquiry as a principle for the students' research. The structure of the programmes requires learners themselves to define the scope and focus of their programmes in which they are able to make significant changes to the practice of their organisations or professional area. The exchange of knowledge between university and partner organisations allows a flow of people and data to develop knowledge and evidence that can benefit students and their organisations/ professional areas (Garnett 2005) as well as contributing to the knowledge base of the university. An important part of the success of the taught Master's programmes and the M/DProf programme is that they meet particular needs of practitioners who wish to study at master and Doctoral level but wish to develop their practitioner knowledge supported by higher level learning and approaches, rather than learn new knowledge from the university. The WBLRC has built its reputation on the role of the university as facilitating knowledge production in contexts outside the university (Garnett 2001, Costley 2001, Armsby et al 2006, Garnett 2007).

It follows that the focus on research became concerned with learning in the context of work and followed a curriculum driven agenda. An important concept for research in this area is to define and clarify exactly what is meant by the term 'work' and what is meant by learning for, in and through work and because the focus has been more towards experienced workers in full time work, the centre has been more involved in learning in work and learning through work. Also, because the centre is concerned with all learning and does not specify a subject discipline or particular profession, the approach taken is transdisciplinary in nature and this has raised broader issues of epistemology (WBL network conference July 07, Costley and Armsby 2006, Armsby et al 2006) and has led to a pan university remit for the research centre.

The Centre has developed much of its curriculum led research with research expertise in accreditation of learning from experience, Thus, for example, Armsby et al (2006) investigated the Accreditation of Prior Experiential Learning not merely as a mechanism of access to learning programmes but as a mode of evaluation and legitimation of tacit professional knowledge. Garnett et al (2004) have written a commissioned report on this subject for UVAC and situate these concerns within a wider inquiry into the capitalisation of knowledge and the formation of new intellectual capital in both the partner organisation and the university in the enabling conditions of WBL programmes, (Garnett 2007).

Ethical issues are a shared concern in the group, especially in relation to the research and development work of the practitioner-researchers who are the main student population for WBL studies and professional studies. Ethical issues are the topic of a series of articles (Costley and Gibbs, 2006, Gibbs and Costley, 2006, Gibbs, 2007).The centre also investigates the nature of its own field of study and practice proposing a critical topology of higher education (Gibbs and Costley, 2006) and the research practices therein. WBL can be understood as a specific field of study (Costley and Armsby 2006) with one of its stronger themes as the epistemological issue surrounding insider researchers (Workman, 2007). The relationship between the context of work with its pressure, tensions and potential for exploitation have been discussed (Gibbs and McRoy, 2006).

The methodologies appropriate to practitioner research in WBL is an important theme for research in the centre (see for example Costley and Armsby 2007) while elearning for WBL is a new and developing area as is structuring, developing and evaluating WBL curricula (Workman 2007). Boud and Costley (2007) have made an extensive study of facilitative teaching 'advising' rather than 'supervising'. Costley (2007) convened a published discussion of assessment and evaluation in WBL, issues of assessment in WBL being the subject of topical debate also addressed in Armsby et al (2006) and Costley and Armsby (2007).

As well as research that relates directly to work based modules, the broader themes that involve more theoretical, policy and paradigmatic issues have also been embraced in the research of the Centre. Researchers have drawn upon relevant research from other academics, internationally, whose interests are in work and learning. For example, the position of WBL as a field, mode and discursive space has emerged since changes in the ideas about research and scholarship (Gibbons et al, 1994, Nowotny et al 2002) have focused more on practice, practice knowledge and the professions. Research in WBL links quite clearly to these broader socio-economic interests in the UK (Research Councils UK 2006) and internationally. Another example of the broader themes of the WBL research centre is in relation to its international work. Developing European WBL Approaches and Methods is a curriculum based project that seeks to share expertise in WBL with countries across Europe. The Developing European WBL Approaches and Methods, Gruntwig funded project researched and developed WBL across countries in Europe with the intention of finding a common European platform for WBL (DEWBLAM 2006).

WBL is concerned with development and change, the generation of new knowledge for practice and new practices. These activities require knowledge that specialises in methodological approaches to development and systematic change. The next section focuses on the practitioner led research that is undertaken by students in the centre on all the WBL programmes. We explain the approach used to preparing people at work to become researchers and show how the issues of reflexivity, insider as researcher and ethical issues in practitioner research have been researched and developed by academics in the WBLRC. Academic advisers/researchers steer learners into producing work based research projects that involve high level judgements and decision making that influences change in complex real life situations (Lester 2004).

Preparing the researcher from within the worker

Research as a way of seeking a truth, albeit a truth relevant to a certain context, is a structured way of enquiry. Indeed research gains its validity in the epistemological worthiness of its claims and as such it is not an extension of everyday working practices. Worker researchers choose to research as an intended activity which has a form determined prior to engaging in a chosen approach to the research activity. The chosen approach is decided upon after studying research methodologies which helps them to understand what methodology can do, what methods to use and what truths it can help to reveal.

As common as this position on research might be, researcher development in WBL at Middlesex extends this to look not just at the technologies that researchers use but also at the ontological transformation of nonresearcher into researcher. Moreover, the evolution of the researcher is embedded within an ethical ethos which recognises the context and its socio-political influences on the well-being of all parties to the research project.

Through the odyssey of becoming a researcher students face many trials upon which they are expected to reflect and embody within their identity as researcher. The journey, unlike that of Ulysses does not end, for the growth within the students is often an identity change where their world view is different after the experience of the research modules than it was before and acts as a trajectory for their future way of seeing the world.

The process of investigation advocated by the Institute for WBL is collaborative with the learning jointly undertaken by student and adviser and might best be described in Hiedeggerian terms as 'letting the student learn'. This is facilitated by textual information and experiential engagement in research workshops, online and real time discussions and the encouragement to link this with independent resources. Such diverse learning facilities involve critical judgements and assessment on data source (guided if needs be by the adviser) but under the direct control of the student.

To support this across cohorts we use the roles of module leader and personal academic adviser. In this way materials and the media that carry them are blended to give a rich approach to research, so it can be assimilated and used by the researchers as they develop their research awareness.

The main form of input to this process is the provision of a handbook which is also available via the dedicated website accessible by the student and the adviser and facilitated by the module leader. This document creates an architecture of research philosophy, methodologies and methods that are related to specific activities intended for students to reflect upon their own learning and that have relevance to their proposed research area. The reflections are prepared in the form of a diary. In addition, students are required to manifest their learning through a portfolio showing how they understand research practice and how they can comprehend what it is to be a worker researcher and the reality this creates for them.

The website provides a forum for discussion wider than the adviser/

student relationship and is also used to offer materials to supplement the handbook. Its purpose is to help students in finding a researcher identity; to find a community of learners and researchers. This material is informative and challenges students to delve deeper into their research understanding and is a stimulus to add materials to their research portfolios and to their growth as researchers. Regular adviser tutorials are advocated and one formative assessment is required prior to the final submission of the portfolio for assessment.

The pedagogical blend advocated is not attractive to all the students. Many do take the opportunity to engage in the journey towards researcher, others become research technicians determined to find any appropriate solution to a research project, follow its procedures and then through this method realise the goal of the project. Using methodology like that is like picking up a hammer and saw, cutting and nailing a box together and passing oneself off as a carpenter. In order to support students there are formative assessment procedures which we feel can reveal such approaches both in the written reflection of the learning diary and in the oral presentation of their projects. In this way, all students are supported to engage with research at a conceptual and indepth level.

A central feature of our research approach is the ethics of insider researchers. We have had some success in developing group teaching (Gibbs et al, 2007) where the ethics is an integrated part of the teaching and learning experience of research methods. In this module we discuss how the ethical constraints for voluntary participation gained through informed consent free of coercion, presupposes a number of basic issues in the research process. First it assumes a participant/object distinction, second it assumes that 'participants' can (at least in certain contexts) act autonomously and that actions, once public, can in some way be cloaked in confidentiality. It assumes that researchers are, for the most part, free to seek outcomes from their research unencumbered by political, economic or social pressures in their quest for understanding, insight and truth.

However, it is debatable whether research has ever been able to be transacted under these conditions (Van Den Hoonaard, 2003) and under the current hegemonic economic context in education, it seems unlikely that ethical considerations are any more than mere rhetorical references to an idealised notion of what it is to research. The university that is driven by research is more than ever reliant for funding from external sources and therefore is directed or guided towards questions which arise outside of the university. This is even more the reality of work based, practitioner led research where academic responsibility must take into account multiple communities of practice, each of which has its own epistemological and power agenda. The researcher is usually involved with what might be the "moral requirements of research once one realises that no set of principles (and thus no moral code) can exhaustively shape the moral deliberation which inevitably researchers are caught in" (Pring, 2001:411–12). The justifications for external criteria for research have been explained adequately, even powerfully, elsewhere (see Pimple, 2002, Jessop and Miller, 2002) and we look at the context in which some researchers attempt to undertake their research in the ethical shadows of these criteria (Costley and Gibbs 2006). We are not claiming that such general safeguards, for example Gregory's "the pillars", for participants against encroachments of researchers are not worthwhile, we just suggest that their effectiveness can be compromised within the hegemony of capital and the compliance to the needs of non-academic interests.

Work based professional researchers, because of their action within the everyday world, can help us to create responsible social meaning and thus blend the notions of ethics, good actions for their own sake with the actions that have an end other than themselves (see Wall, 2003). However, they are vulnerable to the complexity of their research environment in ways that academic researchers might not be (but in similar ways that sponsored researchers could be). We perceive that ethical notions developed within the context of an academic environment, and controlled and managed within the notion of academic freedom, might not transfer readily to a different political environment where the interests of the academic community are not necessarily paramount.

As an example, the work of a practitioner researcher takes place on the inside of the political context of work where the researcher may be in a powerful (or weak) position in relation to the participants of the research. This political context is further problematised when the nature of the learning contract (an agreement between the researcher, the academic institution and the recipient of the research e.g. the researcher's employer) requires evidence of a personal transformation through the process of reflective practice. Gregory (2003) is insightful when he claims that decisions of research ethics are decisions of the consequences of the research for the researcher amongst others. These necessarily make research – at least social research – political.

Drawing on related fields and theories

As a relatively new academic area, research in WBL is often groundbreaking work, although there are many related fields, which can be drawn upon to ground this relatively new area on a theoretical basis.

WBL can draw upon theoretical roots from a variety of sources. Business schools and schools of management have a recent but prolific history in researching areas such as the learning organisation, management and business practices and organisational development. Schools of education have provided a rich literature on action research, higher education practices and pedagogy. Discourses in adult education have provided a particular insight into pedagogical issues that relate to WBL especially in relation to supervisory practices and approaches to knowledge. Professional and vocational areas such as healthcare have a wealth of literature on areas such as assessing and judging capability, reflexive practices and bridging practical and theoretical divides. The various academic literacies, approaches and methods that are drawn from the disciplines, especially social science provide data that informs research approaches both for WBL academics and for the learners who engage in practitioner led research. Practical philosophy and the sociology of work in particular have informed us about the management and philosophy of knowledge and the methodologies and epistemologies that can be drawn upon and developed in relation to WBL. For example writers such as Gibbons et al (1994) in a seminal work suggesting mode 1 and mode 2 forms of knowledge, have raised broad issues about transdisciplinarity, new forms of knowledge and ways of researching that relate to new forms of knowing and the knowledge economy.

Research on work and learning proliferates in conferences and seminars; see especially the conference series 'Researching Work and Learning' which is a key international conference that is relevant to the field. It started in the University of Leeds in 1999 then Calgary, Canada 2001, Tampere, Finland 2003, Sydney 2005 and Cape Town 2007. The sixth conference will be in Copenhagen 2009.

Below we consider writers who have made significant contributions to practice based learning and practice based research which can offer relevant theoretical models that WBL can draw upon. Dewey (1938) provides a logic for action that is opposed to a theory/practice divide. Some of Dewey's ideas are being used to develop positions directly relevant to WBL, for example Hickman (1990) and Burke (1994).

Schon's (1995) ideas around reflective practice and call for "new epistemologies of practice" have led many WBL researchers to consider the characteristics of reflective and reflexive practices. Schon's earlier work on the reflective practitioner developed further the thinking of two way interactions between theory and practice.

Bourdieu's work on social and cultural capital is recast by WBL as the imbalances in society that are reproduced through education are on one hand challenged through possibilities of allowing greater access to HE study but on the other hand perpetuating a system that requires education to follow the needs of the national economy more closely. These ideas provide underpinning theory for many of the approaches concerning inclusiveness adopted to learning at work.

Bourdieu's (1990) work relating to practice identifies an epistemological difference between science and practice that has important relevance to WBL. The difference is based on dispositional logic of practice that is lost through the 'theorisation effect' (1990: 86) and which presents intrinsically coherent practices which function only as long as they function in the sphere of practicality. This approach contributes to a different habitus for the practitioner than for the academic both epistemologically and ontologically. This is potentially critical since the practice of logic cannot be totalised by the theorisation of practice so it is hard to see how WBL can ever fully be part of a conventional approach to knowledge where theorised discourse based upon generalisation dominates academic thinking. WBL can be seen as a way to take action on the reasoning of theorists who identify practice because it can play a significant role in meeting the needs of people in a knowledge driven society. Bourdieu's analysis brings us to rethink the 'theory underpinning practice' model in the conventional sense and to debate whether or not the change in the way concepts arising through the study of WBL are translated into theory constitutes a new paradigm within education (Jary and Parker 1998).

One of the distinctive features of practice is the extent to which practitioners act autonomously, delivering effective services. These activities also offer opportunities for learning. New problems have to be addressed, tried and tested solutions adapted, new approaches devised and appropriate actions taken. These are the kinds of processes informed by theory because practice is not atheoretical, that it is possible to illuminate, practice and assess through WBL modules and/or programmes. WBL students who are workers as well as researchers are enabled to enhance their abilities in for example, how to select and study a phenomenon from their own work situation. WBL seeks to provide an understanding and knowledge in an epistemology of practice where knowledge is created and used rather than codified. Whilst such an epistemology is already understood by professional people at work in their continuing professional development and other reflexive activities, WBL can formalise this thinking.

WBL uses approaches to learning and to knowledge for which there are many parallels that can be drawn from the ideas of post-structuralist thinkers such as Derrida (1986), Lyotard (1984) and Foucault (1976) especially in that knowledge is viewed as inexorably associated with power and is structured discursively. These issues raise contested ideas in relation to the contextual knowledge of WBL and are causing some educationalists to rethink their premises and traditional constructions about learning and knowledge in the field of WBL.

Other thinkers who are able to influence the theorisation of WBL include Habermas (1981) where he construes the solution to technical problems as depending on interactive relationships that require the kind of learning that is often promoted by WBL practitioners as being conducive to

221

successful team work and team learning. In formulating the concept of 'communicative rationality' Habermas asserted that interactive relationships at work involve processes of learning and arriving at mutual understanding.

The acquisition of learning, experience and knowledge are frequently found and articulated as part of formal and informal agendas outside higher education. Learning can be gained through organisations and other experiences through lifestyle practices (see for example Handy 1994).

Aristotle's practical knowledge and Marx's notion of praxis both focus on the legitimacy of knowledge gained through practice. Universities have not controlled such practical knowledge because the expertise lies outside the university in different communities but especially arenas where 'work' is the focus of the activity. WBL is able to address these knowledges because the field is developing a reflective and analytic interrogation of practice assessed by generic, work based criteria.

WBL academics need to critique their own practice and engage in scholarship that will inform and develop the field. To do this effectively, the story of WBL in a higher education setting needs to be told by those who are involved in its development at policy and curriculum levels.

Research funding for WBL

The Research Councils UK (RCUK), following government directives, propose to improve research in the UK to benefit the society and the economy 'ensuring the UK is one of the most competitive locations in the world for research and innovation as global restructuring focuses developed economies towards knowledge-based and high value-added sectors' (RCUK 2006). The Cross-Council Funding Agreement of August 2006 makes significant amendments to their peer review systems and the way research is funded as they do not want intellectual gaps between the Councils' subject discipline responsibilities. At first this seems a breakthough for research in WBL and in many respects it promises to be beneficial for those seeking funding for WBL research with the research councils. However, WBL is not exactly what RCUK have in mind, they are thinking more about proposals that lie between traditional disciplines, rather than research that takes a trans-disciplinary approach.

RCUK do have the notion of multidisciplinarity, which they say 'adopts a single set of imperatives and approaches', and it is from this concept where WBL researchers may start to think that their work may fit into the research councils' structures. However they go on to state that this is done by 'fusing established research disciplines together'. Rather than a generic or horizontal approach to knowledge RCUK are looking at topics such as climate change, design, neuroscience and chemical biology where they can clearly see how the topic includes subject discipline knowledge from more than one Research Council. More hope for WBL research appears when they state that tailored support for multidisciplinary research will be provided but again this is qualified by also stating that this involves 'different disciplinary approaches to be harnessed towards a common research challenge' with examples of genomics, eScience, the rural economy, energy and ageing.

The RCUK protocol aims to:

i.   Ensure that the Councils' structures provide no discouragement to research at the interface between disciplines.
ii. Ensure that there are no gaps between Councils' remits and that interdisciplinary and multidisciplinary research is effectively supported by the Councils, either independently or in partnership.
iii. Ensure that peer review is fair, appropriate and avoids 'double jeopardy' for projects that straddle disciplinary and Council remits.
iv. Minimise consideration by applicants of Council remits.
v.   Neither advantage, nor disadvantage, single discipline research.

RCUK (2006)

These initiatives certainly give WBL research a better chance of being funded and they can be considered as, at the least, being a step towards funding research into the kind of initiatives about which many researchers in the field of WBL are involved. Protocol ii provides the nearest hope but research proposals are still likely to require researchers to specify subject discipline areas even if the list of subjects may be numerous. At a recent meeting with one of the research councils, one of the authors enquired as to the position of WBL research when selecting the required subject discipline/s on the list specified by the councils. The answer came that the researcher would tick the box for the subject discipline within which the researcher him/herself belonged. It does not really seem that this is a viable solution for a researcher in the area of WBL who could have come from almost any subject discipline background. Rather, now the aims of the councils are predicated on research that links to socio-economic benefit through new knowledge that often relates to workforce development and public well being, WBL researchers might ensure that proposals use this kind of language and try to couch it in terms of subject disciplines. If the proposal itself is excellent, then even though it may be hard to locate in a discipline, it would seem that there will now be a greater chance that it may be funded.

Conclusion

The WBL research area is being developed within an international setting with increasing amounts of WBL students, partnerships and consultancy. Future developments are to further inform and evolve an understanding of the field through scholarly work, to theorise and underpin what might be construed as a post-structural field of study and to realise it in an international context that has considerable interest and authority from outside the university sector. Through conceptualising WBL as a field of study, the research centre has contributed much to debates about epistemology and how approaches to knowledge generation and use are changing through theoretical reasoning and ideological standpoints that are placed both within and outside of universities.

References

Armsby, P., C. Costley and J. Garnett. (2006) The Legitimisation of Knowledge: A Work Based Learning Perspective of APEL. In *Journal of Lifelong Learning and Education*. 25 (4)

Boud, D. and Costley, C. (2007) – accepted for publication 'From project supervision to advising: new conceptions of the practice' Innovations in Education and Teaching International

Bourdieu, P. (1990) *The Logic of Practice*. Cambridge: Polity Press.

Costley, C. (2007) 'Integrating Research and Work-force development activities'. In *Incorporating the learning people do for, in and through work into higher education programmes of study* Eds S.Roodhouse and L. Brennan. Bolton: UVAC/ LCCI Commercial Education Trust

Costley, C. (2006) 'Introduction to Assessment and Evaluation of Work Based Learning in Higher Education'. In *Special Edition Assessment and Evaluation in Higher Education* vol 31 no 4.

Costley, C. (2001) 'Employee and Organisational Perspectives of Work Based Learning'. In *The Learning Organisation* vol. 8 no.2 pp 58–63.

Costley, C. and Gibbs, P. (2006) 'Work-based learning; discipline, field or discursive space or what?' In *Research in Post-Compulsory Education* vol 11 no.3 pp 341–350.

Costley, C. and Stephenson, J. (2008) 'Building doctorates around individual candidates' professional experience'. In *Changing Practices of Doctoral Education* Eds. David Boud and Alison Lee, London: Routledge

Derrida, J. (1986) 'The Age of Hegel', pp.1-43 in S. Weber (ed.), *Demarcating the Disciplines: Philosophy, Literature, Art*. Minneapolis: University of Minnesota Press.

Dewey, J. (1938) *Experience and Education*. New York: Touchstone.

Foucault, M., (1980) *Power/ Knowledge: Selected Interviews and Other Writings 1972–77,* Brighton: Harvester.

Garnett J, Portwood D and Costley C (2004), *Bridging Rhetoric and Reality: Accreditation of prior experiential learning (APEL) in the UK*, commissioned report for the Universities Vocational Awards Council.

Garnett J (2005) 'University Work Based Learning and the Knowledge driven project'. In *Work Based Learning in Health Care*, Rounce and Workman (Eds), Chichester: Kingsham Press.

Garnett, J. (2007) 'Employers and University Partnerships'. In *Employers, Skills and Higher Education* pp108–123Eds Roodhouse S and Swailes S Chichester: Kingsham Press

Gibbons, M., Limoges, C., Nowotny, H., Schwartzman, S., Scott, P., and Trow, M. (1994) *The New Production of Knowledge: The Dynamics of Science and Research in Contemporary Societies* London: Sage.

Gibbs, P. and Costley, C. (2006) 'Work-based learning; discipline, field or discursive space or what?'. In *Research in Post-Compulsory Education* Vol 11 No.3 pp 341–350

Handy, C. (1994) *The empty raincoat*. London: Hutchinson.

Hickman, C.R. (1990), *Mind of a Manager Soul of a Leader*, New York: Wiley.

RCUK (2006). http://www.rcuk.ac.uk/aboutrcs/stratsci/default.htm

Downloaded 1st May 2007

Jary, D. and Parker, M. (1998) *The New Higher Education; Issues and Directions for the Post-Dearing University*, Stroke on Trent: Staffordshire University Press.

Lester, S. (2004) 'Conceptualising the practitioner doctorate'. In *Studies in Higher Education* 29(6): 757–770.

Lyotard, J. F. (1984) *The Postmodern Condition: A Report on Knowledge* Manchester: Manchester University Press.

Nowotny, H., Scott, P. and Gibbons, M. (2001) *Re-thinking Science: knowledge and the public in an age of uncertainty*, Cambridge: Polity Press.

Schmidt, R. (2006) *DEWBLAM; The social and educational challenge of Work Based Learning in European higher education and training. Results of a pilot experience* Firenze, eform

Schön, D. (1995) Knowing-in-action: the new scholarship requires a new epistemology. Change, November–December.

JWPL (2007) *Journal of Workplace Learning*, Vol. 19 (3) Special Edition http://www.emeraldinsight.com/Insight/viewContainer.do?containerType=Issue&containerId=24925

AEHE (2007) *Assessment & Evaluation in Higher Education*, Volume 32 (1) Special Edition http://www.tandf.co.uk/journals/spissue/caeh-si.asp

TLO (2001) The Learning Organization, Volume 8 (2) Special Edition http://www.emeraldinsight.com/Insight/viewContainer.do?containerType=Issue&containerId=19929

WBL e-journal (2007) http://test.cy-designs.com/middlesex/index.html

RPCE (2007) Research in Post-Compulsory Education, Volume 12 (3)

http://www.informaworld.com/smpp/title~content=g781987115~db=all

WBL network conference July (2007) http://www.middlesex.ac.uk/wbl/research/uall07.asp

Workman, B. A. (2007) 'Casing the joint: explorations by the insider-researcher preparing for work-based projects'. In *Journal of Workplace Learning*, Vol 19, No 3 146–160

19
Contributing to the Intellectual Capital of Organisations

Jonathan Garnett

***

Introduction

The rise of an information age and a post industrial knowledge economy is widely acknowledged (Castells 2000, Abell and Oxbrow 2001). The McKinsey global management survey on knowledge management (Kluge et al, 2001) identifies a historical transition from the three concrete production factors of land, labour and capital to the far more intangible factor of knowledge. Knowledge is seen as essential in making operations effective, building business processes or predicting the outcome of business models.

Stewart (1997), Edvinsson and Malone (1997), Burton-Jones (1999) and a growing host of others argue that in the new knowledge economy it is intellectual capital which is the true measure of the wealth of an organisation. The importance attached to the concept of intellectual capital is indicative of a revolutionary shift from the company as a place of production to being a "place for thinking". At one level this could be thinking to improve what is already being done or at a deeper level a fundamental change in what is being done. The economic importance attached to knowledge and learning has impacted upon and challenged the role of the university (Barnett 2000) and the rise of the "Corporate University" is a potent symbol of the extent to which Higher Education institutions are losing influence (Jarvis 2001). The role of university courses in the "knowledge age" is still typically seen as developing the individual for employment or continuing employment rather than developing the intellectual capital of organisations.

This chapter draws upon the work based learning (WBL) experiences of Middlesex University, featured in earlier chapters of this book, as well as knowledge management literature, to identify the potential of higher education WBL programmes to contribute to the intellectual capital of organisations.

Distinctive features of University Work Based Learning programmes

University WBL in the UK developed from a range of Employment Department funded initiatives in the early 1990s (Brennan and Little, 1996). By 2001 Boud and Solomon (2001:1) were able to draw upon evidence from Australia and the UK to argue that WBL could be seen as "one of the very few innovations related to the teaching and learning aspects of post secondary education that is attempting to engage seriously with the economic, social and educational demands of our era". The preceding chapters have explored distinctive features of WBL:

- partnerships between an external organisation and an educational institution specifically established to foster learning (see Hodgers, chapter 12, and Rounce chapter 14).

- Learners are employees or have some contractual relationship with the external organisation, and negotiate learning plans approved by the educational institution and the organisation (see Rounce, chapter 14).

- The programme followed derives from the needs of the workplace and of the learner rather than being controlled by the disciplinary curriculum (see Critten, chapter 3; Durrant, chapter 2 and Portwood, chapter 10)

- The starting point and level of the programme is established after a structured review and evaluation of current learning (see Costley and Armsby, chapter 9).

- A significant element of the programme is WBL projects that meet the needs of the learner and the organisation (see Critten, chapter 2; and Hodgers, chapter 12).

- The educational institution assesses the learning outcomes of the negotiated programme with respect to a transdisciplinary framework of standards and levels (see Workman, chapter 16).

At the heart of the distinctive nature of university WBL programmes is the interaction between the needs of a specific learner, their work and the university. This contests the supremacy of the role of the university in curriculum design, delivery and validation of knowledge (Jarvis, Op. Cit) and suggests that university WBL should seek alignment with thinking and practice relating to knowledge creation and use in the workplace.

Key factors for enhancing intellectual capital

Consideration of knowledge management and intellectual capital literature, suggests that in order for knowledge to contribute to the intellectual capital of the organisation the following are key factors:

1. Knowledge must have a performative value in relation to the achievement of organisational objectives in order to contribute to the intellectual capital of the organisation.

For knowledge to be of value to the organisation it has to contribute to the aims of the organisation (Rohlin et al, 1998:39). Leaders should develop structures (formal and informal) to ensure that the business aims of the organisation are clearly defined and understood so that knowledge production can be focused and applied to achieve them (Stewart 1997). This places an emphasis for the organisation on identifying, utilising and measuring the performative value of knowledge. In the context of the organisation the value of knowledge is performative rather than intrinsic.

2. Individual knowledge is a key component of intellectual capital, recognition and transfer of individual knowledge is thus a key concern of the organisation

Knowledge is possessed by individuals and enables them to make sense of data and information received. Mayo (2000:523) argues that "all intellectual assets are maintained and governed by people". Individual knowledge forms the basis for communication of information to others who will then make sense of it in the light of their own personal knowledge. It follows that a key concern for organisations must be the facilitation of the recognition of knowledge, for example through reflexive practice and the reduction, as appropriate, of barriers to the socialisation of knowledge, that is, making tacit knowledge explicit. For individual knowledge to become organisational knowledge, and thus fully contribute to the intellectual capital of the organisation, it must be shared and accepted by others (Eden and Spender 1998:216). Sharing will often involve codification of some sort, for example, entry into a database under certain fields, submission of a formal report.

3. Organisations need structures to facilitate knowledge development and transfer at the level of the individual and the group

Stewart (1997:108–109) outlines the significance of structural capital, which he describes as including not only technologies and inventions but also strategy and culture, structures and systems, organisational routines and procedures. Central to the value of structural capital to the organisation is that it can help individuals develop their personal knowledge, store and transmit the information derived from it and access information provided by others. The dilema for knowledge management is how to apply structural capital to facilitate the creation, recognition, transfer and use of tacit knowledge which by its nature is intangible (Myers 1996:4). Tacit knowledge can be learned by example, as in the case of the apprentice learning from observation, and may be shared by whole communities of practice. The knowledge of teams may be more than the sum of the individual parts due to partial and complementary knowledge (Choo 1998:118). The use of reflexive practice (eg Baumard 1999, Moon 1999) has been advanced as the key to revealing tacit knowledge by thinking about one's own actions and analysing them in a critical manner, with the purpose of improving practice. The difficulty of this process is compounded by the organisational context described by Baumard (1999:12) as "fragmented and multi-dimensional operative fields with their own ceremonial conformity". Structural capital needs to take into account such "cognitive bulwarks and territories" (Baumard, 1999:14) within organisations if it is going to be effective in enhancing intellectual capital.

Explicit knowledge also requires the deployment of structural capital to facilitate production, dissemination and use. Without the use of structural capital as a planned strategic intervention to leverage intellectual capital knowledge generation and validation would be largely at the whim of individual managers. Explicit knowledge held in common within one department of an organisation is not of value if it is needed but yet unknown to another department. Explicit knowledge may be a barrier to progress, thus a key function of structural capital may be to initiate and action review and replacement of existing explicit knowledge. Combining or reconfiguring existing explicit knowledge can lead to the transfer of new explicit knowledge (for example the formal learning in schools) (Choo 1998:124). Structural capital must facilitate such combination. Nonaka and Nishiguchi (2001) emphasise that it is equally important to be able to internalise explicit knowledge in order to translate it into implicit knowledge, so that, for example, individual behaviour conforms to principles and procedures by habit as under some circumstances this may be necessary for high levels of performance.

The individual and social dimensions of both tacit and explicit knowledge mean that knowledge is a difficult resource for the organisation to manage. Nonaka and Nishiguchi (Op. Cit.) have contested whether knowledge can be managed and believe that knowledge must be nurtured rather than managed. The role of managers is to facilitate "knowledge emergence", through the creation of "ba", a platform in space and time where knowledge is created, shared and exploited. In this model tacit and explicit knowledge are vital as they are complimentary. Nonaka and Nishiguchi believe " what knowledge management should achieve is not a static management of information or existing knowledge, but a dynamic management of the process of creating knowledge out of knowledge" (2001:13). The role of the manager is one of nurturing knowledge by creating conditions conducive to the provision of all of the different forms of "ba" by, for example, not only providing physical space but also by promoting interactions and fostering autonomy, trust and collaboration. This approach is indicative of a movement away from seeing knowledge management primarily in terms of technology driven data storing and information sharing to a greater emphasis on the critical importance of facilitating direct human interaction to create, share and apply knowledge.

The nature and lasting value to the organisation of structural capital is hinted at by Edvinsson and Malone (1997:11) when they define structural capital as "all the value that remains when the lights are turned out at 5pm". In this sense structural capital is the only asset which belongs to the organisation rather than individuals or groups within it. Stewart (1997:132) identifies codification of bodies of knowledge and connecting people to data and expertise as the two main purposes which structural capital should serve. Stewart (Op. Cit.:110) argues that structural capital is vital and should be managed in order to promote "rapid knowledge sharing, collective knowledge growth, shortened lead times and more productive people". An example of structural capital working this way would be standard procedures and an organisational culture which encouraged the reporting of defects in a construction process so that the construction company could learn from experience and adjust future action to become more productive.

4. The performative imperative of knowledge closely links it to organisational decision making and thus to bounded rationality

Choo (1998) draws upon the work of Simon on "bounded rationality" to point out that the rationality of decision making in organisations is bounded as knowledge, and anticipation of the consequences of a decision can never be complete, and only a limited number of possible alternatives can be considered, hence optimising is replaced by satisfying. For example pressure of time may mean that a professional judgement is made based upon only a fraction of the potential evidence available and a critical part of the decision making process is determining whether there is sufficient evidence available upon which to base future action. The importance of ideological, political and personal preferences come to the fore in organisational decision making and feature strongly in "post-rational management theory" (Burgoyne and Reynolds 1997:164). Nonaka and Nishiguchi (2001:41) note that "occasionally, groups of experts keep secrets, they will protect explicit knowledge from other groups in order to keep their power". All of this is not to downplay the importance of knowledge but to emphasise that in the social context of the organisation knowledge creation, recognition and use is not a neutral or objective undertaking.

Consideration of the factors discussed above suggest that if university

WBL is to enhance the intellectual capital of organisations it needs to:

- Focus on organisational objectives to ensure that the knowledge it develops has a performative edge and is thus of value to the organisation.

- Develop strategies within the WBL programme for working with tacit knowledge.

- Fully exploit the structural capital of partner organisations in fostering knowledge recognition, dissemination, creation and use and seek to enhance the structural capital of organisations.

- Explore the nature and implications of the apparent linkage between WBL, knowledge creation, organisational decision making and bounded rationality.

These are considerations far beyond graduate employability and pose a considerable challenge not only to providers of WBL programmes but to the intellectual capital of the university.

How might University Work Based Learning contribute to Intellectual Capital

The following discussion explores how WBL programmes of the types discussed in section 2 of this book relate to the four key issues identified above and thus to the potential to enhance the intellectual capital of organisations.

1. Focus on organisational objectives and the performative edge of knowledge.

The inclusion of the negotiation of a learning agreement as a key part of a learning programme to achieve customisation at the level of the individual and to promote individual empowerment is well documented (for example Anderson et al, 1996). University WBL programmes seek to extend the use of the learning agreement to include the organisation as a third party to the proposed learning programme (Boud and Solomon, Op. Cit.). The learning agreement provides a mechanism for identifying and reconciling the interests of a range of stakeholders (at a minimum the individual programme participant, the university and the employer) and involving them in planning WBL (Osbourne et al 1998). This significantly extends the scope of the learning agreement to include access to learning resources held by the organisation and critically an explicit focus on the aims of the organisation. In knowledge management terms the learning agreement has the potential for acting as a key mechanism for the sharing and use of knowledge to attain organisational objectives.

One way of regarding such a three way learning agreement is that the individual is proposing how she is going to use the intellectual capital of the university and of the employer. In the case of the university it is clearly the use of human capital (the knowledge and skill of the programme adviser and project supervisors) but this is only made possible by the structural capital of the university. In the case of the employer there is also potential for a human capital (such as expert or general advice) and structural capital (for example education and training support infrastructure, access to records) dimension. In addition there may be instances where, due to the importance of the project to the organisation, external expertise (such as professional market researchers) will be bought in to support a WBL project.

In practice it appears that this range of benefits is going to be difficult to achieve unless the rationale for the programme in terms of business benefit is accepted by an appropriate decision maker. The negotiation of effective learning agreements for WBL programmes requires understanding on the part of the individual participant and the university of the work context and may have to be extended so that it reflects the interests of multiple work stakeholders (for example the central training department and local business manager) (Garnett 2000).

2. Develop Strategies for working with tacit knowledge.

Universities have long had mechanisms for the formal recognition and evaluation of learning from experience (known as APEL in the UK). APEL often involves the university providing a facilitative structure for the identification and accreditation of learning from work (paid and unpaid) of individuals and requires the application of reflection to experience in order to identify learning. Participants undertaking APEL as part of the Middlesex programme are asked to reflect upon the APEL process and often make statements like " it helped me to think about what I had done and how I had done it and to set it out logically (Hawkes, 2002). This is potentially a knowledge creation as well as a knowledge capture exercise as it can facilitate the conversion of tacit knowledge to explicit knowledge which can then be shared. However the narrow use of APEL to determine advanced standing on predefined university programmes has meant that this potential has rarely been realised. APEL at Middlesex is offered as a module which provides structured support for individuals to review their experiences, including paid and unpaid work, leading to identification of their own areas of learning. The process starts with the participant producing an expanded resume and job description which is to help the participant, in consultation with their university programme adviser, to identify their own "areas" of learning. Each area of learning is described in terms of acquisition and application. Knowledge and skills attained and exercised are described and evidence is used to illustrate their application.

Each participant submits a portfolio that includes several areas of learning. The focus on the facilitation of a participant led learning review leading to general credit has freed the traditional APEL process from the limitations of only recognising learning which closely matches existing validated programmes (Garnett 1998). This is highly significant as it provides for fuller recognition of high level learning achievement which is external to the university and may often be highly personal to the individual as it is the product of their particular range of experiences.

The general credit approach approach to APEL has been further developed to achieve customisation to the needs of the employer organisation through the alignment of areas of learning to organisational core competencies. This involves taking statements of behavioural indicators and articulating and evidencing the knowledge and skills required to exhibit competent performance. In this way reflection is focused upon knowledge and skills which the organisation has determined are key to business performance and thus relate directly to organisational appraisal and performance management systems (see Garnett, Comerford and Webb, 2001). Province and national APEL practice in Canada and France respectively illustrates how APEL can be developed to serve the needs of a wider group of stakeholders, for example, unions and employers. Garnett, Portwood and Costley (2004) have argued that in order for APEL to be taken up more widely and to serve the interests of a wider group of stakeholders there needs to be a fundamental shift from seeing it purely as a mechanism to facilitate entry with advanced standing on a course to using it as a developmental tool for learning recognition and development which has the potential to combine with organisational learning and performance management systems. The potential to link individual reflection to change in organisations is explored in "Productive reflection at work" (Boud et al, 2006).

3. Fully exploit and enhance the structural capital of organisations.

The WBL programme offers the employer the opportunity not only to develop an individual member of staff but also, through the work based project to focus university critical thinking (Barnett 1997) and expertise upon a real life work issue.

Table 19.1: Example Middlesex University Work Based Learning Studies Masters Projects.

PROJECT AIM	MAIN METHODOLOGY	IMPACT ON STRUCTURAL CAPITAL
A joint project (two participants) to provide a framework to enable managers to determine the competencies of posts and assess the competencies of individuals within the Department	A survey approach to the problem definition and intervention design stages of action research	A framework in the form of a handbook for managers was produced and recommendations for the use of competencies made. The Department has subsequently implemented these
To improve feedback on tendering	Action Research	Improvements were made to the tender documentation and feedback process
A collaborative project to learn from the experience of construction defects in order to reduce defects and thus improve productivity and customer satisfaction	Survey	Six recommendations considered and partially implemented
To produce a guidance note for Chief Officers/ designated managers on the establishment of a workplace register of relevant environmental legislation.	Action Research	The guidance note was put out for formal consultation across the Authority

Table 19.1 above illustrates the potential of the WBL project to contribute to the structural capital of the organisation (Garnett, 2005). WBL programmes at Middlesex use the learning agreement as a device to focus accredited learning on future project activity. Over a fifteen year period Middlesex has developed a range of work based research and development methods modules to equip participants to undertake projects of a research and development nature in their own workplace. The nature of action research projects (change projects undertaken by those able to make change) means that in terms of impact upon the organisation it is a highly effective approach. In the case of the project to improve the procurement and tendering processes the participants concerned had authority within their organisation to implement change. The collaborative project which surveyed the reporting of construction defects is particularly interesting as it was commissioned by the head of the relevant department and thus the recommendations were made direct to senior decision makers within the company. The Centre for Excellence in Learning and Teaching and growing

experience in the Corporate sector have highlighted the need for further radical development in this area to fully utilise the research and development project to draw upon and contribute to the structural capital already in the workplace (see Hodgers chapter 12).

4. Explore the nature and implications of the apparent linkage between WBL, knowledge creation, organisational decision making and bounded rationality.

"What counts as timely action in a given setting depends not only on past-oriented norms and on attention in the present, but also on the personal intentions and collective visions of the future" (Chandler and Torbert 2003:138). Working with this complex situation is core to the ability of higher education to directly contribute to the intellectual capital of organisations and thus to the ability of a higher education institution to engage with employers (Garnett, 2000). It suggests that WBL must develop to harness higher education level critical thinking to enquiry of a highly pragmatic and performative nature. In such an approach the high level skills developed and recognised by higher education will be acquired and demonstrated for, at and through the complex and time bounded requirements of work.

Conclusions

Current WBL practice, including the distinctive Middlesex approach as a field of study suggests that WBL has the potential to focus upon facilitating knowledge creation, recognition and use at, through and for work rather than just knowledge transfer from the university to the individual student.Existing features of a university WBL programme could be developed to relate explicitly to enhancing the intellectual capital of organisations. Accreditation of Prior Experiential Learning has the potential to be developed into a tool to make tacit knowledge explicit and to enhance awareness of the pre-understanding of real life project teams. The focus of programme planning should be broadened beyond the quality assurance needs of the university to alignment with the business focus and structural capital of the employer partner. Work based research and development methods should explicitly plan for knowledge creation/capture utilising and enhancing the structural capital of the work organisation. Work based projects leading to knowledge creation should draw upon the structural capital of the work partner and be disseminated and thus contribute to the structural capital of the workplace.

Developing the linkage between university WBL and the intellectual capital of organisations would represent an important evolutionary stage in combining individual learning with organisational development. Such an approach to WBL would transform the basis upon which higher education could engage with employers.

References

Abell A and Oxbrow N (2001) *Competing with Knowledge*, London: Library Association Publishing.

Anderson G, Boud D and Sampson J (1996) *Learning Contracts – a practical guide*, London: Kogan Page.

Barnett R (2000) *Realising the University in an age of complexity*, Buckingham: SRHE and OU Press.

Baumard P (1999) *Tacit Knowledge in Organizations*, London: Sage.

Boud D and Solomon N (Eds) (2001) *Work-Based Learning: A New Higher Education*, Buckingham: SRHE and OU Press.

Boud D, Cressey P, Docherty P (2006), *Productive Reflection at Work*, London: Routledge.

Brennan J and Little B (1996), *A review of Work Based Learning in Higher Education*, London, DFEE.

Burgoyne J and Reynolds M (1997), *Management Learning*, London: Sage.

Burton-Jones A (1999) *Knowledge Capitalism*, Oxford: Oxford University Press.

Castells M (2000) *The Rise of the Network Society*, 2nd Edition, Oxford: Blackwell.

Chandler D and Torbert B (2003) 'Transforming inquiry and action'. In *Action Research*, Volume 1 No 2 (pp 133–152).

Choo C (1998) *The Knowing Organization*, Oxford: Oxford University Press.

Costley C and Portwood D (Eds) (2000) *Work Based Learning and the University: New Perspectives and Practices*, Birmingham: SEDA Paper 109.

Doncaster D and Garnett J (2000) 'Effective Work Based Learning Partnerships: two case studies from Middlesex University', In *Education through Partnership*, Volume 4 No 1 (pp 18–24).

Eden C and Spender J (1998), *Managerial and Organisational Cognition*, London: Sage.

Edvinsson L and Malone M (1997) *Intellectual Capital*, London: Piatkus.

Garnett J (1998) 'Using APEL to develop customised work based learning programmes at postgraduate level'. Beyond Graduateness, South East England Consortium for Credit Accumulation and Transfer, Page Bros.

Garnett J (2000) 'Organisational cultures and the role of learning agreements'. In Costley and Portwood (Eds) *Work Based Learning and the University: New Perspectives and Practices*, Birmingham: SEDA Paper 109.

Garnett J (2001) 'Work Based Learning and the Intellectual Capital of Universities and Employers'. In *The Learning Organization* Volume 8 Number 2 (pp 78–81), MCB University Press.

Garnett J (2005) 'University Work Based Learning and the Knowledge driven project'. In Work Based Learning in Health Care Rounce and Workman (eds), Chichester: Kingsham.

Garnett J, Comerford A and Webb N (2001) 'Working with Partners to promote Intellectual Capital'. In Boud D and Solomon N (Eds) *Work-Based Learning: A new Higher Education*, Buckingham: SRHE and OU Press.

Garnett J, Portwood D and Costley C (2004) *Bridging Rhetoric and Reality: Accreditation of prior experiential learning (APEL) in the UK*, A report for the

University Vocational Awards Council, Bolton: UVAC.

Garrick J and Rhodes C (Eds) (2000) *Research and Knowledge at Work*, London: Routledge.

Hawkes J (2002) 'How is the accreditation of prior learning customised by Work Based Learners'. In Holifield (Ed) *Knowledge, Work and Learning*, Proceedings of the UACE WBL Network Conference, UWIC.

Jarvis P (2001) *Universities and Corporate Universities*, London: Kogan Page.

Kluge J, Wolfram S, Licht T (2001) *Knowledge Unplugged- the McKinsey and Company Global Survey on Knowledge Management*, Basingstoke: Palgrave.

Mayo A (2000), 'The role of employee development in the growth of intellectual capital'. In *Personnel Review*, Vol 29 No 4, 2000 pp521–533, MCB University Press.

Moon J (1999) *Reflection in Learning and Professional Development*, London: Kogan Page.

Myers P (Ed) (1996) *Knowledge Management and Organizational Design*, Boston: Butterworth-Heinemann.

Nonaka I and Nishiguchi T (Eds) (2001) *Knowledge Emergence*, New York: Oxford University Press.

Nyhan B, Cressey P, Tomassini M and Kelleher M (Eds) (2003) *Facing up to the learning organisation challenge*, CEDEFOP Reference Series 41–I, Luxembourg: Office for Publications of the European Communities.

Osborne C, Davies J and Garnett J (1998) 'Guiding the Student to the Centre of the Stakeholder Curriculum'. In *Capability and Quality in Higher Education,* Stephenson J and Yorke M (Eds), London: Kogan Page.

Rohlin L, Skarvad P, Nilsson S (1998) *Strategic Leadership in the Learning Society*, Lund: MIL.

Stewart T (1997) *Intellectual Capital*, London: Nicholas Brearley.

Biographies of contributors

***

Dr Barbara Workman

Director, Centre of Excellence in Work Based Learning (WBL).

Barbara has a background of nursing and teaching with expertise in accreditation of organisational and individual experiential learning, and facilitation of work based learning across all higher education levels. She is committed to sharing, spreading and facilitating good practice in WBL across a range of Higher Education activities.

Prof Jonathan Garnett

Jonathan is Professor of Work Based Knowledge and the Director of the Institute for Work Based Learning at Middlesex University. Jonathan has sixteen years experience at the leading edge of the development of work based learning programmes with public and private sector organisations in the UK and internationally.

Prof Carol Costley

Carol is Head of Work Based Learning Research Centre (Reader in Work Based Learning) at Middlesex University. She works with individuals and organisations in the private, public, community and voluntary sectors internationally in the teaching and learning of work based programmes, particularly in Cyprus where she has developed the Work Based Learning and Doctorate in Professional Studies programmes since 1996.

Research interests include examining methodologies and epistemologies in work based learning, particularly work based learning as a field of study, especially issues relating to trans-disciplinarity, equity, ethics and practitioner as researcher.

Carol is the convenor of the Universities Association for Lifelong Learning, Work Based Learning network (1998–present) and executive member of UALL.

Alan Durrant

Alan is Arts and Education Coordinator for The Centre for Excellence in Work Based Learning. He is a Principal Lecturer and Programme Leader for MA Professional Practice at Middlesex University. His academic background has been in educational and curriculum development and teaching in art and design.

He has worked professionally as a designer and craftsman in the jewellery and spectacle industries and as a games designer. Research interests include learning and teaching development in higher education, the role of student feedback in developing academic programmes and the role of work based learning in the creative and cultural sectors.

Dr Peter Critten

Peter is a Principal Lecturer in the HRM Academic Group at Middlesex University Business School and coordinator of Work Based Learning in the Business School. He was formerly Programme Leader for the Business School's Doctorate in Professional Practice and teaches a range of subjects on the MAHRD programme including Organisational Learning and Knowledge Development, Facilitating Organisational Change and Transition, and Management and Leadership Development.

He has been with the University for 18 years and previously had a career in training and development in both the private and public sectors. His main research interest is the role of 'Practitioner Research' in work based learning and how work based learning can bring about organisational change through the learning process.

Dr Muthana Jabbar

Postgraduate Programme Leader – Middlesex University, School of Computing Science

Muthana trained in physics and electronics and undertook postgraduate and postdoctoral work in electrical engineering and electronics for industry in the UK. Teaching, research and work experience includes telecommunications, computer networks, network security and network management, industrial and project planning and management, and innovation and total quality management (TQM). He consults to various UN organisations on information and communication technology (ICT).

Dr Katherine Rounce

Katherine was Head of the Work Based Learning and Accreditation Unit in the School of Health and Social Sciences at Middlesex University where she has been involved in WBL since 1995. Katherine has extensive experience of working with organisations, particularly in the public sector, to translate their aspirations from workforce development into academic programmes or activities that can be awarded academic accreditation. Katherine led the development and implementation of the Doctorate in

Professional Studies in Health and the Doctorate in Professional Studies in Environment. Katherine's interests are in management and leadership and in the development and implementation of accreditation and its use in academic programmes of study.

Dr Philip Frame

Philip is a Senior National Teaching Fellow. He is a Principal Lecturer in Organisational Development. Philip's first degree in Social Anthropology was followed by eight years with the Race Relations Board. He subsequently obtained an MSc in Organisational Development and a PhD in Management Studies. He is a Fellow of the RSA and the Higher Education Academy, and co-chair of SEDA's publishing committee. He has published on student induction, learning from part time work and consultancy, and managing diversity.

Dr Gillian Hilton

Gillian has worked in Teacher Education for many years and is now Head of Education at Middlesex University. She has a keen interest in education in Europe, particular teacher education in the Baltic States. These European connections have aided her specific research interests in teacher education, gender and education and in PSHE, in particular sex education. She has undertaken a considerable amount of fieldwork in the area of SRE, particularly related to the needs of boys. The Department of Education at Middlesex has been successfully running work based courses for several years including Foundation Degrees and now the NPQICL and EYPS programmes, and she has been closely involved with the planning for and implementations of these developments.

Molly Bellamy

Molly is Director of Work Based Learning studies programmes.

Dr Pauline Armsby

Pauline is the Director of Masters/Doctorate in Professional Studies Programmes at the Institute for Work Based Learning. She gained her MPhil (1986) and PhD (1996) in occupational psychology and she holds a Post Graduate Certificate in Post Compulsory Education (1995). She also achieved post graduate level accreditation through Work Based Learning Studies and is a Chartered Psychologist. Her research interests include examining methodologies and epistemologies in work based learning and looking particularly at work based learning as a field of study; professional doctorates, including parity and difference with PhD study, quality assurance issues and the use of accreditation of prior and experiential learning (APEL).

Professor Derek Portwood

Derek is Emeritus Professor of Work Based Learning at Middlesex University where he founded and was the first Director of the National Centre for Work Based Learning Partnerships. Currently he is an academic consultant and writer on work based learning, specialising in the development of professional doctorates. This includes playing a leading role in the DPsych at Metanoia Institute.

Annette Fillery-Travis

Annette is an experienced education coach and researcher working with the Professional Development Foundation. During a successful and highly published career as a research leader in food and nutritional science she undertook a work based Masters in management science and has developed that further within her second career. She is now programme director for the work based Masters programme in professional development through PDF. Her pedagogic interests are focussed on the design and delivery of work based learning programmes to facilitate the development of reflective practice and writing, specifically the blending of resources such as learning sets, virtual learning environments and workshops in a paced and well managed manner. Predominantly her research has covered the application of coaching and its link with the learning organisation and knowledge management within organisations. Specifically, she is interested in the results that can be achieved by this intervention and how it differs from conventional learning and development options.

Professor David A Lane

David is Research Director of the International Centre for the Study of Coaching at Middlesex University and contributes to leading edge research in coaching as well as supervising leading coaches undertaking Doctoral research with the Centre. He is Chair of the British Psychological Society Register of Psychologists Specialising in Psychotherapy and convenes the Psychotherapy Group of the European Federation of Psychologists Associations.

Dr Andrew Hodgers

Andrew is a highly experienced consultant in Organisation Development (OD) and Work Based Learning with many years of international experience. He has worked with multinational corporations in Europe and Asia and has been involved in numerous OD, strategic business development and business performance improvement projects. He is also an expert adviser to management candidates in multinational corporations pursuing Work Based Learning programmes at Masters and Doctoral level.

Nick Hodgers

Nick is a director and co-founder of the Irish Centre for Work Based Learning Partnerships. He has been Chief Executive officer of many multinational companies as well as chairman and director of companies in the USA, Ireland, France and Germany. He has also served as an expert adviser and member of the European Union 'COMET 1 and 2' Pan European Educational Integration Programmes expert committee for many years.

Dr Barbara Light

Barbara has significant expertise in the field of work based learning in higher education, working as a senior tutor at Middlesex University, and as a consultant advising European universities and other educational institutions on the implementation of work based learning approaches and systems, holding regular seminars and workshops. She has also developed university accredited programmes specifically for the Small and Medium Enterprise sector aimed at enhancing management competencies, and has worked for many years in the field of organisational and management development with specific focus on behavioural change.

Dr Paul Gibbs

Paul is Reader in IWBL and interested in work based practice, Heidegger and philosophy of higher education

Index

Abo Akademi 174
academic accreditation at
    Middlesex University
    link tutor role 165-6
    overview 169-71
    partnership working 165
    procedure 164-5
    see also Local Authority
        academic accreditation
        case study
access, practice-based arts
    courses 18
accreditation of prior
    experiential learning
    (APEL) 5, 232-3
    research into 215
accreditation of WBL
    see academic accreditation
    at Middlesex University;
    Local Authority academic
    accreditation case study;
    Masters in Leadership and
    Management Practice
    (WBL) for Lloyds TSB
    Asset Finance Division
Action Learning Questions
    (ALQs) 31
Action Learning Sets 137
'action research' approach 30
adult learning theories, in
    MU WBL programme
    189
ALQs (Action Learning
    Questions) 31
Annual Monitoring Report
    165
APEL (accreditation of prior
    experiential learning) 5,
    232-3
    research into 215
Armatage, Judith 31
Articulation Cycle 64-5
articulation of learning
    case examples 69-71
    heuristics to aid
    identification of learning
    64-8
    'Learning from Part
    TimeWork' module 62-4
    learning from routine
    71-2
    overview 62, 72
ASKE Typology of Learning
    Domains 65-6

'ba' 177-8, 229-30
Belgian Katholieke
    Hogeschool, Limburg
    173-4

best practice 44
blended learning 45
Bologna Process 173
bounded rationality 230-1
Bourdieu, Pierre 91, 220-1
bridging modules, FD to BA
    (Hons) 82-3
Business School see Middlesex
    University Business School

CEEDR (Centre for
    Enterprise and Economic
    Development Research)
    links with MU Business
    School 36
Centre for Excellence in
    Teaching and Learning in
    Work Based Learning
    (CEWBL) 5
Centre for Vocational
    Excellence (COVE) 77
CertAVP(Vet GP)
    development 135
    discussion 139-41
    history 131-2
    methodology 136-7
    reflective practice 133
    research activity 137-9
CEWBL (Centre for
    Excellence in Teaching and
    Learning in Work Based
    Learning) 5
Chartered Institute of
    Personnel and
    Development (CIPD)
    recognising the value of
    learning from experience
    29-30
Children's Workforce
    Development Council
    (CWDC) 84
CIPD (Chartered Institute of
    Personnel and
    Development)
    recognising the value of
    learning from experience
    29-30
collaboration, within DPscyh
    125-7
Collingham, Bob 32-3
Communities of Practice,
    psychotherapy 122
computer science
    academic field of 39-40
    appropriateness of APL
    38-9
    cultural changes 42-3
    disciplinary transformation
    41

professional context 40-1
    technological changes
    41-2
Computer Science, School of
    overview 43, 50
    proposed WBL MSc
    programme in computing
    49-50
    WBL rationale 43-9
Consalia 33
Continuing Professional
    Development see CPD
COVE (Centre for
    Vocational Excellence) 77
CPD (Continuing
    Professional Development)
    as a means of improving
    practice 132
    for the Vet General
    Practitioner 136
    frameworks for 132-5
CPD links 36
criterion referenced
    assessment level descriptors
    195-200
Cross-Council Funding
    Agreement (August 2006)
    222
curriculum
    core 5-6
    potential of WBL for
    postgraduate provision 16
    WBL programme at MU
    191-2
CWDC (Children's
    Workforce Development
    Council) 84

day release, problems with
    75-6, 78
Design for All project (DfA)
    47-9
DEWBLAM project
    common European WBL
    platform 183-6
    context 174-6
    development process
    179-83
    internal project
    environment 176-8
    overview 173-4
    potential impact 187
    tensions within 176-9
Dewey, J. 220
DfA (Design for All project)
    47-9
Doctorate in Psychotherapy
    see DPsych
domestic activities 3

DProf (Masters/Doctorate in Professional Studies) Programme 30, 33–4, 44
administration 104–5
assessment 105–6
challenges 113–15
context 108–10
flexibility 107–8
history 102
impact of student doctorate in work sphere 106–7
literature in 111–12
overview 102–8
publications concerning 214
research resulting in 214–15
student characteristics 102–4
support for candidates 107
teaching and learning 110–13
DPsych (Doctorate in Psychotherapy)
candidate collegiality 128–9
context 118–23
external relations 129–30
links with professional bodies 119
overview 118
professional knowledge 122–7
professional practice 127–30
relationship with Middlesex University 119–20
staff team 127–8

e-portfolios 35
Early Years practitioners, Middlesex Foundation Degree
creation of 75
learning and teaching strategies 78–85
Work Based Learning in 77–8
elitism, practice-based arts courses 18
Elton-Wilson, Jenifer 120
emancipatory standpoint, as WBL project approach 92–3
employer involvement
lack of paid day release 75–6
problem in Early Year Foundation Degree 77
English skills, problem for SME managers 157

epistemologies, transformation of 174–6
ethical issues, research into 215
European WBL see DEWBLAM project
external examiners, problems finding, for D Psych 120
external support matrix 67–8

Fachhochschule Aachen 174
FDs see Foundation Degrees
Feedback surgeries, 'Learning from Part TimeWork' module 64
field of study approach 3, 88–92, 96–7, 204
financial provision for students, FD for Early Years practitioners 78
foci of learning 66–7
Foundation Degrees (FDs) 73–4
bridging module to BA (Hons) 82–3
for Early Years practitioners 74–7, 78, 79
see also Early Years practitioners, Middlesex Foundation Degree

GC (Global Campus) 45
general credit 191, 233
Gibbons, M. 110, 158, 171, 216, 220
Global Campus (GC) 45

Habermas, Jürgen 221–2
Hale, Richard 31
Health and Social Science, School of 51–61
continuum of WBL use 53–5
history with WBL 51–3
nursing programmes WBL components 56–61
subject areas 56
HET system 175
Ho-shin planning 148
Hodgers, Andrew 144
Hodgers, Nick 144

insider research
into management 148–9
research into ethics of 218–19
Institute for WBL (IWBL) 4–5
Institutional Audit 205–6
intellectual capital
key factors for enhancing 227–31
models of 134–5
overview 226

potential contribution of university WBL programmes 231–5
Irish Centre for Work Based Learning Partnerships
client focus 145–6
history 144–5
overview 143–4, 149–51
ISO9000:2000 Management Systems Standard 145–7
IWBL (Institute for WBL) 4–5

Kaizen 148
knowledge based economy 86
knowledge brokerage 156
knowledge driven economy 86

Lane, D. 139
lean manufacturing 148
learning age, the 86
Learning Agreements 94–6, 231–2
in Local Authority academic accreditation case study 167
learning analysis matrix 66–7
learning cycle, and WBL curriculum framework 192
'Learning from Part TimeWork' module 62–4
learning logs 35
Learning Objectives Profile 28
Learning Sets see Action Learning Sets
learning transferability matrix 68
lessons learned 44
level descriptors see criterion referenced assessment level descriptors
link tutors, role of 165–6
Living Theory 32
Lloyds TSB Asset Finance Division 31–3
Local Authority academic accreditation case study
background 166
discussion 169
effects 168
outcomes 168–9
overview 166
programme process 166–8

MA Professional Practice see MAPP
Management Practice Programme (MPP) 144
management research, by insiders 148–9

managerialist standpoint, as
WBL project approach 93
MAPP (MA Professional
Practice)
Academic School context
20–1
elitism/access 18
overview 16–17, 25
practitioner-teachers 23–4
professional practice 19
student perspectives
19–20
valuing practice 24–5
Margersion, Charles 31
Masters in Leadership and
Management Practice
(WBL) for Lloyds TSB
Asset Finance Division 32
Masters/Doctorate in
Professional Studies see
DProf
MBS (Middlesex Business
Studies) modules 28–9
Memorandum of Co-
operation 164
Metanoia Institute 118,
120–1
Middlesex University, history
in WBL 2–4
Middlesex University
Business School
ethos for WBL 28–9
examples of WBL
improving professional
practice 30–4
future developments 34–6
overview 27–8, 37
recruitment of new tutors
30
'Theory/Practice' divide
29
mode of study, WBL as 87–8
Moore's Law 41
MPP (Management Practice
Programme) 144
MProf 44
see also DProf
Mulcahy, Noel 144

National Centre for Work
Based Learning Ireland
144
NCWBLP (National Centre
for Work Based Learning
Partnerships) 4
Nursing Studies, BSc (Hons)
56–8

overseas students
local attitudes and
educational policy 104
proportion in MU
Business School 27

PD (Professional Doctoral)
study, in UK 109
positionality as 'point of
entry' into knowledge
claim 93–4
practice-based arts education
disciplinary cultures in
21–3
practice/theory separation
23–4
see also MAPP
practitioner research 45
practitioner-teachers
and theory/practice
separation in practice-
based arts education 23–4
motivations 22
need for involvement for
practice-based arts
education 16
professional bodies, and
academic requirements
29–30
Professional Knowledge
Seminars 124
professional practice, practice-
based arts courses 19
Programme Plans 95
psychotherapy, field of 121–2

quality assurance
development of the
understanding of quality
210–11
discipline audit by Quality
Assurance Agency 205–6
HEFCE consideration for
award of Centre for
Excellence in Teaching and
Learning 207–8
MU Enhanced Review
206–7
MU Review of Academic
Provision (RAP) 205
overview 201–2, 204, 211
themes and issues 208–10

RAL (recognition and
accreditation of learning)
89
RAP (Review of Academic
Provision) 205
RCUK (Research Councils
UK) 222–3
REC (Recruitment and
Employment
Confederation)
MU Business School
designed Foundation
Degree 30–1
recognition and accreditation
of learning (RAL) 89
Recruitment and
Employment

Confederation see REC
Ree, Jonathan 91
reflection
in MU WBL programme
189
within DPscyh 125–6
reflective practice, within
Cert AVP GPVet 133
Research Challenges module
124–6
Research Councils UK
(RCUK) 222–3
'research informed teaching'
development funding 23
research into WBL
developing worker
researchers 216–19
drawing on related fields
and theories 219–22
funding 222–3
overview 213–14, 223–4
see also WBLRC
research methods module,
MAPP programme 17
Revans, Reg 144
Review of Academic
Provision (RAP) 205
routine, articulation of
learning from 71–2

scholarly professionals 54
Schön, D. 55, 90, 134, 189,
193, 220
SECI knowledge conversion
model 176–7
Senge, Peter 144
Sets see Action Learning Sets
sign-off sheet, in Local
Authority academic
accreditation case study
167–8
Six Sigma 148
SME sector work based
management programmes
context 153–4
issues 157–8
key features 154–5
participant profile 155
pedagogic approach
155–7
specific credit 191
Squire, Philip 33–4
standpoint as 'point of entry'
into knowledge claim
93–4
structural capital, importance
in knowledge transfer
228–30
student selection, FD for
Early Years practitioners
79
students
becoming better qualified
than their managers 76–8

financial provision for FD
for Early Years
practitioners 78
'personae' used when
writing claims 89–92
see also overseas students
Sure Start endorsement 75

teaching staff
use of FE staff 80
see also tutors
technological support for
WBL 34–6
'Theory/Practice' divide
Middlesex University
Business School 29
practitioner-teachers in
practice-based arts
education 23–4
transdisciplinary skills,
practice-based arts courses
19, 22
tutors
recruitment of 30
see also link tutors, role of

Universidad de Granada
174–5
Università di Firenze 174
Université des Sciences et
Technologies de Lille 173
University of Lille 175–6
university WBL programmes
distinctive features 227
potential contribution to
intellectual capital 231–5
see also WBL programme
at MU
university–workplace
relationships 158–60
Univerzita Karlova Praha 174
unpaid activities 3

Value Projects Ltd (VPL)
31–2
veterinary profession 135
see also CertAVP
Virtual Learning
Environment 105
VLRC (Virtual Learning
Resource Centre) 45
voluntary activities 3
VPL (Value Projects Ltd)
31–2

WBL (Work Based Learning)
and industry 147–8
as field of study 3, 88–92,
96–7, 204
as framework for CPD
133–4
as mode of study 87–8
definitions of 4, 183–5
distinctive features of

University programmes
227
WBL Centre for Excellence
214
WBL programme at MU
assessment 193–5,
197–201
core components 190
curriculum 191–2
quality assurance 201–2,
204, 211
student advisers 194
see also university WBL
programmes
WBL projects
approaches 93
standpoint/positionality as
'point of entry' into
knowledge claim 93–4
WBL Research Centre
(WBLRC) 214–16
WBLA (Work Based
Learning and
Accreditation Unit) 51–3
WBLRC (WBL Research
Centre) 214–16
Welch, Jack 148
Work Based Learning *see*
WBL
Work Based Learning and
Accreditation Unit
(WBLA) 51–3
worker researchers 216–19
workplace–university
relationships 158–60